Is *Lying* sometimes the Right *thing* *for an HONEST* *person to do?*

Is *Lying* sometimes the Right thing for an **HONEST** person to do?

How Self-Interest and the Competitive Business World Distort Our Moral Values— and What We Should Do About It

Quinn G. McKay

Executive
Excellence
Publishing

Executive Excellence Publishing
1344 East 1120 South
Provo, UT 84606
phone: (801) 375-4060
fax: (801) 377-5960
e-mail: execexcl@itsnet.com
web: http://www.eep.com

First printing: May 1997

Printed in the United States of America
10 9 8 7 6 5 4 3 2 1   02 01 00 99 98 97

ISBN: 1-890009-12-1

Cover design by Ginger McGovern
Printed by Publishers Press

This book is dedicated to the most important associates in my life: Shirley, my wife of unquestionable devotion, and my children:

Shirene and James Bell
Cathy and Richard Salisbury
David McKay
Maryann and Daniel Goodsell
Rebecca and Jay Meyer

Acknowledgments

As I HAVE READ the acknowledgments pages of other books, I have often felt that they were gratuitous in thanking people who were only involved on the fringes of the project. "How could so many people participate in a book?" I wondered. But now, after weathering the experience of writing a book, I feel very different. If other writers are like me, their gratitude goes far more understated than overstated. Nevertheless, I feel that even though my thanks may be brief and limited only to the most prolific contributors to this book, I need to make my thanks a matter of public record. I truly could not have produced a book of this caliber on my own.

I owe a great debt of gratitude to my family—seven brothers and sisters and their spouses—for their tolerance in the face of my incessant discussions of ethics and values over the years: Donna and Gunn McKay, Lucy and Monroe McKay, Elaine and Barrie McKay, Ann and George Downs, Mary and Jerold Stirland, Elizabeth and Brant Seamons, Willamena and Del Richardson, as well as some 50 nieces and nephews. Most of the time I'm sure they thought I was just playing mental games, but their responses and challenges helped me greatly to mature ideas that would have been much less without them.

Also, my professional partners at Synthesis Consulting Group— Bruce Bennett, David Tippetts, Glade Tuckett, Chris Marshall, and their wives—gave unusual support not just as sounding boards, but with their professional encouragement, including freeing me from other duties while I completed this book. My former associates at Vitality Alliance Consulting Group of Provo were also helpful to inquire of the book's progress and to provide much needed incentive. They contributed valuable ideas and anecdotes.

I thank my table partners at the Salt Lake Rotary Club, who week after week endured my obsession with the project in cheerful repartee and gave me real insight into the complexity of the practical application of ethical principles in the workaday business world. Other professionals were particularly helpful: Claude Smith, Ivan Radman, Arland Larsen, Cyril Figuerres, and Alan Tingey, who explored concepts with me and motivated me with the periodic prod, "When is that book going to be finished?"

Many students I have had over the years pushed back on their professor to clarify ideas that initially were vague and unfocused. Many other longtime associates, professional and casual, have shared experiences and anecdotes and have helped me test the application of ethics and moral values in the business world of the 20th century.

Three special people not only did the yeoman work of typing up my ramblings to make them useable, but also edited and lent me that essential encouragement to keep moving when the project became tiresome or I sensed that people were not interested. These were Kelly Cowser, David McKay, and Sandi Ercanbrack. In the end, Kelly particularly carried the heaviest load of meeting deadlines, always with cheerfulness and professionalism while she simultaneously cared for a husband and three children (with one on the way). By the way, her children added to the pleasantness of the team effort.

At Executive Excellence, Trent Price and Ken Shelton made major contributions to the manuscript and in many other ways shepherded this neophyte through the demanding publishing process. Their hours and hours made the very best book possible from the raw material I provided. Ken gave invaluable coaching in the early stages and gave vision and confidence that I initially did not possess.

Several authors and publishers have been more than generous in allowing their materials to be used in this work, including quotes, anecdotes, cases, and studies. Excerpts from their works—and in T. V. Newmark's case the entire work, published here for the first time—have added immeasurably to making this writing much more than it would otherwise have been. I insisted that my publisher include endnotes to make sure that each author was credited properly and completely.

When it comes to the bottom line, however, the responsibility for the concepts, the interpretation of the materials I have borrowed, and the conclusions reached rest with the author. And, if no other value comes from writing this book than simply that it has been the stimulus for others to develop better ideas of their own, my effort has been worthwhile.

Table of Contents

Introduction

A Matter of Trust

"The system of American business often produces wrong, immoral, and irresponsible decisions, even though the personal morality of the people running the business is often above reproach."

—John Z. DeLorean[1]

I HAVE NEVER met a dishonest or unethical person. Several years ago, I presented a half-day program on business ethics to an executive development program at a university in Texas. At the start of my program I asked a few questions, sort of a pre-test so I could find out generally where the group stood on the subject. The first question I asked the 29 top executives was, "How many of you consider yourself an honest person?" All 29 hands went up. Then I asked, "How many of you engage in dishonest business practices?" No one raised a hand. And finally, "How many of you have encountered dishonest people in the course of your work?" All 29 hands were raised again.

For about three hours, the group wrestled with actual business situations. The executives were asked to judge whether some common business practices were "honest" or "dishonest." They were able to identify cases of deception: the deliberate misleading of customers, competitors, and creditors; the withholding of information to avoid a true impression; consciously delaying payment to creditors beyond the agreed upon due date, and so forth.

At the conclusion of the session I again asked the participants, "How many of you consider yourself an honest person?" Three hands went up, and then I followed, "How many of you engage in dishonest practices?" And 26 hands went up. It was interesting to see the change. Without hesitation, the whole group initially had been able to spot the dishonest tendencies and behaviors of the people we discussed, but they had not yet found those same tendencies dishonest in their own behavior. So when I asked how they could reconcile such apparent incongruities, many responded with something like, "I just

11

hadn't looked at it that way before," or "I just wasn't aware that it was dishonest before."

Who Is Honest?

Recently, in a university class on business ethics, I asked my students to define what it means to be an honest person. A feeble mental struggle ensued. Do we have to be 100 percent honest to merit the title? Honest 95 percent of the time? Will 75 or 51 percent do? We agreed not to use the term "honest person" until the class had devised a definition. Three months later when the class concluded no student was willing to use the term.

Just like my students, most people are simply unaware of the nature of unethical behavior. Often, they don't even have a definition of honesty. In my experience, there are few "crooks" in business. I do not question the sincerity of executives or doubt their good intentions with respect to honesty, but I feel the trouble comes more from naivete and lack of awareness about the nature of ethical behavior. It is somewhat analogous to a medical doctor telling a patient to "quit being unhealthy—go out and be healthy" without explaining the cause of the disease. Good physicians, after a thorough diagnosis, first determine the causes of an ailment, and only then can they prescribe an appropriate antidote. If polluted water is the source of a fever, ice packs are not nearly as effective as finding a source of pure water.

As a result of this pervasive unawareness, the disease of unethical behavior is spreading dangerously. Almost daily the media exposes unethical and illegal activities on the part of executives of various organizations, large and small. Even highly respectable corporations such as General Electric, General Dynamics, and E. F. Hutton have admitted in public court to unethical and illegal practices. The losses in dollars are immense.

Most people who are caught in unethical behavior either maintain their personal innocence or make statements of justification: "I didn't know it was happening in my organization," or "Everybody does it," or "I was only trying to save my investors' money," or "I honestly don't know how such a thing could have happened," or "I did nothing illegal."

Moral Values a National Concern

During the 1996 Presidential election, concern about moral values rose to the top of the electorate's concerns. A poll presented some interesting questions and answers:

- "Which concerns you more, the nation's moral problems or the nation's economic problems?" 53 percent said moral; 38 percent said economic.
- "Overall, how would you rate the state of moral values in this country today?" 78 percent said very weak or somewhat weak.
- "How important are the Presidential candidates' stands on moral values in deciding your vote in this year's election?" 87 percent said very important or moderately important.
- "Have moral values in the USA become stronger or weaker, or have they stayed about the same in the past 25 years?" 76 percent said weaker.[2]

Clearly, morality is a problem of major concern to many people.

Executives Exert the Greatest Influence

The importance for business managers to discuss matters of ethics cannot be overstated. I argue that, as a group, managers and executives have a greater influence on society's ethics than any other group. They even have more impact than educators, politicians, or the clergy. There are at least two major reasons for this: First, managers maintain a pervasive daily influence over the lives of employees and their families. Often, 40 or more hours a week of an employee's life fall under a manager's direct control. Second, and more important, an employee's livelihood hinges on the wishes of a manager who has the power to make employment and promotion decisions. This strong dependency makes employees vulnerable to the subtle influences of managerial power.

Indeed, this thesis receives strong reinforcement from at least three different studies, which were summarized by Warren Schmidt and Barry Posner:

> It was surprising, then, to find out that the "behavior of superiors" and the "behavior of one's peers in the organization" were felt to contribute the most to "unethical behavior or actions by managers." These choices were ranked first and second, respectively, by the majority of respondents from all levels, regardless of age, education, or gender.[3]

Over 35 years ago, Raymond Baumhart surveyed over 1,500 *Harvard Business Review* readers about the factors that influence executives to make unethical decisions. He found that "the behavior of one's superiors" was cited as the primary influence. This finding was replicated in another survey of *HBR* readers 16 years later by Steve Brenner and Earl Mollaner: "The behavior of one's superior is the primary guidepost for unethical behavior." Superiors and peers had more influence than "society's moral climate," "personal financial need," "formal organization policies," or "ethical practices of one's industry or profession."[4]

Managers and executives, because of their extensive control over economic resources, can have significant impact on other major influences. They exert a powerful control over campaign funds that can influence politicians as well as charitable donations that can sway the clergy. They have a disproportionate impact on education and educators. Businesspeople permeate society and its values as no other group does, and therefore, they shoulder a greater responsibility for setting and maintaining society's ethical standards.

Unethical Behavior Triggers Legislation

The urgency of this subject is further heightened by the seeming cry from some quarters for more legislation or regulation to curb wrongful behavior. The threat of additional legislation has been a valid threat to executives in the past. Most of them already complain that the government has heaped upon them too many regulations. And every law that is passed creates restrictions on someone's behavior. However, too many laws also result in limiting the free environment that is essential for a highly productive system to thrive. Therefore, the desire of executives to see decreased legislation is a valid one.

But, how can these executives thwart the government's constant pressure to pass another law? Often, the first reaction of executives is to bolster their lobbying power in Washington or in state legislatures. Or, they may initiate crafty public relations campaigns to "educate the public." These efforts may all be well and good, but generally the best way for executives to curb the legislation passed against them is to curb their own wrongful behavior within their industry.

If, in the banking industry for instance, executives refuse to refrain from deceptive advertising and partial explanations about interest charges, they can expect that sooner or later someone will promote a "truth in lending" bill, with all its accompanying requirements for record keeping, reporting, inspections, audits, and so on. The best way to thwart such regulation is for the executives to restrain themselves from unacceptable behavior. To accomplish this feat industry wide, they must establish commonly accepted standards of ethical behavior and develop the individual commitment that will cause each executive to abide by the established standard.

While I was having lunch one day with a senior executive of a large oil company, the subject of business ethics came up. He spoke to me at length about how his company had made almost a fetish of honesty. At one time, he explained, external interests had started to compromise the morality of the organization's conduct. So, the corporation's executives had initiated a three-year public relations program to inform the public of its high standards.

After his extensive explanation, I asked him what he thought of the conduct of one of his major competitors, which had recently acknowledged its practice of bribing foreign government officials to the tune of several million dollars. "Oh," he remarked, "in those countries that's just the way you do business."

I then asked, "Did you know that every one of those countries has anti-corruption laws and is trying to stamp out bribery?"

"They do?" he responded. "Well, anyway, that's often the only way you can get anything done." Here is an example of a good man who thought his company and his competitors were doing nothing wrong because they were naive—unaware.

Not Even Once?

In another exchange I had with a recently retired executive, who had spent many years with one of the best-known retail chains in the United States, the man insisted, "In my 43 years with my company, I have never engaged in one unethical act, nor has my company."

When I asked, "Do you really mean that neither you nor your organization have ever done one unethical thing?" he responded, "Not even once."

The conversation continued for another 20 to 30 minutes, during which time I presented several business situations with multiple ethical dimensions, and I asked him what he would do. He was able to recall in detail some of the past practices of his company, and we discussed some relevant ethical principles. Near the end of our discussion, he volunteered, "Well, I had never thought about our activities in that way before. I guess I will have to go back and do some rethinking about ethics."

This man was no scheming or conniving "dishonest" manager. He had only been the apparent victim of the "what we are doing is ethical" trap: We are seduced into believing that our actions are ethical because someone in power over us says that it's fine. It seems that in many cases people reason, "I am an honest person; therefore, what I do must be honest and ethical."

During a discussion about bribery in a business ethics class, a woman who held a supervisory position in a government office told the other class members how the rules in her office were so strict that no one was allowed to accept any gifts. "We can't even accept so much as a calendar," she said. She continued by sharing her strong personal endorsement of the rule, emphasizing her own high standards of ethics. However, later in the same class, the discussion turned to the ethical problems in obeying or not obeying the law. Most of the students felt that disobeying the law was generally to be considered unethical behavior. At this point, the woman who would not accept a calendar as a gift told the class that she and her husband regularly and knowingly hired illegal aliens to help out in their small home-based business. She justified herself by saying, "It's ethical to give these people an opportunity to make a living."

Awareness Is the First Step to Improvement

I cite such incidents to point out the need to develop a greater awareness of some of the subtle or hidden aspects of ethical conduct as an important first step to improving the situation.

When enough people become aware of what is polluting the stream that nurtures ethical behavior and begin to recognize that their own thinking and behavior may be contributing to that pollution, the ethical world will begin to right itself. With this in mind, I hope that the concepts in this book will help you see that much of your own behavior may need correcting—not just the other guy's behavior. Without recognizing the need for change in ourselves, little of substance will be accomplished to establish a more ethical environment. But, when the revelation dawns that causes a person to say, "That's right. I can see now where I have erred, and I can work on that myself," positive forces will begin to rise up to correct the wrongs.

By identifying the root causes of unethical behavior, even though ready solutions may appear impossible, we can better concentrate in the right areas until useful solutions can emerge. Contrast this with the current sloganeering, which results in ready agreement by most everyone, but ends up with business as usual.

Ethics are a key, a guide or pattern of behavior that allows people to relate more effectively in their families, neighborhoods, organizations, or social circles. These ideas and concepts will help business managers and their employees function more effectively in their sphere of responsibility.

Confusing and Conflicting Messages

Organizations and their leaders often send confusing and conflicting messages about ethics, honesty, lying, cheating, and even about stealing. How often do leaders, managers, and parents preach one value and live another? They talk about honesty, but they reward those who cut corners. Rewards come, even when a person uses questionable methods to attain a goal. And because achievement and results are so highly prized, most leaders often do not even question how the results were accomplished. We admonish our children to obey, and then we consistently exceed the speed limit.

Sometimes these conflicting messages are even formalized. Take the example of the subsidiary of a nationally known and respected company: All the employees receive a two-page document entitled, "Policy on Ethical Standards." One of the items, number 12, states:

> It is your responsibility as an employee of this organization to report immediately any and all irregularities of which you become aware, which might indicate the actual or suspected loss, fraud, embezzlement, or similar impairment of the company's funds or property. Such irregularities include, but are not limited to, any facts such as the use by anyone of improper operation procedures (**even if directed by a superior**), suspicious activities, or the presence of suspicious persons in the company. [The bold print and underlining were in the document.]

The employees also received another document entitled "Rules and Regulations," which spelled out specific behavioral do's and don'ts. Number 7 says, "Follow instructions received from supervisors. Insubordination will not be tolerated."

Any employee who is fully aware of these two rules would see some potential confusion. On one hand, number 7 says that employees are to follow supervisors' instructions under any circumstances. Insubordination is the refusal to carry out instructions from one in authority, and such actions are not tolerated by the company. Yet, number 12 instructs employees to be insubordinate: There are some things they must refuse to do, even if "directed by a superior." So, if a superior instructs an employee to carry out a procedure the employee suspects is improper, what should the employee do if "insubordination will not be tolerated"?

Many might say that this is just an inadvertent oversight. Someone must have failed to edit the documents properly. But, even more likely, the company's management means just what it says: The company doesn't want insubordination, but it also wants employees to report suspicious activities, even when a superior instructs them not to. It's not a matter of editing; management is simply unaware of the potential conflict it has caused.

Cynics might argue that this is done deliberately and knowingly for management's benefit. Their logic suggests that if something goes wrong, management has a way out. If something goes wrong because an employee followed irregular instructions, then the employee is responsible for not reporting the suspicious or irregular procedures. And if something goes wrong because an employee refuses to follow instructions, then the employee is insubordinate.

Or, management may argue that such a scenario would never arise. But if management doesn't think such a conflict would ever arise, then why is the clause "even if directed by a superior" balanced with the insubordination clause? Which clause should be removed, if any? How would you write the two policies?

A Climate of Trust

For many years, I have conducted culture assessments for a host of different companies. A culture assessment involves setting up interviews with the employees of a company. The assessment is different from a survey in terms of what is discussed. A survey tries to get people to respond to a predetermined set of questions or examples that the surveyor feels is important, but a culture assessment allows employees to focus on what they feel is important. I find it intriguing that in every culture assessment I have conducted, trust surfaces as one of the top concerns. Employees don't trust management, or management doesn't trust employees, or employees don't trust each other.

Establishing a climate of trust requires a concerted effort. Then, maintaining an atmosphere of trust requires unusual alertness and attentiveness. Giving into one temptation to step over the ethical line causes damage to the trust of an institution, organization, work group, or family. Trust and respect are not like gold—once obtained, gold can be locked up, preserved, and counted upon indefinitely. But no one can order other people to be trustful and respectful. Trust and respect are more like delicate flowers, requiring constant care and attention, or they wither and die. Neglect can also cause the blossom of trust to wilt. Bruisings received in the rough and tumble game of business cause the petals to turn brown and drop. Carelessly falling into the traps of unethical behavior can cause the plant to die altogether. The destructive weeds of distrust begin to grow, and as they flourish, all the negative outcomes of distrust destroy the healthy, positive aspects of personal relationships.

Root Causes of Dishonest Behavior

This book will look at the overall health of ethical behavior in business—sort of a microscopic view of the ugly bacteria, microbes, and other hidden forces that cause many of the inflammations, infections, and life-threatening disorders to the body of the ethical business world. Hopefully, by identifying the causes of these ethical infections, or at least by noting the conditions that create the fertile ground for such diseases and the atmosphere that leads to proliferation, we can take a first step toward removing the germs, changing the undesirable conditions, developing helpful treatments, and thus nip these diseases in the bud. If enough effort is concentrated on the causes, maybe even some vaccine can be found in the form of controls, rules, policies, or laws that will help eliminate certain kinds of unethical behavior.

Discussing morality in general terms is easy because, most often, agreement occurs almost automatically. I think most people like books that reassure them that they are pretty much okay as they are. And, when the books also reassure readers that their judgments about their enemies or competitors are valid, then that is better still.

Platitudes that are general enough so each can respond, "That's me" seem to be most popular: "Be honest," "Live the Golden Rule," "Don't lie," "Honesty is the best policy," "Respect others," "Be loyal," "The only way you get ahead in business is by just being honest," "Ethics pays," or "Keep promises and be honest." Few people will oppose such statements, and it's hard to argue with such basic, black-and-white moral simplicity.

Feel-good statements like these will likely change very little over time, but prattling platitudes will just not cut it. It's like admonishing a sick person to "Be healthy—good health pays." Such pithy advice bears little fruit if unhealthy people do not recognize the factors that cause poor health or lead to greater health. Glossing over the real challenges of ethics with vague generalities, in the same way, does not help society's ethical body, either. Only when people are faced with the here and now, and when they can see the things they need to do, is there hope for change and improvement. The devil is in the detail, it is said, and the application of these agreed-upon slogans is what I am aiming at.

Varied Opinions

For many the ethical line is not clear, and people often disagree on where the ethical line should be drawn, or even if it is to be drawn. From where I stand, some people overreact even to seemingly trivial matters, and others claim there is nothing wrong with certain kinds of statements and behavior that I would consider ethically questionable or even outright wrong. On the other hand, I am sure that others have thought that some of my actions were questionable.

Other people seem only concerned about the legal line, and I think many people believe that the legal line generally reflects, or at least should reflect, our concern about the ethical line. I don't claim to know all the right answers or even the appropriate strategies for all situations, and I'm sure the government doesn't know, otherwise the lines would all be clear and there would be no need for legislatures. Although I think I know what I would do in many instances, I don't always know if that's the "right" thing to do. And yes, I have deeply held personal standards of right and wrong—but that's just the problem. Everyone has different standards and opinions, and yet we all would like to believe that we are "honest people," at least generally.

One of the problems is that we tend to judge other people based on their actual words and actions as we interpret them, but we judge ourselves based on our intentions and desires, which does not always take into account our actual words and actions. Which method is best? Who knows, but the conflict is a real one and the discrepancies between the two can be huge.

Matters are complicated when people are faced with dilemmas, enticements, and pressures to step over the ethical or legal lines. Who is to say that a person is evil or wrong who succumbs to such weakness? Or, who is so righteous that they have carefully contemplated how they would act in each such situation? My main purpose with this book is not to pontificate any precise and pat answers to complex ethical dilemmas, tell you what is or isn't moral, or supply you with "Six How-To Steps" for ethical behavior. Instead, I hope to help you as you wrestle with the challenges of becoming a more honest and moral person and as you work to make your families and organizations more ethical.

Practicing the Art of Honesty

Honesty is an art that requires great knowledge and skill, and it is only with long practice that we can begin to master that art. Therefore, I only hope I can stimulate some meaningful dialogue that will help you clarify your thinking on these issues, and hopefully, you can help yourself and your family and organizations to raise awareness about how your words and actions may be interpreted by others—or by God, if you believe that the opinions of others shouldn't matter—and how (or even if) your intentions and desires to be honest are reflected in your words and actions.

This book will explore and bring into sharper focus the underlying causes and forces that lead to unethical conduct. Particularly, it will show the power conflicts that business managers and executives must deal with and explore how such pressures can actually force people to engage in questionable behavior. Without attempting to be psychoanalytical, some of the psychology that allows leaders to behave dishonestly while still considering themselves honest people will also be presented. In raising such issues to a conscious level, I hope you will take, and encourage others to take, a courageous first step in correcting the actions that so frequently do violence to our society and lead to increased regulation.

In my consulting group, just in the past few months as this manuscript has been circulating around the office, I have heard the principals of the company and some of our clients say things like, "Does this convey an honest impression?" "Are we withholding pertinent information?" "Are we using gaming ethics instead of personal ethics?" "Have we made a promise, and are we keeping it?" or "Does our client believe we have incurred an obligation?" In most companies, questions such as these never come up. But for us, this has become a common part of our conversation and helps keep our ethical conscience alive. I like to think that this book had something to do with that.

Contrast this with the story about a young man who is asked by his employer to "pretend to be a potential customer" while speaking to a competitor to find out the prices of certain services. The young man explains how he "felt guilty and like a spy." I do not intend to say whether or not he should feel that way—that is up to you to decide for yourself, and for your family or group or company or association to decide for itself in a discussion. Try to find out how others would act, react, or feel in the situation—from the point of view of both the employee and employer, as well as from the point of view of an outside third party such as a company president, a competitor, or a customer.

For me, I believe that just starting the discussion and allowing the conflicts, dilemmas, and circumstances to settle upon your mind will do more good for you than a thousand-page book of "how-to's" for honesty—even if by reading this book you come to the conclusion that you aren't, or at least haven't always been, honest. Change is easier when you know what to change, but denial has caused many people to fall into invisible, and sometimes invincible, moral traps. Hence, the importance of understanding this subject and its many implications. So I hope that you will discuss these concepts, dilemmas, cases, and insights in your team meetings, board meetings, living room chats, and dinner-table conversations where they can work to increase your awareness, stimulate your emotions about unethical behavior, and cause you to improve your own behavior though increased practice. I further hope that the ideas in this book will contribute additional light on what is generally recognized as a national concern.

Applies to Everyone

At first, I began this book to focus exclusively on the ethics of business executives. But it soon became evident that nearly everyone, in any organization, faces the same problems that executives face—either because of having to work under executives or because of the universality of the ethical traps identified in this book. A little more contemplation revealed that the families of employees also commonly face the same traps, seducements, and enticements to cross ethical lines. For this reason, I have broadened the focus of the book to include everyone: executives, employees, and their families.

Although most everyone will find that this book strikes familiar bells in their personal lives, many of the situations will be placed in an organizational setting, especially business. This is for two main reasons: First, most people function within one or more organizations for a healthy portion of their lives (i.e., work, family, church, club, school, or political community). Most of our ethical challenges occur within these organizations. Second, business executives have an inordinate influence on society's moral values.

Awareness of the traps and seductions that cause these dysfunctional relationships will go a long way toward attaining and maintaining a climate of trust and respect. The first section sets the groundwork for awareness, including the skills and strategies you need to avoid unethical situations, and the second section explores the dilemmas—traps or seductions that cause people to either jump or be pushed over the ethical line. Helping you to understand, or at least be aware of, these traps is the primary object of this book. The third section guides you toward what to do once you have greater awareness; nine practical suggestions for improving ethical behavior are set forth in Chapter 15.

Case studies at the end of each chapter will challenge you in your thinking. At first glance they may seem simple, but let the dilemmas stir up the memory of similar circumstances in your own life. How would you handle these situations, and how could you have handled them in more ethical ways? You likely will find that there are no quick and simple answers. Any answer will generate only more questions.

I hope that by the time you have finished reading this book you are more aware of the ethical challenges everyone faces, and that you will no longer treat honesty as a "simple" matter, laced with simple black and white, right and wrong logic. I hope you will discover that it takes great effort, over time, to master the skills and insights necessary for honest behavior, and that you will learn to recognize and then effectively deal with the dishonesty you find around you—in your own behavior and in the behavior of others.

CASE: Cash on the Catwalk

The Martin Company, a variety store, closed at 9:00 p.m. At 9:40 p.m. the burglar alarm went off. The police arrived promptly. The store manager was called in, and he arrived at the front door of the store in just a few minutes. He let the police in.

As they walked up and down the aisles, they found the man who triggered the alarm hiding in the hardware department. He said his name was Peter, and he claimed that he had been inadvertently locked in at closing time.

The police were suspicious of his claim, and they made a thorough search to see if he had stashed any contraband hoping to retrieve it later. Their search turned up an interesting discovery: $900 in cash was found on the catwalk wrapped in the bank bands of the store's former owner, The Easy Shop.

Three months earlier, The Easy Shop had sold the store to the Martin Company chain. At the time of purchase, Martin Company executives had asked that The Easy Shop manager discharge a certain employee, who had formerly worked for the Martin Company, who had been suspected of dishonesty. At that time, The Easy Shop manager informed the new owners that during the previous year the store had mysteriously lost $34,000, presumably to theft.

The Martin manager now surmised that an employee of The Easy Shop had taken the $900 and had hidden it on the catwalk, hoping to retrieve it later, but never found an opportunity to do so before the store was sold.

The hiding man was let go since the police could find no evidence that he had stolen anything.

Questions:

1. Whose money is it—the Martin Company's or The Easy Shop's?

2. Assuming it would be legal to keep the money, should the Martin Company manager keep it or return it to the former owners?

3. Should he keep the money if it would help his bottom line and improve his opportunity for managerial bonuses?

4. What is the ethical thing to do?

Section One

Awareness

Chapter 1

Was He Pushed or Did He Jump
(Over the Ethical Line)?

*"The things we admire in men—kindness, generosi-
ty, openness, honesty, understanding, and feeling—
are the concomitant of failure in our system. And
those traits we detest—sharpness, greed, acquisitive-
ness, meanness, egotism, and self-interest—are the
traits of success. And while men admire the quality of
the first, they love the produce of the second."*

—John Steinbeck[1]

"IT'S GETTING HARDER for the good kids to compete with the
cheaters," reported Barbara Wood, director of competitive events at
the Tulsa State Fair in March 1994. She was speaking of 4-H Club
and Future Farmers of America livestock shows. According to Wood,
"Youth livestock shows have been infiltrated by adult breeders who
use these shows as marketing tools."

Apparently, some farmers and ranchers had become very creative
in their marketing ability:

> They are producing animals almost exclusively for
> club show projects. They are manipulating the kids
> and driving this excessive competitiveness. They are
> cheating by altering the animals to be more attractive
> to the judges. This includes pumping steers with air
> or oil to fill out depressed areas on their bodies, feed-
> ing them steroids to bulk up their muscles, removing
> the ribs of lambs to make them appear to have longer
> loins, and gluing sawdust to the legs of steers to make
> the legs appear large or eliminate knock knees.[2]

The pressure to step over ethical and legal lines in our economic
system is all-pervasive. Nearly everyone crosses the lines at some
time. Frequently, it's hard to tell whether a person jumped or was

pushed over the lines. But the result is the same—unethical or illegal behavior.

Self-interest in a competitive system provides constant pressure and motivation to step over the lines. Exhibit A diagrams the conflict between self-interest and ethics in an environment of competition:

Self-Interest and Ethics
Under Competition

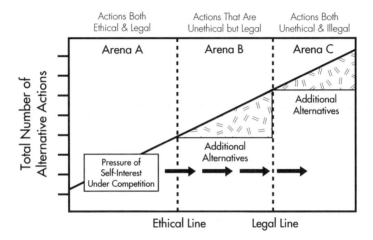

This graph shows three categories of business practices: Arena A represents actions that are both ethical and legal; Arena B includes actions that may be unethical, but they are still legal; and Arena C shows actions that are both unethical and illegal. The shaded areas represent the additional opportunities available to people who decide to cross the "ethical" or "legal" lines. Such opportunities may represent increased income, improved status, or simply the unwillingness to "lose"—the grass does, indeed, look greener on the other side. The same shaded areas also represent the perceived risk to credibility or discipline, but the actual risks to personal and organizational integrity and moral character begin at the ethical line.[3]

The actions that fall in Arenas A and C should be self-evident. Inherent in Arena B is the idea that many actions that take place within the law or rules are, nonetheless, dishonest and unethical. For instance, those who maintain the Golden Rule as an ethical standard will regard it unethical to take advantage of a customer's ignorance to make a sale, although it may be perfectly legal or within the rules to do so (*caveat emptor*—buyer beware). Telling a supplier that a check is "in the mail," while holding the check for a few more days for funds to arrive may be legal, but it is hardly honest or ethical. At the Tulsa State Fair, mentioned earlier, no law or rule specifically stated that pumping animals with air or oil, or feeding them steroids, was illegal. But it seems that the people in charge and the participants who didn't win the competition regarded those actions as highly unethical—"cheating."

Interestingly, many maintain a philosophy with no ethical lines and perhaps do not realize it. Others, who advocate that it's okay to take advantage of "all the law or rules will allow," have done away with a separate ethical line. They make the ethical and legal lines into one and do away with Arena B. To them, everything that is legal is also ethical, and only illegal behavior is unethical. So, they claim, if there is no explicit rule against removing a lamb's rib to make it look better, then there is nothing wrong with doing so.

I argue that in both theory and practice, there is an "Arena B" that represents actions that are legal but unethical. If this were not so, the word "ethical" would be redundant. *Ethical* would be just a synonym for *legal*.

The idea that actions can be legal but unethical is widely held in American society. For instance, in paying taxes we are often told, "You would be a fool not to take advantage of all the law will allow." Ironically, those same people may feel it is wrong for athletes to take steroids, even if there is no rule against it. And even though there is no stated rule against gluing sawdust to a steer's legs, there is a sense, a feeling, that this is wrong. This is ethics: applied morality, sometimes beyond what the law requires.

In fact, the fastest way to get a new rule or new law passed is for athletes, taxpayers, or business executives to fail to act "ethically." Often, citizens and business executives only have themselves to blame for the burden of new laws and additional red tape. When they will not voluntarily refrain or police others from pouring toxic waste into streams, they should not be surprised when a new law, with all its paperwork and inspections, gets passed.

The problem arises when competitors operate in Arenas B and C. Can an individual or business continue to act in Arena A and still compete or even survive? The competitive pressure constantly pushes people to step over ethical and legal lines.

Self-Interest Pushes People to Jump

Self-interest is the force that causes people to "jump" or be "pushed" over the ethical and legal lines. It is like a prevailing wind that is so constant, persistent, and intense that the trees and shrubs in its path become permanently bent, their growth distorted by the pressure. Likewise, people's moral and ethical standards become permanently bent and distorted by the constant pressure of self-interest, causing them to overstep the ethical and legal lines.

Understanding three aspects of self-interest is helpful. First, self-interest is *all-pervasive.* It can be argued that all human actions are motivated by self-interest. With that logic, even acts of "charity" occur so the giver will feel better or assuage a guilty conscience or set a good example in groups that advocate charity. Second, self-interest is *constant.* Whether it is exhibited for survival or to gain approval, recognition, or power, it is a persistent force.

Third, self-interest is often *intense* and *compelling.* People tend to work harder and longer hours when they see something in it for themselves, other than just working for the other guy. In most societies, money is the single best representation of what will satisfy most people's needs and wants. When a situation holds out the possibility for a substantial financial reward, people are usually willing to invest great effort in terms of work, thinking, designing, and scheming. Often, the carrot of a significant reward can stimulate such intensity that the results can be described as nothing less than greed or avarice. Hence, an economic system based on the opportunity for each individual to gratify a desire for money and all that money represents is really capitalizing on the universal, constant, and often intense or compelling motivation of self-interest.

Ethical Behavior—A Serious Disadvantage

Why does this drive place constant pressure upon us to cross ethical and legal lines? When we decide to stay well within Arena A and avoid the very appearance of unethical behavior, we commit ourselves to a serious disadvantage in a competitive system. How so?

People who are willing to play near the ethical line and even step over it occasionally increase the number of alternatives available to them. This nearly always gives a competitive advantage. The more alternatives available, the greater the ability to compete. Further, people who are not only willing to step over the ethical line, but who also play right up against the legal line (all the law will allow) in Arena B have a great advantage over people who stay well back of the ethical line in Arena A. Playing right up against the legal line to the right of Arena B nearly always results in occasionally stepping over the legal line just to grab one or two additional alternatives, giving a slight edge over competitors who are ignorant of the alternatives or who are unwilling to indulge. Hence, the urge to step over the line can be strong in a competitive environment.

In business, that extra gift or entertainment, exaggeration, or dropping a negative hint about a competing product could make the difference in winning the contract or closing the sale.

In sports, the rewards for stepping over the ethical line can be great. One hundredth of a second can be the difference between gold, with its glory and thousands of dollars in endorsements, and nothing. Doing steroids, blood doping, or taking cheap shots can be so tempting. For example, basketball used to be referred to as a non-contact sport. Now, players who try to avoid contact are pushed off the floor.

In a recent review of the fellowship applications of medical students, 29 percent of the applicants were found to have lied about their research, presentations, and articles. The reasons cited: "intense competition," "Everyone is doing it," and "Why should I be at a disadvantage by being honest?"[4]

Even in the Olympics?

Another example comes from the business world surrounding Olympic sports. In June 1985, representatives from four U.S. cities were making bids to the U.S. Olympic Committee, hoping to be selected as the United States' nominee for the 1992 Winter Olympics. Anchorage, Alaska, won the decision over the three other cities: Lake Placid, Salt Lake City, and Reno-Lake Tahoe. A few days after the committee announced its decision, a Salt Lake City newspaper reported six lessons that the Salt Lake Winter Games Organizing Committee learned from the experience. Lesson two was "Olympic rules are apparently made to be broken," suggesting that the drive of self-interest pushes people to overstep the lines. While Olympic organizers in Salt City and Reno-Lake Tahoe did not understand this, boosters from Anchorage and Lake Placid did.

"We were naive," admitted one member of the Salt Lake committee. "We thought you played by the rules. The rules said 'no direct lobbying of U.S.O.C. members,' and we honored the rules. But we learned that Anchorage had a direct mailing go out to all U.S.O.C.

members and that [Ted] Stevens [a U.S. Senator from Alaska] contacted upwards of 40 delegates."

Tom Welch, chairman of the Salt Lake committee said, "If we did one thing wrong, we followed the rules too closely. Anchorage and Lake Placid lobbied U.S.O.C. members directly—contrary to U.S.O.C. rules."[5]

The number of reports in the press of people and companies overstepping ethical and legal lines is likely very small compared to the total number of incidents that actually occur. This tip-of-the-iceberg image suggests that overstepping is not uncommon, and more often than not such actions go rewarded rather than punished.

Difficult to Contain Self-Interest

Competitive sports clearly demonstrates the horrendous problem of containing the pressures of self-interest within appropriate bounds. In American football, for example, the rules of acceptable and unacceptable behavior are well-known to all participants. Each participant makes an individual, overt, prior commitment to abide the rules. The field of play is small (300 feet by 160 feet), and the actions to monitor are few—at least when compared to the real-world geography of business and the many kinds of business an individual or organization can undertake to do. (The complete rules of football can be condensed into one handy volume, albeit a thick one. But the laws and regulations of American business are strewn throughout massive, multi-volume sets in thousands of national, state, county, and local archives, including federal, state, and local laws, and judicial precedents—not including internal company policy guidelines, handbooks, memos, and unwritten codes or international and common laws.)

To enforce the rules in football, seven referees are assigned to watch 22 players—a ratio of roughly one to three. These officials literally watch over the shoulders of the participants to keep behavior within the established bounds. Yet, even with all the enforcers, clear rules, small playing field, simple activities, and the ostensibly intrinsic pride of every participant to "play by the rules," the pressure of self-interest is still so intense that frequent gross violations of both ethical and legal behavior occur (holding, unnecessary roughness, interference, fakes, reverses, intimidation, etc.).

If abuses of self-interest cannot be controlled within the closely monitored competitive arena of a football field, imagine what happens in the business world where the rules are not so clear, not always agreed upon by participants, and not monitored except by a few very remote referees (civil servants). Surely the ethical and legal lines are much more likely to be crossed in this case.

My Experience with Self-Interest

Shortly after I entered college, I gained part-time employment as an accountant with the State Road Commission. This paralleled very nicely with my major field of study—accounting. I worked half days during school times and full-time during the summer. I was assigned a desk and work area in the district office where a small cadre of engineers and office workers was staffed.

The state was divided into six districts. Our district was responsible for maintaining the highways and roads in the northern part of the state (repairing signs and guardrails, clearing rocks from the roads and drains, patching and resurfacing roads, and removing snow). The work was carried out by groups of workers assigned to various "shops" placed in strategic locations around the district. The employee roster was made up of 60 to 100 outdoor laborers and equipment operators.

One summer, the state governor began to take a personal interest in the U.S. Savings Bond payroll deduction plan. He had discovered that the number of state employees who had signed up for the plan was low, and he determined to change it. His staff prepared a special packet of instructions for each district, which included a letter over the governor's signature along with sign-up forms and brochures that gave reasons why everyone should sign up for the payroll deduction plan.

The governor's letter asked that each district designate a person to be responsible for the bond drive. The district superintendent asked me to be in charge. I suggested that because I was a junior employee and only temporary, I would not be a wise choice, but he insisted. After all, we were neighbors, and he said he would help me. One phrase in the letter struck me as odd, but it later became very useful: "When the drive is completed, please send directly to me a list of names of those who did not sign up for the U.S. Savings Bond payroll deduction plan."

The district office where I worked sent a packet similar to the governor's to each employee in the district, which included all the information from the governor's office plus a letter from the district superintendent indicating that I had been placed in charge of the drive. However, the superintendent was skeptical that these hard-bitten, outdoor workers would be interested in the payroll deduction scheme. So, to increase our chances of signing up more people, he wrote in his letter that I would be paying each of them a personal visit.

At first I was reluctant to take the assignment because I felt it was hypocritical to ask people to sign up for the plan when I didn't intend to sign up. I needed to save all the money I could for my school expenses. Still, I couldn't turn down the superintendent, for he was the one who got me the job and who had been sort of a personal mentor to me. I hoped that by just passing out the information I could get by. But, as we discussed that method, he convinced me that these maintenance men were a skeptical lot and would just as soon not be bothered by handouts or mail.

We designed a campaign to overcome the resistance. The superintendent had a no-nonsense leadership style, and everyone knew that he was a political appointee. In addition, the people who worked for him knew that he controlled their jobs largely at his pleasure. In our campaign, we were to use this information to our advantage: A critical part of our strategy was that I would personally accompany the superintendent to each work site in his truck. While he took care of his regular business, I would speak to each employee personally. The intent was that if the workers saw me get out of the truck with the superintendent, they would think twice before turning down the invitation to sign up. We supposed that if they gave me a hard time, they would think I would report the conversation to the superintendent as we drove off.

When I approached the first workers, I could sense a grudging deference toward me when I stated my mission. One man brought me up short when he challenged, "Yeah? How much have you signed up for?" I was on the spot. In the crisis of the moment, I said, "I'm signing up for the recommended amount." I think he assumed that I had signed up, which I hadn't. I did nothing to correct his conclusion, for I didn't want to reduce my already limited authority to influence. So, the way he understood my comment made me untruthful. After the fact, I corrected the situation by returning to the truck and filling out a payroll deduction slip for myself.

Now I was trapped. I had been forced, by not wanting to lose face, to do two things I did not want to do: be deceitful, and sign up for the payroll deduction plan. From then on I would speak honestly about my own position.

Although the positive arguments for U.S. Savings Bonds in the brochure didn't do much to overcome the workers' evident reluctance, the subtlety of me stepping out of the superintendent's truck seemed to help a lot. I heard casual comments like, "You must be the boss's drinking buddy," or "How come you're in so good with the boss?" If that didn't carry the day, I would casually mention the governor's statement of wanting a list. In my mind, that was not a threat. My rationale for using it was, "I just didn't think it would be right to go behind their backs and send in their names without letting them know up front." Usually just a comment about the governor's statement was enough.

Things had gone so well that near the end of the drive all but three men had signed up for the plan. When I reported the results to the superintendent and other key people in the office, the 100 percent fever began to rise in the office. "Wouldn't it be great to get 100 percent? No other district is going to do it. We would be the only ones." We huddled and conspired—excuse me, I mean "strategized." We decided that the superintendent would call the three men and appeal to their loyalty and team spirit. "Look, we are so close to 100 percent, please don't let the team down." None of them budged.

More strategizing. People in the office began to reiterate what a shame it would be if we didn't get 100 percent—we were so close. We just couldn't stop now. What a feather in our cap we would have if we could get those last three. Everyone in the Road Commission would recognize what we had done. Surely it would not go unnoticed in the governor's office either, because there would be few, if any, 100 percent departments. We decided that I should go back to visit with the men one more time.

By this time, I noticed that my personal reputation had a chance for major upgrading. If I could pull this off, I reasoned, I would be seen as someone who "knows how to get things done," even though I was still quite young. My name would be on the final report that goes personally to the governor: "Governor, we are happy to report that we have 100 percent subscription in our department"—and then my signature.

My personal energy, commitment, and creativity were now fully combined. Along with some suggestions from the people at the district office, I set out on my appointed mission determined to reach the new goal. With the first man I pleaded, cajoled, and mildly threatened that others in the district might regard him unfavorably for letting the team down, and I again reminded him of the governor's statement. After my reminder, he paused a minute as he tried to assess the possible implications, and then he shook his head no.

In my mind, I now believed that this would be good for the district and also very good for him. After all, he was not a saver, and this would be an important start for him. With all this moral justification and reasoning on my side, in desperation I pulled out of my folder a letter that I would be sending to the governor that showed his name among the three lonely names standing out on the page surrounded by a sea of white. As I pulled it out I thought to myself, "I do not want to put undue pressure on him." My only desire was to give him all the information possible so that he could make an informed decision. After all, I was only trying to look out for *his* interests.

He took the letter from my hand and studied it for some time. Finally, he set the letter down, and in a very resigned voice said, "All right, what's the minimum amount?" He then filled out the sign-up slip. Then, conspicuously and with a broad smile, I took a pen from my pocket, and with a larger than necessary motion I crossed off his name. He didn't seem all that happy, but he did seem somewhat relieved.

With the second man, I repeated the same sales performance, except now the governor's letter showed only the two names with another name crossed out. Reluctantly, he signed up for the minimum. Then he asked, "How long do I have to wait before I can cancel this deduction?" I was now beaming. Only one more to go!

The last man twinged my conscience a little because he had a large family, and it was hard for him to make ends meet. But, for a true salesman like me, caught up in the 100-percent fever, I rationalized that with his big family, it was even more important for him to save. It was the best thing for him, even if he didn't realize it. When I showed him the letter with only his name on it, he paused for a moment, but he still balked. Then still aching for that 100 percent goal, I remembered the previous man's question and proposed, "Look, why don't you just sign up for the minimum, and then after you get your first check with the deduction, you can call up the office and cancel the deduction? This will save us from sending your name in to the governor [pause] . . . and you won't be an embarrassment to the team by single-handedly keeping them from reaching 100 percent [pause] . . . and, you'll be out practically no money at all [pause] . . ." I pushed the sign-up slip toward him already filled out, only wanting a signature.

He stared at it for a moment. Then he said, "Oh, what the hell." He took my pen, scribbled his name on the slip, pushed the pen and paper back, stood up, and left. Again, I felt a little twinge of something—but only for a moment until I could sense my success.

"Yeah! 100 percent!"

The report went in. Recognition came back, even more than we had expected. The other districts in the state inquired, "How did you do it?" We received a personal letter from the governor. The superintendent was overjoyed. And, I had learned how to sell successfully.

But did I do it ethically? At the time, I was confident that I did. It was just good ol'-fashioned American can-do know-how, right?

Since then, I have had many second thoughts about that experience. No one asked a single question about the propriety or ethics of my methods. Most people were simply awed by the skill and competence of a good young man. It was mostly a matter of laud and fame for me. Well, some of the employees may have felt that they had been unduly influenced. Maybe they were the victims of some subtle trickery and even subterfuge. I have often wondered how the last three men had interpreted the experience. Was it ethical? I wonder if they might even have a legitimate claim that they had been blackmailed.

In hindsight, it now seems obvious to me that the not-so-subtle pressure of the 100-percent fever and the seduction of success first pushed me over the ethical line and maybe even the legal line. Blackmail is illegal. The most embarrassing aspect about that experience now is that, at the time, in the heat of the battle, I didn't see any of those questionable things but for a brief moment. The reflections coming off the gold pot of success overwhelmed all those other little subtleties. Does the pressure of self-interest push us over ethical and legal lines? Or, does the seduction of desirable results cause us to jump? Regardless, the result is the same—we find ourselves trapped in unethical and sometimes illegal behavior.

Creative Marketing

A business professor in a management seminar once shared another interesting example of the pressure to overstep ethical lines. In a discussion about creative marketing techniques, he told attendees how, during a sabbatical leave from the university, he had discovered a company in Chicago that hired select college educators for six- to twelve-month internships. The company provided a hands-on business experience to the teachers, who, in turn, would give the students a more real-world understanding of how business works in the American economic system and, hopefully, recommend a good student or two to work there. He applied and was accepted by the medium-size manufacturing company that was well-known nationwide.

Near the end of his nine-month internship, the company's public relations department approached a major Chicago radio station. As a result, the professor, along with another teacher from another company, was invited on the show for an interview to discuss the teacher internship program. The people at the radio station explained that the show was to be a discussion about a unique community interest education program, not advertising for a specific company.

However, he explained, in a preparation meeting at the company prior to going to the studio the public relations director told him, "Although this is supposed to be a community interest program, it provides us with an unusual opportunity to support the company's marketing effort. So, for every time you mention the name of the company during the interview, we will give you $50. It will surely be worth that much to us in advertising."

He explained to the seminar attendees, "I came away from the experience with a tidy bonus. I also learned that, with the right motivation, marketing people can be made very creative. With that motivation, I surprised myself with how many ways I could bring the company's name into the conversation."

The wishes and guidelines of the radio station were well understood, but the pressure on the public relations director to promote the company's interests pressed him to find a way to step over the intended line and operate in Arena B. No one did anything illegal, but it seems evident that both the director and the professor deliberately breached the ethical understanding regarding the rules of the interview and operated in Arena B. And in so doing, their self-interests were, indeed, well served.

Ethical Lines Are Often Unclear

This constant pressure of self-interest to overstep ethical and legal boundaries heightens when unscrupulous practices on the part of one competitor go unpunished by the business community, often causing others to step over the lines to maintain their competitive positions. In industries, markets, or geographic areas where most competitors operate in Arena B, up against the legal line, it is extremely difficult for companies to operate well within Arena A and also stay in business. This problem is compounded in that the legal line often lacks a point of clear demarcation as to where illegality begins. The ethical line is even less clearly defined and is thus more vulnerable to overstepping.

In nations where bribery is a common practice, it is often difficult for companies with overseas operations to get their share of the business without also operating in Arenas B or C by giving bribes. Additional pressures to edge over the legal line also occur when corporations hire top attorneys to find "loopholes" in the law that allow them to do many things that their "less informed" competitors may consider illegal. Further, when the law is unclear, "good attorneys," who have the mission to help their companies obtain "all the law will allow," can often assess the risk of their behavior: what the chances are that they will be "found out," what the combined damages and penalties could be, whether or not the action can be successfully defended in court, whether chief executives can be shielded from the burden of responsibility, and so forth. All of these procedures demonstrate the constant, often intense pressure not only to overstep the ethical lines, but also the legal lines.

So, when competition is intensifying, most of the decisive plays in Arena A are up against the ethical line where, from time to time, players step over into Arena B. When competition is very intense and Arena B is the primary playing field—all the law will allow—we see the same effect: Most major actions are up against the legal line, which means from time to time the players spill over into Arena C— illegal activities.

When pressures become intense, rationalization often sets in, either justifying unethical actions for a higher good or reasoning that the actions really aren't unethical after all because everyone is doing them, or they only hurt a few people, or the actions help them, or whatever. I am not trying to imply that all managers overstep ethical or legal lines all the time, but the pressures to do so are constantly present to a lesser or greater degree.

The Need for Counter Forces

With such constant pressure to break through the structures and barriers that uphold, support, and reward ethical and legal behavior, some very strong counter forces must be applied to reinforce them and keep them in place. Without significant pressure from the other side, these safeguards can collapse very easily, leaving little or no protection. How strong must these counter forces be? In physics, there is a law that says for every action there is an equal and opposite reaction. So, in recognizing how forceful the pressures are to overstep ethical and legal lines, we have an idea of how strong the counter forces must be to be effective.

So, in competitive business, what forces exist to counter the pressures to overstep the lines? Are they adequate to support and reward ethical behavior? What should we do to reward ethical behavior, strengthen ethical and legal lines, and reduce the frequency of their breach?

A first step is to *recognize that people and companies face constant pressure to overstep ethical and legal lines in a competitive environment* and, subsequently, fall into the dishonesty trap. Although the intensity of that pressure may vary, the forces are like prevailing winds constantly blowing in the same direction and distorting ethical standards just like persistent winds can distort the growth of trees.

As in all problem solving, recognizing and understanding a problem and its cause are an important first step to solving the problem. But until we can agree upon a cause, little appropriate action will happen. On the other hand, the mere awareness of the nature of self-interest pressures can provide the motivation and insight that lead to solutions. In this book I hope to help you become aware of some of the traps, enticements, and seductions that lead to unethical behavior. These include instances in which people fail to:

1. Maintain a working definition of telling the truth.
2. Understand and avoid the four devilish devices of deception.
3. Recognize honesty as an important skill that must be practiced.
4. Make sure that noble means are always used to achieve noble ends.
5. Think beyond the "everybody does it" logic.
6. Be aware of the law of obligation.
7. Apply personal ethics over gaming ethics.
8. See how moral principles often conflict with each other.
9. Blow the whistle on unethical behavior when necessary.
10. Keep promises and honor contracts.
11. Apply properly the Golden Rule.
12. Notice the subtle effects of the "frog principle" in the progression from money to power to influence to corruption.

A second step, whenever possible, is to *eliminate the source or reduce the intensity of competitive pressure.* As one executive rightly said, "If there is plenty of cash in the bank and profits are rising, it's not hard to be ethical." When profits are up; when the company faces no crisis in meeting payroll; when there is no criticism from shareholders about company performance; when no one is threatening a hostile takeover—pressures to step over the lines are not absent, but they are reduced. But managers do not always have control over these sources of pressure. Nevertheless, managers can at least recognize the need for greater attentiveness to the ethical and legal lines—the need for strong counter forces.

A third step is to *establish very clear and high personal standards for ethical behavior*. This requires two key elements: (1) Businesspeople must clearly determine and delineate for themselves what is ethical and what is unethical, and (2) they must make a strong personal commitment to abide by ethical standards even in the face of danger. That is, they must be willing to endure any negative repercussions that may result from maintaining high ethical standards: poor results, diminished competitiveness, embarrassment, etc. Within the organization, top management must be willing to give positive reinforcement to those who abide by proper principles, even in the face of disappointing results.

Fourth, within the organization, *build a system of rewards that supports ethical and legal behavior and punishes unethical behavior*. Such a system would implement performance criteria that not only determine that desired results were attained, but also find out how well proper ethical procedures were followed or enforced. Too often in business, ethical issues are only discussed when the actions are so outrageous that the press or some outside group is likely to raise the issue and expose the wrongdoing.

A fifth step is to *deliberately establish long-range strategies to ensure that ethical standards will eventually become automatic to the corporate culture* and will become self-sustaining because the workers believe in and adhere to the standards both personally and professionally. Any corporation that has survived for any length of time has an ethical aspect to its culture. Companies would be wise to begin by carefully evaluating their culture—not in a witch hunt to root out past offenders (who may have been going along with the company's tolerance for unethical behavior), but in a focused effort to establish new working principles and procedures based on ethical practices.

Sixth, *companies should employ, either as a member of the board or as an internal consultant or advisor, someone to be responsible to ride herd on ethical and legal issues*. Many organizations already have attorneys, accountants, human resources staff, and other "compliance officers" to help keep executives out of legal trouble. However, ethical watchdogs would need different qualifications and relationships. These will be discussed further in Chapter 15.

We have learned that self-interest and competitive pressures often combine to create difficulties and at times wreak havoc with ethical standards. These pressures exert almost a constant temptation to over-step ethical and legal bounds, expand the arenas of action, and increase the number of available options. Following the above six suggestions for establishing strong counter forces against those pressures within companies will go a long way for creating a more ethical business environment.

CASE: *Stanley Mudrak and the Accounting Statement*[6]

After graduating from college, Stanley Mudrak spent five years with a reputable public accounting firm. His good work with the firm led to the break he hoped for: an excellent position in the Jason Manufacturing Company. During the first few months with his new company, Stanley watched the sales and profits of the company decline rather drastically. He was confident, however, that the decline was only temporary and that in another month or two the market would adjust, the marketing campaign would run its course, and the company's sales and profits would be better than ever.

While this situation existed, the company president called Stanley to his office. Evidently disturbed, the president told Stanley that the board of directors had just informed him of an unscheduled meeting for the following day. In the meeting, the president was to present the company's financial statements as of the end of the business day. The president knew that he was not the cause of the company's recent poor performance, but he feared that the board of directors would blame him, or at least hold him partially accountable for the slow turnaround. Like Stanley, he was confident that the firm's condition was temporary and would soon improve, but he felt that he might not convince the board on this point either. Accordingly, he requested Stanley to fix up the profit and loss statements to show a much smaller dip than had actually occurred. After all, he argued, better times were definitely coming, and no one would be hurt if the statistics were altered.

Stanley knew the president to be a hard-driving but competent man, and he feared that the president would probably be hurt if the statistics were not altered.

Questions:

1. If you were in Stanley Mudrak's position, what would you do and why?

2. What are the implications of questioning a leader's directions, knowing that most leaders prize unquestioning followership and loyalty?

3. If Stanley refuses to go along with the president, how will it impact his career?

Chapter 2

To Tell the Truth: A Definition

"For the merchant, even honesty is a financial speculation."

—*Baudelaire*

THE FOLLOWING STORY serves to illustrate that telling the truth implies more than just saying things that are true.

Treasures of Provence[1]

The old man was just taking a swig from the bottle when he heard the car pull up. A British license plate, he saw. Quickly he put the bottle away in the cupboard, wiped his stubbly chin with the back of his hand, wiped the back of his hand on his faded blue tunic, and lumbered across the room to open the door.

He saw a middle-aged Englishman with an owlish face and a fresh complexion. He was wearing a light summer jacket and beautifully creased trousers and was carrying a rolled up newspaper.

"Good day, monsieur," the man said, first smiling, then frowning through his glasses as he carefully composed his French. "Is it Monsieur Roulon to whom I have the honor to address myself?"

The old man nodded.

"My name is Spooner. I saw your advertisement in the paper." There was no response so he tapped the paper vigorously.

The old man peered down as if he had never seen a paper before.

"Yes. Isn't this you? Antiques for sale?" said Spooner.

"Ah. Pardon, monsieur. Enter . . ." the old man said as his arm swung from his shoulder. "Enter, if you please. Forgive me. I am old; I forget. I never go out. No radio . . . no television."

"You're certainly isolated. Have you lived here long?"

"All my life, monsieur. And my father. And my grandfather. And my great-grandfather."

"Really." The visitor looked around with the eager eye of an amateur, which soon glazed over in disappointment. For a cottage in Provence, the room was remarkably unattractive, poorly and sparsely furnished, and everything was old, dilapidated, and dirty.

The owner appeared to be oblivious of all that. "Pray, take this chair, monsieur. But be careful: It is . . . antique," he said as he gestured around him. "Everything here . . . is very, very antique. Monsieur is interested in such things?"

"Oh, I collect things, as a hobby. And I was just passing through on holiday when I saw your advertisement in the local paper."

"Monsieur was lucky. I have treasures here. For example . . ." He shuffled over to a drawer, took out a small object, and placed it on the table. "This."

"This?" Spooner stared in disbelief.

"You have not seen the like?"

"It looks to me like a pepper pot."

"It is a snuff pot."

"Snuff pot?" said Spooner. "As far as I know, no one ever shook snuff from a pot. They pinched it from a box."

"You are sure? My grandfather always said . . ." The old man's voice trailed off.

"I'm sorry. Perhaps you have something else?"

The old man roused himself with effort and looked around the room. "Ah yes. That stool."

"But that's an ordinary milking stool."

"Milking stool, yes. Ordinary, no. My grandfather told me it belonged once . . ." he leaned forward and tapped Spooner on the knee, "to the Queen—the Queen Marie Antoinette! It came from the royal estate."

"How do you know?"

"You see this hole? That is where was stamped the royal arms. But the Revolution came . . ." He drew a finger across his throat, "Dangerous!"

"So the hole was made to cut them out?"

"Exactly."

Spooner stood up, smacking the newspaper against his leg. "I'm sorry, Monsieur Roulon, it isn't quite what I was looking for." He was on his way out when he noticed an old walking stick next to the door. "This is rather nice."

"Ah yes, monsieur. That is . . . very antique."

"How much do you want for it?"

"I regret, monsieur, that I cannot sell it. It has sentimental value."

"A present?"

"To my grandfather, monsieur. It was given to him by a man who stayed here one summer. He was very poor. Sometimes he could not even pay the rent. So, he left his stick. Ah, but that was not all. He was an artist—a painter—I remember, and my grandfather liked his paintings. Me, I thought they were terrible."

"You haven't still got them?"

"Perhaps one or two in the attic. There used to be many, but he could never sell them so he left them all when he went. We used them for mending the chicken house. The canvas was good."

"Pity. I'd like to have seen them."

"Oh no, monsieur, he was no good. Never sold one. My grandfather took a liking to him, but most people thought he was mad."

"Ma-ad?" The word rose sharply.

"But really he was drunk. Drunk nearly all the time." His hand, making circular movements as he crossed the floor, alighted on a bottle in the cupboard. "Permit me, monsieur, to offer you a glass of wine."

"Oh, thank you. That's very kind of you." Spooner took a sip, trying not to show how horrible he found it to be.

"Our local wine," the old man said. "Some find it a little sharp."

"Not at all. Not at all."

"Others cannot have too much. He, by all accounts, was one of them."

"Where was he from? A local man?"

"No! From up north, I believe—he was not even French."

"Not . . . French?"

"I believe he might have been . . . Another drink, monsieur?"

"Thank you, thank you." Spooner finished his wine and held out the glass, his hand trembling.

"No, I don't think he was French," the old man repeated. "I think he might have been . . . Belgian."

"He wasn't . . . Dutch?" Spooner asked.

"Dutch?" The old man brooded on the idea as he rubbed his finger down his long, sharp nose. "He might have been Dutch. Monsieur has some reason to think . . . ?"

"Not at all, not at all," Spooner said. "But what was his name?"

"You know, we never knew his name."

"You must have called him something."

The old man smiled. "We called him something all right. A nickname. Everyone knew him by his nickname. He even used it himself. You see, he liked his wine. It was not one glass with him. Not one, not two. Not six, not twelve. It was said he could drink *one hundred* glasses of wine in a single night. One hundred glasses! And that is how he got his name. You guess now?"

"No-o-o."

"Wait." He stood up. "I will see if I can find one. One moment, monsieur. And I beg you . . ." He indicated the bottle as he disappeared upstairs.

Spooner poured himself another glass without thinking and began to pace back and forth, muttering over and over to himself: "A hundred glasses—*cent verres* . . . cent verres—cent verres *de vin* . . . cent verres de vin—cent . . . *vin* cent . . . **Vincent!**—Vincent Van Gogh!" He clapped his hand over his mouth. While the old man rumbled overhead in the attic, Spooner gulped down two more drinks, then sat with clenched fists and teeth, forcing himself to calm down.

Monsieur Roulon clumped down the stairs with a canvas rolled up under his arm. "You are lucky, monsieur. Here, I show you. The picture is no good. It is old, dirty, but you will see . . ." Holding the canvas to his chin he let it unroll while he kept his eyes on Spooner's face, watching the struggle of expressions as the Englishman gazed on the unmistakable cornfield, cypresses, and sunlight beneath the dust and grime.

"Now you see."

"Yes. Yes." Spooner stood transfixed.

"I mean the signature, monsieur."

"The . . . ? Oh, I see. Vincent. That was his name?"

"Vincent. 'Hundred wines.' I told you—he used it himself."

"Oh yes. Yes, of course." He suddenly noticed that the old man had started to roll up the canvas. "Wait a minute."

"You like it?"

"Well . . ."

"But no. He was just an amateur."

"All the same, I think it's not bad. I like it. In fact, I'll buy it."

"Monsieur—I will give it to you."

"I couldn't possibly . . ."

The old man waited for the psychological moment, just before the protest would have petered out. "Very well. We make a bargain. I give you the picture. You buy these . . ." His eyes swivelled around to the stool and what he called the "snuff pot."

Spooner bowed and spoke with careful precision. "You know, I think I was wrong. I see now: They are both valuable antiques."

"I was sure monsieur had good taste."

"How much?"

"Ten thousand francs."

"Ten thou . . . ?" Spooner nearly dropped his wallet.

"Each. As you said, monsieur, they are very valuable antiques."

Spooner squinted along the rolled canvas and up at the fixed grin on the grizzled face. Then he quickly counted out the money, grabbed the canvas, and picked up the stool and the "snuff pot." He walked rather unsteadily to the door. "Au revoir, Monsieur Roulon."

"It was a pleasure." The old man shook his hand and bowed him out, waiting till he heard Spooner's car start up and move away. Then he took another swig from the bottle, loped across the room with unexpected agility, and bellowed into the kitchen, "Marie! Another one!"

The stout woman, all in black, came in and looked at him accusingly. "Gaston. One day you will get caught."

"For what?"

"Fraud. And forgery."

"What fraud? I did not sell the picture. I gave it away. And I told him it was no good. Is it my fault," he asked as he threw out his arms, "that none of them believe me?"

Is Monsieur Roulon an honest man? For most people the initial reaction is an obvious no. They just feel or know that in this story Gaston, as the old woman calls him, pulls off a blatant scam. He lies. Yet when asked, "Where in the exchange, exactly, does he lie?" most people would be hard-pressed to discover the answer. This is a challenging test.

Can we not argue, likewise, that Gaston is, in fact, a very honest man? He is so honest he actually refuses to sell the paintings—he refuses to take Spooner's money for the paintings. He never once mentioned the name of Van Gogh—that was Spooner's conclusion. Here is a man who has a chance to make some money on a worthless painting, but he refuses to take money for it. How honest can you get? As he tells Marie, "I did not sell the picture. I gave it away." Is it Gaston's fault if Spooner will not believe him when he says the picture is no good?

This story illustrates a very important aspect of honesty: Sticking with "the facts" or "technical honesty" is wholly inadequate as a guide for telling the truth. But, if stating "the facts" is not a valid guide and measure for telling the truth, then what is? We need a definition of truth that we all would agree is more watertight than simply "the facts." Gaston is a pretty good manipulator of "the facts," and legally he seems to be on pretty solid ground.

Gaston is able to carry out his scam—his lying—by using subtle nuances. Beginning with his visual image of appearing rather uninformed, Gaston creates a type of "trust" on Spooner's part. He further crafts that image by sharing generous amounts of good country hospitality—wine—to loosen Spooner's ability to make judgments. Then he guides Spooner down a carefully planned series of assumptions: He alludes to a "Dutchman" without ever naming the country. He leads Spooner to think of Van Gogh without ever saying his name—describing someone who was "mad," who "never sold one," and who went by the nickname "Hundred wines." (*Cent verres de vin*, in French, means one hundred glasses of wine.) He guides and allows Spooner to believe a lie without ever stating it. Fascinatingly, Gaston is able to claim a technically correct position of strict "factual" honesty. As Gaston says, "I refused to take money for the painting."

On the other hand, how honest is Spooner? Well, he lied about how he liked the wine. But, although that may be forgiven as an act of charity or kindness towards a gift, he begins to craft a much larger deception as greed gets the best of him. He assumes Gaston may have a priceless Vincent Van Gogh painting that only Spooner knows about, and so he tries not to let on that he thinks the "Dutchman" may have been Van Gogh. Then, although he feigns reluctance when Gaston tells the price of the other items—a negotiating tactic—he is actually trying to purchase a multimillion-dollar painting for twenty thousand francs. He seems to justify the unreasonable purchase of the stool and the snuff pot as an act of offering at least something to the old man for giving him such a priceless treasure for the asking.

But, we ask, if Spooner knows he's dealing with someone who is apparently less than honest, is it appropriate for him to behave in kind? Is negotiation just a game? Whether or not Gaston is trying to get Spooner to buy his junk at overinflated prices, and whether or not his con is to use a supposed Van Gogh painting to achieve that goal, we must eventually admit that Spooner lied, too, and is not entirely blameless in the transaction.

Many people feel that, deep down, everyone knows the difference between truthful statements and lies. Others say that if you do not tell the whole truth, asked for or not, you are being dishonest. But the problem is, people use different measures for determining truth. Some say that you are honest if you answer everything you are asked in a truthful manner. But what if you are not asked specific questions? How many questions must be asked? How much information must you divulge?

Facts Are Not Enough

If "the facts" are not enough to measure truth telling, what definition of truth can we use to guide ourselves and condemn the crafty schemers and scammers?

In this book I will use the best definition I know. It is given by Robert Louis Stevenson in a short essay entitled, "Truth of Intercourse" (a discussion of social relationships): "To tell the truth, rightly understood, is not just to state the true facts, but to convey a true impression."[2] I am sure that with a little thought, nearly everyone can recall an incident in which strict adherence to facts still conveyed a dishonest or untruthful message. It is possible to stick to the facts but still lead someone to believe something very different from the truth.

Take, for instance, the statements, "Well, isn't that a masterpiece," or "Isn't she a beauty," or "Boy, isn't he fast." These exact same words can be understood to be complimentary or, with a different inflection in the voice, can convey criticism or sarcasm.

Truth telling is not just a statement of facts as many think, but it involves skill. It must be exercised regularly or it will be lost, particularly when competitive pressures tend to push the truth off track. Most people want to be honest, but few know how.

Sincerity Is Not Enough

Some people attempt to reassure themselves that they are truth tellers by saying, "But, I really *do* believe this is the best product," or "I really didn't believe we had a deal." This leads us to ask, "Can we be truly sincere and still convey a falsehood—tell a lie?" If we say, "The world is flat," and we really believe it, does sincerity make the statement true? Isn't the statement still false—a lie? So, enthusiastic believers must always suspect themselves if they really want to merit the label "an honest person." To consistently ensure that we are telling the truth, we must earnestly ask ourselves questions such as, "Is this conveying a true impression?" "Should I make more inquiry before declaring it the truth?" "Should I indicate that this is only my belief or opinion so others do not accept it as a true impression?" "Should I emphasize the negatives a little more so people do not draw the wrong conclusion?"

The idea that truth has not been told until the correct impression is conveyed may, for many, seem to be a very high or even impossible standard. Perhaps this is true. On the other hand, whether it is achievable or not, it sets a standard by which we can measure our words and behavior. Without such a common standard for honesty for judging and debating, the air can get filled with charges and counter-charges—accusations of dishonesty and claims of honesty which seldom lead to fruitful dialogue. But, with an agreed-upon standard, we can transform accusations into building blocks of understanding. When someone says, "I stated the truth," and another person argues, "It was a lie," a debate may follow. But, if the second person asks instead if the first person conveyed a true impression, the question can often bring the discussion into focus.

An agreed-upon, working definition of truth telling can serve as an important bridge to understanding. Without such a definition, claims and accusations can be flung endlessly back and forth, seldom resulting in better or more effective interpersonal or group relationships.

The Magic of 9s

Many people are simply unaware about when they are being untruthful. Let's look at one common business practice in light of our definition, which requires us to convey a true impression. How often do you see items on display in a store priced at $1.00, $20.00, $100.00, $20,000.00, or some other number rounded to the nearest dollar? Most often, we see prices such as $.99, $19.99, $99.99, or $19,995.00—we even see gasoline priced at $1.19 and 9/10. Why is this? Is it because in adding up and calculating taxes the 9s are easier to handle than the 0s? Why do we tolerate this cumbersome number system? Surely, when we buy gasoline, the actual difference between $1.19 and 9/10 and $1.20 amounts maybe to one or two pennies per tank at the most and does not justify the complication of all those 9s.

I would argue we use this system because it works. Otherwise, we would quickly go for the more efficient and convenient system of zeros. Marketers know that most people tend to look only at the first digits in a number when they are making a decision based on price.

Emotionally, consumers feel that $19.99 is closer to $19.00 than it is to $20.00. The method conveys the impression that $.99 is significantly less than $1.00, and people are led to believe that they are paying less, or at least not more than the rounded amount, which is a mental barrier. Consumers tend to drop off the last small 9s in their mind as they compare prices.

Would you like to test the idea? Think of the last time you or a member of your family saw the price of gasoline on a sign that said "$1.05 9/10" but actually reported it as "$1.06." Most people would report it as "$1.05," wouldn't they? So, merchants gain almost one additional penny on each gallon of gas without the additional customer pain of an additional penny, or they gain almost an additional dollar or more of income on other products without any additional customer pain.

Some people counter that the method is truthful: All the facts are there—all the little 9s. No one is getting ripped off, right? But remember, truth telling means conveying a true impression, not just stating the facts.

Some may scoff that this example is such a little matter. But I am trying to establish the subtle and delicate nature of truth, and this is one of the best visual examples I can find. Gross lying usually begins with small things like this and grows into progressively more vicious lies, and then people wonder how it came to be. Small matters like pricing create the fertile environment that nourishes creative people in a competitive climate to grow small, questionable behaviors into blatant lies, letter by letter, syllable by syllable, word by word, and sentence by sentence, without ever becoming aware of it.

Consider what happens when the pricing example is combined with the previous chapter's discussion of the pressures of competition and self-interest. When other vendors are pricing with 9s, the vendors who price with 0s, to convey a true impression, soon find themselves at a disadvantage. Either they lose out on an extra 95 cents, or they don't get the sale because products are perceived to be more expensive. So the vendors end up going along with this less-than-honest practice, justifying themselves by saying, "All the facts are there. See those little 9s? It isn't my fault if people don't pay attention to them."

Get Rich Quick

I recently heard a similar deception in a radio advertisement. An announcer in a standard 60-second spot encouraged people to invest in an investment commodities plan wherein "If you only invest $10,000 or $15,000 now, your investment is projected to grow to $100,000 to $200,000 over the next three to five years." The advertisement urged listeners to call a toll-free telephone number to take advantage of this great opportunity. During almost the entire ad, an enthusiastic voice proclaimed how great the returns *could* be—implying to the listener, "would be." But, near the end, one short sentence was inserted in a more subdued voice, saying, "Investors should be aware that they could lose their entire principal." This was followed by another reassuring statement of the great opportunity to get rich.

Was this a truthful message? Technically, yes. Did it convey a true impression? Not to me. It conveyed the impression that there was a 90 percent chance you could get rich and a small 10 percent chance you could lose all your money. But, in my experience, the odds of getting rich in such investment schemes for the lay person are 50–50 at best, and often much worse.

In a highly competitive world, honesty does not come naturally. Conveying a true impression to avoid stepping over the line can be an awesome challenge. I was raised with the impression that truth was bold, bright, shining, and readily recognized by almost everyone, and that lying was dark, dirty, sinister, and easily recognized by regular people. It is just not so.

When my family lived in Africa, we were warned not to go out at night without a flashlight so we could see the snakes. At first, whenever we went out, we had our eyes peeled for large spitting cobras, puff adders, and black or green mambas—all deadly snakes. The small ones did not merit our attention because they looked more like worms. Finally, one day we became aware that the little worm-size snakes were just as deadly, if not more so. Our unawareness and inattention could have wreaked deadly results on us and our children.

So it is with truth and lying. They are not bright and bold or black and dirty. The truth is not always easily recognizable. Rather, *truth is a subtle, delicate, and fragile thing that must be handled with great skill, dexterity, and constant vigilance*. The simplest things—tone of voice, facial expressions, or even slight pauses—can destroy truth. Imagine how the delicate truth must suffer among the flailing elbows and knees and the pushing and shoving of the competitive world, along with the constant pressure of self-interest to step over ethical and legal lines.

A True Impression

An important first step in affirming our individual standards of honesty and establishing an environment of truthfulness in business is to be aware of the subtle and fragile nature of truth. We should ask ourselves things like, "Did I convey a true impression to the boss in my last report?" "Did the company's annual report convey a true impression to the stockholders?" "Did I convey a true impression to that client about the risk of this investment in both my sales pitch and my advertisement?" "Did I convey a true impression to my competitor about why I wanted the information I was seeking?"

I do not expect every businessperson to become completely truthful overnight. But I believe that just raising the issue will nudge you and the people in your organization to reach a more noble level of honesty, rather than just ignoring the issue.

CASE: The Faulty Transmission[3]

Bill Goebels proudly whirled his new car up to the gas station. Station attendant Harry Smith admired it as he filled the tank.

"It's a lovely car," Harry remarked, "and you were smart to get rid of that other heap before the transmission went out on you. Like I told you last time I worked on it, it might last one more day if you were lucky. Did they catch it at the agency?"

"No. I got a nice trade-in on it. The sales manager just looked at the rubber on it, took a good look inside, said it looked like a real clean car, and made me a nice offer—no questions asked. I guess he really wanted to make a sale. I'd hate to be the guy who buys that jalopy, but I figured it wasn't up to me to teach that character at the agency his business. If I'd been dealing directly with a private customer, it might have been different. Anyway, the transmission may still last for a while. Besides, nobody else gave me a break like that."

Questions:

1. Is Bill Goebels an honest person? Did he tell the truth?

2. Should Bill have pointed out the defect to the buyer at the agency? What if he had been dealing with a private buyer?

3. Does his final remark make any real contribution to your reasoning?

4. Is the principle of *caveat emptor*—"let the buyer beware"—a morally good one? If not, how much does the seller have to inform the buyer?

5. Is there any difference in the obligations of physicians, insurance agents, or store clerks to the buyers of their products or services? If so, why?

Chapter 3

Four Devilish Devices of Deception

"We often do not expect people to accept our words literally. When we speak, we are confident they won't."

—*Anonymous*

For a long time, one of Tylenol's advertisements proclaimed, "Doctors recommend Tylenol more than all leading aspirin brands combined." The copy went on to tell how "Tylenol is safer than aspirin" and "just as effective."[1]

What is the message of this advertisement? Apparently most people understand this to mean doctors recommend Tylenol more than aspirin. Tylenol is safe while aspirin is not always safe. Tylenol does everything aspirin can do. Is this honest advertising or a case of deception?

It appears the makers of Tylenol were trying to capitalize on what is known in marketing as the "bandwagon" effect: Everybody is doing it. In the advertisement, they claim that most doctors think Tylenol is best. So, based on the working definition of truth telling presented in the previous chapter, "To tell the truth is not just to state the facts, but to convey a true impression," does the Tylenol advertisement convey a true impression? What impression do the advertisers intend to convey? If the advertisement does not convey a true impression then it must be deceptive, and possibly even fraudulent.

Executives at Bayer, a major aspirin manufacturer, recognized the ad as deceitful. In an advertisement designed to attack and expose Tylenol's dishonest ad campaign, Bayer blasted, "Makers of Tylenol, shame on you!" Although Bayer acknowledged that Tylenol's statement "Doctors recommend Tylenol more than all leading aspirin *brands* combined" was *technically* correct, it reasoned, "Just think how many times doctors say 'take aspirin' without mentioning a specific brand." According to Bayer, the real truth is that "Doctors recommend aspirin more than twice as often as they recommend Tylenol."[2]

So it appears, based on our definition, that Tylenol engaged in deceptive advertising. Ostensibly, the ad was designed to lead people to believe that doctors recommend Tylenol more than aspirin when in fact doctors recommend aspirin twice as often as Tylenol. The company launched a campaign "to cause people to accept as true or valid that which is false or invalid," which is, by definition, *deception*.[3]

Bayer also pointed out that Tylenol's claim to being safe was misleading because "Leading medical experts have expressed great concern about the occurrence of liver damage with acetaminophen (an ingredient in all Tylenol products)." In addition, Bayer stated that Tylenol's claim to being "just as effective" as aspirin was also deceptive, for "inflammation can be a major cause of pain, and Tylenol does nothing about inflammation. Absolutely nothing."[4]

I remember being particularly interested in that last claim. Not long ago, when a visit to the doctor revealed I had contracted Bell's Palsy—a paralysis of the face caused by the inflammation of a nerve—the doctor instructed me to take aspirin to clear up the inflammation. He specifically clarified his instruction, "Not Tylenol."

Therefore, we can conclude that Tylenol was lying. But that sounds so harsh. Surely, we reason, it wasn't that bad. But I believe that we often tend to avoid being so direct as to call such behavior dishonest or deceitful or to label the outcome as a lie. So we engage in euphemisms by calling it puffery or a little distortion. Sometimes we call it clever or effective advertising. Nevertheless, if we are really concerned about honesty in business, we would do well by being truthful in calling things as they are, as a step to strengthen morality.

In this chapter I will attempt to show how many businesspeople, and particularly executives, frequently, if unwittingly, engage in dishonesty, approve of deceptive behavior, or do not even recognize dishonesty because it has become so commonplace in their environment that familiarity has made it acceptable. In order to help you get a better handle on the problems of deception and fraud in the world of business, I will (1) explore the four main devices of deception, (2) examine the special phenomenon of the cover-up, and (3) look at the process that leads people from honesty to fraud.

Four Devilish Devices of Deception

Most forms of deception are centered around manipulations of the communication process. This can be done in four basic ways:

1. Stating things that are just not so—outright lying.
2. Overstating or exaggerating a situation or condition.
3. Understating circumstances.
4. Withholding important or helpful information.

Outright Lying

The first major device of deception, stating things that are not so, is regarded as blatant lying and is commonly accepted as dishonest. Stating a parcel of land has water rights when there are none; saying a check is in the mail when it is still sitting on the desk; claiming you have no knowledge of an action when just yesterday you participated in a meeting about it; insisting you have never been convicted of a felony when you have, or writing a resume that shows a college degree when you never enrolled in college are all examples of blatant lying.

Even though most of us recognize that saying things that are not true is outright lying, many still engage in this type of dishonesty. Often, the lies are told in an effort to avoid trouble, get out of a tight spot, gain a sale, or avoid embarrassment or being caught in wrongdoing.

Exaggeration

The second device of deception—overstatement or exaggeration—is probably the most often used of the four devices, particularly among people who work in the role of persuader. The great persuaders include people who make their living in sales, marketing, advertising, public relations, journalism, politics, law, negotiation, and religion. When selling an item or promoting a cause persuaders have a great tendency to exaggerate the benefits of the things they are espousing, as well as the negative aspects of competitive products or causes. Tylenol, for example, implied that its product was more approved by doctors than aspirin and that it was just as effective. A grocery store in a major city claims the "lowest prices in town," but an independent study shows that, on average, it is the highest priced among the large supermarkets. In another city, three automobile dealers concurrently advertise that they have the lowest prices.

In Maryland, advertising among banks for I.R.A. accounts demonstrates the deception often employed in the practice of overstatement and exaggeration. Newspaper advertisements placed by local banks contained two important features: the "bonus rate" placed in very large print, and the regular base rate printed at one fraction the size of the bonus rate. One bank advertised:

25% Bonus Rate for 2 Months

10.87% after April 16. Annual compounding.

Another bank advertised a 15 percent bonus rate for two months, accompanied by a regular base rate of 11.5 percent for 28 months. The large-print emphasis on the bonus rate, which was only available for two months, was an exaggeration by both banks. The actual effective annual yields, which were never disclosed in the ads, were quite different from the overstated bonus rates. Which was the best deal? Annual effective yields were actually 12.31 percent for the first bank (compared with a bonus rate of 25 percent) and 12.39 percent for the second bank (compared to the bonus rate of 15 percent).[5]

Recently, I received in the mail an 8″ by 11″ envelope with big bold declarations on the front and back such as "Guaranteed and Bonded," "Sweepstakes" (in red), "Prize Eligibility Notice," "No Cash Award Less Than $1,000"—all in boldface letters. Also, on the front in bold black ink on a light gray background appeared:

Winning Numbers Have Been Selected— Quinn G. McKay

Inside, an official-looking certificate with six "Exclusive Numbers" asked me to sign and indicate whether I preferred the "cash prize" or "merchandise option." I suppose the multiple numbers were there to suggest increased odds of winning. The package also included eleven pages of "information." The pages mentioned a Grand Prize of $1,666,675—and printed the specific figure ten different times. Prizes of $100,000 were mentioned eight times, and $25,000 nine times. The copy also told me that "hundreds more free prizes" were available. "No prize less than $1,000—over 10,000 prizes yet to be awarded totaling $1,937,675."

After going through the material, it appeared to me that I had a good chance of winning something. The company had personalized the document with my name, given me an extra set of exclusive numbers for good luck, and promised that thousands of prizes would be awarded (including the grand prize worth over one million dollars and all other prizes worth at least $1,000 each). The word "guaranteed" added further emotional reassurance. It's not a slam dunk, I reasoned, but it was surely worth the time to respond.

I should have been more skeptical when I was confronted with a page and a half of text that described the joys of owning a subscription to *Travel and Leisure* magazine. But, a trial subscription was a small price to pay for the chance to win such big prizes.

In the interest of research, I took the time to read another third of a page that I found on the back of the very last page of the packet in tiny print. The section was titled, "Official Rules—No Purchase Necessary." I learned that of the 10,006 prizes available, 10,000 were worth only $10 each—not the $1,000 minimum amount I had read about earlier. I also discovered that I had only a 1 in 12,000 chance to win even $10, and that the odds of winning any one of the six big prizes were 1 in 120 million. Fat chance.

I was particularly disappointed, not because it was such a long shot to win, but because I had always held the sponsoring company in such high esteem. I had never known such a highly regarded and trustworthy company to engage in such gross deception. Now, for the most part, the company technically stated all the facts (except for telling me that every prize was worth at least $1,000 when over 10,000 prizes were worth only $10), but by overstating the chances of winning, the company violated the truth by conveying the wrong impression.

Of course, if we assume that this is just a competitive game where deliberate deception is acceptable then nobody should be upset or accuse the company of being dishonest. In such a context, deliberately misleading people is just part of the game—no different from a bluff in poker or a fake handoff in football. But somehow, deep down inside, I expected better treatment from such a reputable financial company. I thought that company would operate on higher moral ground.

What kind of a message does this send to young people, employees, etc.? That shading the truth is okay? That deliberately misleading others is okay? After all, if a credible financial company among the *Fortune* 500 can manipulate the truth to its advantage, despite its formal and rigid ethical code, it must be acceptable, right?

Overstatements, often called puffery, are used widely to deceive not only in advertising, but also in selling, negotiating contracts, seeking leverage, and in many other activities, especially in the pressure of highly competitive circumstances. Jane Bryant Quinn accurately describes the problems of exaggeration in business: "In the fight against the tendency of the overblown to overstep, nice guys finish last."[6]

Understatement

The third device of deception, understatement, to some degree is simply the mirror image of exaggeration and overstatement. While persuaders tend to be guilty of overstatement, defenders are usually more prone to use understatement to get their way. Defenders include people who make their living in fields such as finance, accounting, banking, medicine, insurance, human resources, and manufacturing. You have likely heard statements such as, "There is really very little risk," "He'll only be gone a few minutes," "We have had very few complaints," or "That was really out of my hands," which are all classic examples of understatement.

Deception by understatement is often found in labor-management negotiations. Management typically understates how much it is able or willing to give while labor overstates its minimum acceptable amount. However, these forms of deception often do more to build distrust between the two great groups rather than encourage their cooperation.

In selling, the negative aspects of a product or service are generally minimized or understated. Those who promote financial investments frequently stress that "risks are minimal" or that their investments are "safe." The victims of many recently exposed financial scams report how their suitors assured them that there would be little or no risk—even though the promised returns were extravagant. Such deceptive understatements have proven to be financially disastrous for many individuals who lost their savings.

Sometimes good wordsmiths can use language to gloss over or understate the negative aspects of a situation. In the modern vernacular, "spin doctors" are the professionals at this task, especially in a political setting. Coming up with the right words or statements can understate, mask the negatives, and in some cases even turn negatives into positives.

Several years ago, a major aftershave lotion manufacturer surveyed its users to find out what they liked best and what they disliked about the company's products. The survey showed that users definitely did not like the way the product stung their faces when the lotion was applied immediately after a shave. The combination of the razor blade nicks and scrapes and the alcohol in the lotion made for an uncomfortable and sometimes even painful stinging sensation.

What did the company do to solve the problem—bring in brilliant chemists to change the ingredients and make a more pleasing formula? No. Instead, it brought in top advertising executives and spin doctors to come up with a clever and highly successful advertising slogan. The new advertisements admonished users to splash the aftershave lotion on their faces and notice "the wake-up tingle." After all, a "tingle" is much better than a "sting," they seemed to say. So, it appears that in our world, understatements and the clever use of words are more successful than telling the simple truth.

I heard another good example of the art of the clever understatement in a story about Winston Churchill that I was told when I lived in England. According to the story, one afternoon when Churchill was giving a speech as a young parliamentarian, he had been speaking for several minutes, when suddenly one of his opponents openly accused him of lying. Throughout the remainder of the afternoon, Churchill adamantly denied that he had lied, but his opponent just as adamantly accused him.

Early the next morning as the next day's session was getting underway, Churchill arose and asked the Prime Minister if he could address the parliament as a matter of personal privilege. After he was granted the chance to speak, Churchill is reported to have addressed his fellow parliamentarians by saying, "I would like this august body to know that this member does not lie. He did not lie yesterday; he does not lie today, nor will he lie tomorrow. He, however, arises on this occasion to acknowledge that yesterday he did indulge in a terminological inexactitude." Surely that does not sound as audacious as lying, but he describes the same thing.

In our society, it seems that entire professions have honed their skills in the English language, not to make things more clear and truthful and to enhance the skill of truth telling, but to obfuscate, mislead, deceive, and otherwise lie in ways that give the appearance of truth. We often admire such efforts in commerce and social intercourse as clever. And, people who can do this effectively—coin a phrase, create a label—are rewarded very well in our society with high pay and ample recognition. The understatement is one of the most frequently used and effective devices of deceit. It involves the art of conveying misleading ideas without blatantly lying—but it has the same effect.

Withholding Information

The fourth device of deception, withholding information, in some ways has become the most accepted, apparently because many people are not aware that it is a form of deceit. In a court of law, if an attorney is aware of important and relevant information in a case and fails to disclose it to the court, the case may be dismissed or the attorney may be held in contempt. Contracts can be invalidated if one of the parties learns that important information was deliberately withheld that would have changed the terms of the contract or that would have influenced the party to not sign the contract. Withholding information is nearly always a key factor in fraud. At one time or another, nearly everyone has been offended or deceived by someone who withheld essential information.

In the past, horse traders developed reputations that caused people to be wary in doing business with them. Much of this hesitation had to do with traders who not only failed to reveal that their horse balked or had respiratory problems, but who often went to great lengths to cover up defects and preclude prospective buyers from discovering problems until after the sale had been made.

Today, persuaders and defenders alike nearly all engage in the practice of withholding information. Salespeople who deliberately point out a product's defects or who let their customers know that the products can be purchased elsewhere at a lower price won't likely win sales rep of the year or endear themselves to their employers. If executives at Tylenol had proposed that the company's advertisement plainly state that liver damage might arise from the ingestion of one of Tylenol's ingredients, or that the product doesn't treat inflammation, a major cause of pain, the comments would undoubtedly have been frowned upon. *Caveat emptor,* "let the buyer beware," still plays an important role in business activities. Legally, it is the primary responsibility of the buyer to find out the adverse aspects of a deal, and it is not the responsibility of the seller to volunteer the information.

Michael Deaver, an assistant to President Ronald Reagan, explained that in public relations, the practice of withholding strategic information is helpful for maintaining a good public image. He said, "When you're talking to the media, be a well, not a fountain."[7] Incidents such as the famous leak at the Three Mile Island nuclear power plant have often caused me to wonder how the presidents of these organizations react to such a crisis. Do they immediately call in the public relations team and say, "Now whatever you do, be honest with the public. Don't deliberately withhold information from them"? It seems that many organizations will go to great lengths to assess how much bad news they can suppress without negative consequences.

On the other hand, many people would rightly argue that, for the good of the company, the employees, or the public, it is sometimes necessary to withhold information. The withholding of information is acknowledged as a common and acceptable practice, suggesting that in the game of business there are times when deception is all right. Gaming ethics certainly allows for the practice. So, when is deception by withholding information acceptable, and when is it not? If people, especially executives, fail to establish proper guidelines and live by them, then more legislation gets enacted such as the Truth in Lending Act, the Truth in Advertising Act, and so forth.

Withholding information as a device to deceive is frequently exercised by people who find themselves in the position of either "persuader" or "defender." Those who desire to maintain their character and honesty when engaged in such roles should be doubly cautious of the temptation to withhold information.

Low-Balling

Another aspect of deception by withholding information is what is commonly called "low-balling." Tom L. Beauchamp, who I quoted earlier in this chapter, explains that low-balling always involves withholding information in a more or less "intentionally ordered interaction":

> This tactic [low-balling] typically involves revealing certain less favorable or unfavorable aspects of an agreement to a person only *after* the person has already made an *initial* decision to perform some action . . . [but] unlike most ordinary uses of withholding to deceive and manipulate, in low-balling the withheld information is revealed to the manipulee *before* the manipulee makes an *irrevocable* commitment by, for example, actually signing an agreement. . . . [In] a case from retail sales: A salesperson is concluding negotiations with a customer for the purchase of a set of automobile tires. After a quarter of an hour of discussion, the customer agrees to purchase two brand X tires for $150. After the sales clerk has written up the first half of the receipt and has [the customer's] credit card in hand, he observes that the $150 price does not include three forms of tax, and then casually mentions that charges for mounting the tires and balancing the wheels are extra, as is the cost of an extended warranty policy

that is highly recommended for these tires. The total
charge for all goods and services, including sales tax,
is $202.50. The clerk asks if the customer still wants
the tires and, if so, which of the additional services is
desired. Meanwhile, the clerk is poised to complete
the receipt and credit card form.[8]

Thus, "low-balling" involves withholding information until an
initial decision or tentative commitment has already been made.

The Cover-Up

A cover-up is defined as "a device or stratagem for masking or con-
cealing." Ever since Watergate, the cover-up has become a synonym for
"dishonesty at the top." Most people imagine cover-ups to be limited to
top political figures or powerful corporate officers who have undertak-
en some massive dastardly undertaking and now want to suppress all
knowledge of it, but actually cover-ups are so common that they are
practiced almost universally in a major or minor way by everyone.

Cover-ups employ all four of the devilish devices of deception
and are undertaken regularly by people both in the most respected
ranks and the lowliest. The pressure to engage in a cover-up is often
intense, and it often spawns from noble objectives such as the desire
to be loyal, which seemed to be the case with junior Nixon administration aides in the early 1970s. Other motivations also drive people
to cover up: fear of reprisal, fear of loss, and most commonly, fear of
embarrassment. It seems almost innate that when people are caught
in a mistake or ethical blunder, or when they are caught doing something they know is wrong, they react instinctively with a cover-up.
They either state something that is not so, understate their role in the
matter, or withhold information that would confirm their guilt.

The Francis Gary Powers U2 spy plane incident over Russia is
one of the best-known and blatant attempts at cover-up. During
President Dwight D. Eisenhower's presidency, the Soviets announced
that they had shot down a U.S. spy plane over their country.
Eisenhower adamantly proclaimed to the public that no such thing
could have taken place because the U.S. had no spy planes over
Russia. Of course, admitting to the illegal flights would have been a
public embarrassment. When the Soviets finally presented the evidence, a very red-faced administration was forced to admit that the
illegal espionage flights had been carried out deliberately over an
extended period of time.

Another form of cover-up was discussed in an article in the *Wall Street Journal* in 1983, which discussed the controversial practice of off-balance-sheet financing, an accounting tactic designed to hide corporate debt from unaware bankers and investors to enhance borrowing power.

> Consider Avis Rent-A-Car, a subsidiary of Norton Simon, Inc. In 1980, Avis set up a trust to borrow money to buy automobiles, which it then leases to Avis for its rental fleet. Because the trust is separate from Avis and Norton Simon, the trust's debt is not on their balance sheets. The result: Norton Simon kept $400 million in borrowings off its balance sheet for the year ended June 30. Robert D. Walter, Norton Simon's principal accounting officer, says the trust arrangement held Norton Simon's debt down to 56 percent of equity at June 30, rather than the 140 percent that it otherwise would have been.
>
> One of the big advantages of off-balance-sheet financing, Mr. Walters concedes, is that "it permits us to make other borrowings from banks for operating capital that we couldn't otherwise obtain." He adds that Norton Simon didn't give details of the trust in its annual report because that would have required a report "as thick as a Sears Roebuck catalog."
>
> However, Gerry White, a securities analyst who teaches financial analysis at New York University, calls the tactic a "subterfuge." Avis, he says, isn't leasing the cars but really owns them.[9]

Cover-ups are carried out by most people at one time or another. If you hope to maintain a reputation for honesty, this is one area that will need your special attention. Otherwise, things could get out of hand, just as they have for many people in the past. After all, cover-ups are only undertaken when people feel that damage to that reputation could be severe. On the other hand, news of a cover-up could be doubly devastating. So, you had better cover up your cover-ups, too, right? Of course, for those whose philosophy embraces bluffing or "gaming ethics," this is just another part of the game, and the more skilled one becomes at cover-up the more successful that person will be in the game of big business and politics.

Washington, D.C., is certainly a hotbed of cover-ups, but government officials by no means have an exclusive on them. Just consider how many legal investigations are being carried out by the justice department, or how many congressional committees are engaged almost full-time in trying to find out what the executive branch or a member of Congress is withholding from them.

Promotion Versus Honesty

Most fraud is carried out by withholding select information, not by blatant misstatements of fact. In fact, we might ask: If exaggeration, understatement, and withholding information are forms of lying, how can anyone be a great salesman, promoter, or campaigner, and still be an honest person? Answer: Perhaps no one can do both. And since our economic, political, and religious institutions are so reliant on promotion and salesmanship, what can we do to maintain those institutions and still promote a moral and honest society?

First, we can begin by acknowledging that many of our common practices really are dishonest. Until this honesty with ourselves takes place, not much progress toward becoming a more moral society will ever take place. As long as we continue to justify ourselves, make excuses, or rationalize that lying is not lying, nothing will change.

Second, we can apply one of two different strategies to address the problem: (1) We can begin to teach that, yes, lying *is*, or at least may be, sometimes the right thing for an honest person to do, and we can devise a new definition of truth telling—one that never requires us to convey a true impression, but only requires that we say truthful things, however clever and crafty those things may be. Then we can argue that, in marketing, advertising, selling, and other noble cover-ups for good causes, certain forms of lying are justified, or at least permitted. We can then standardize our "real-world" curriculum to engrain in our young students that, indeed, buyers must beware—*caveat emptor*. And, like the Romans of ancient times, our children will be less susceptible to the con artist and the clever sales pitch, knowing that only the ignorant fall prey to such petty devices. At a minimum, we can be honest with ourselves, even if we find it justifiable to lie to others. Or, (2) we can go in the opposite direction and establish heavy penalties for those who use any of the tools of deception and substantial incentives for people who can establish a reputation for rigid honesty, warts and all.

Of course, both of these approaches have problems. The first one seems much too liberal for our Judeo-Christian psyche, despite the fact that we already live and breathe this strategy in our minds as a general rule. The second one seems far too Puritan, and may even require some kind of "big brother" technology and euphemistic political correctness that we, as a nation, claim to detest. But, in fact, many honest citizens already purchase and vote based on their judgment of honesty, many businesspeople make an excellent living by maintaining their reputation for honesty without attempting to cover up mistakes, and political correctness and "watchdog" technology have certainly left their mark on twentieth century culture. It seems the balance lies somewhere between crass manipulation and self-righteous hypocrisy.

CASE: Fire Insurance[10]

Oswald Meyer owned and operated a large and flourishing waste paper and scrap metal business. He had recently renewed his fire insurance on both of his warehouses. At the time, his agent, with whom he had been doing business for years, told him he could substantially reduce his insurance premiums by installing a rather expensive electrical precautionary appliance that had recently appeared on the market. Meyer promised to install the device within a week, and his agent completed the insurance renewal forms including the lower premium. Meyer fully intended to make the installation promptly, as he had promised, but the press of other business caused him to forget. The agent, who always had known Oswald Meyer to be a man of his word, thought no more about the matter.

Within a month, a fire completely destroyed the paper warehouse. Meyer suddenly remembered his promise to install the electrical appliance, and thought with horror of the crippling loss he could suffer if he failed to collect on the insurance. From the look of the damage, it seemed clear that the fire would have started and spread whether the electrical appliance had been installed or not. And, because of his long friendship with the insurance agent, Meyer was sure that the inspection would be rather perfunctory and that he would collect in full on the insurance policy if he simply kept quiet. Further, he reasoned, he had been paying high premiums for years, and this was his first fire.

Question:

1. What would you have done in Oswald Meyer's place? What should he do now? Why?

2. If he shares the information with the agent, what should the agent do?

3. If the insurance company finds out about the case, what do you think it will do? How should Meyer respond to the insurance company's action?

Chapter 4

Desire Alone Does Not an Honest Person Make: The Skill of Honesty

"Intention is not enough. The honest man suspects himself always. He knows honesty is a skill that must be exercised always. Most of us want to be honest, few know how."

—S. Leonard Rubenstein[1]

MANY PEOPLE SEEM to think that the only thing needed for honesty is just the desire to be honest. According to this logic, the cause of dishonesty is simply that people desire to be dishonest. This talk suggests that if someone is dishonest, it is because of some willfully and consciously despicable act. Therefore, to correct the backward slide of morality in our society we only need to motivate more people to be honest—if people have the desire to be honest, they will be honest. That's all it takes, they reason—just desire and motivation.

The argument is carried even further when people equate sincerity with honesty. As long as people are truly sincere, then they are honest as well. Granted, anyone who is insincere, manipulative, or scheming obviously would be regarded as dishonest.

However, heartfelt sincerity and the simple desire to be honest do not make people into honest, truth-telling saints. Someone may sincerely believe that the world is flat, but no matter how earnest and heartfelt the claim, it is still an untruth—a lie. A salesperson may convince himself or herself and sincerely believe that the company's product is, indeed, the best product on the market, but that belief, alone, does not make the salesperson honest. A broker may sincerely believe that there is no downside risk to the investment he or she is selling, but that belief does not make it so.

Well-Intentioned Insurance Scam

Several years ago an insurance salesman tried to persuade me to convert my almost paid-up life insurance policies to a new, improved policy. Instead of holding $20,000 in paid-up insurance, this new plan would provide me with up to $40,000 of paid-up insurance without any additional cost. The salesman assured me that changes in interest rates could possibly reduce the policy's value to $34,000 or $32,000, but I would still be way ahead of the $20,000 face value I currently had. The agent seemed so sincere, convincing, and confident that I accepted his proposal to improve my financial position. Obviously, I reasoned, he is a trustworthy person. I felt he really believed that what he was telling me was the truth. Besides, he represented a reputable and trustworthy firm.

A few years after our conversion, I began to receive premium notices from the insurance company. When I called my agent, he comforted me by saying, "Just let it go. It will build up a little debt of 'premium due' that will reduce your final face value a bit, possibly down as far as the $34,000 or so that I mentioned could happen. But you will still be way ahead."

After two or three years the debt of premium due was building up so fast I began to worry that, unless I died pretty soon, I could end up with no insurance at all. I called my agent and expressed the concern I had about losing my financial nest egg. He told me the interest rates had changed so much it was hard to predict what could happen, but that losing the principal amount was, indeed, a risk. "But," I said, "you assured me that I would still be left with $32,000 to $34,000 in insurance face value, even with the declining interest rates."

"Well," he responded, "you can't always predict these things, even though we were very confident at the time that the assurances we gave you about the range of possible risk fluctuations were valid."

"So, what do I do now?" I asked. "Do I just wait until all my face value disappears?"

"You could live with that possibility, hoping interest rates will turn around," he said. "Or, you could convert it back to what you had before with a locked in, paid-up value."

"If I did that, how much insurance would I have?" I asked.

"I'll calculate that for you and get back to you," he promised.

He did get back to me: Instead of $20,000 of insurance, I now had $16,000. Although I knew that he likely had been motivated by the commissions he would gain by converting my insurance, I also believed that he had been truly sincere about the promises he made. Nevertheless, his sincerity and belief about how much the conversion would benefit me did not make it so.

Sincerity does not an honest person make. Desire and motivation do not produce truth tellers. To put it bluntly, a sincere person can still be a blatant liar.

The Essential Skills of Truth Telling

Besides the desire or motivation to be honest, it takes highly developed and finely honed skills to be a truth teller. Telling the truth is not a natural, innate instinct that simply abides dormantly in all of us, only waiting to come out. It is more like a skill, like mastering the piano, operating a computer, playing tennis, cooking, or performing a financial analysis.

Beginning piano players do not simply express the will to become great concert pianists and then set out immediately to arrange concert bookings for the following weekend. Such expectations are ridiculous to even think about. Although top piano players must begin with a strong desire to master their talent, they must still apply great effort, often over the course of many years, to develop the skills necessary to become concert performers. They must first learn the concepts, theories, and principles of music. They must learn the fine nuances of stroking the keys in different ways to create different tones and dynamics and to evoke different feelings in their listeners. They must learn the elements of composition and about the different styles and tonal qualities of various pianos. Such knowledge doesn't come from attending a one-day seminar by a professional piano teacher who urges you to become a good pianist. It comes from extensive personal study and practice. It involves testing different ideas, theories, and principles in the effort to find your own individual voice in the art form and then selecting the best way to combine all the elements in the most effective way for different audiences.

To extend the metaphor even further, even though the desire to become a concert pianist can be equal in two different people, the results of practice can be quite unequal, depending upon several elements, including the amount and quality of practice and instruction. So, the desire of one person may lead to the person searching out the best instruction and applying a rigorous practice discipline and routine, resulting in great piano techniques and occasional critical acclaim. Another person may end up with poor advice and guidance, learn faulty or limiting techniques, or engage in practice habits that result only in mediocre renditions, and therefore never get the same results as the first person. The second person may impress any group of friends with a jazzed up version of "Chopsticks," but when faced with more complex music, he or she can only blunder through it haphazardly without any sense of dynamics.

So it is with truth telling. The people who are willing to put in the effort to develop the skills of an honest person are more likely to become expert truth tellers than those who fail to recognize the necessity of cultivating those skills, or those who recognize the need but fail to develop the skills. As a result, many of us are like the person who claims to be an expert piano player, but who only has the skill to play "Chopsticks." We claim to be truth tellers, but we have only developed the skills for a very basic level of performance. When circumstances are simple—we say things like black and white, right and wrong, cut and dry—we can express the truth very efficiently. But when we face more complicated situations—the so-called gray areas—we become major blunderers. We often end up saying and doing things that have little resemblance to truth or honesty.

Back to the piano for a moment: Good piano playing requires many skills, such as hand-eye coordination, hand dexterity, a sense of rhythm, the ability to read music, distinguish different pitches, transpose keys, and so on. Likewise, several skills are needed for the art of honesty. There are two general skills: First, the ability to identify what is truth and what is not. Second, the ability to convey that truth. Later in this book, I will identify some helpful additional skills in each of these two categories.

Determining the Truth

Let's first look at the challenge of determining the truth. It seems obvious that we would be hard-pressed to tell the truth unless we were aware of what the truth is regarding a given matter. Many people who desire to be great truth tellers often blunder and fall short because they have not developed or used the necessary skills to determine the truth of a matter. If they are not simply too embarrassed to admit that they don't know the truth, then they draw conclusions that fit preconceived ideas, goals, or objectives, and advocate those conclusions as fact or truth. They become so caught up in obtaining a goal—winning an election or a case in court, making a sale, concluding a contract, or making a convert—that they don't take the time or apply the effort to determine and then state the truth.

Also, people often fail to determine the truth because they lock on to some conclusion, or opinion, and then treat that conclusion as a fact or as the truth. Those who are skilled in truth telling are good at separating facts from conclusions, while others often mistake conclusions for facts. Here is one example of how unskilled people can fail to determine the truth by locking on to some conclusion and then treating it as fact or as the truth:

> John was walking along slowly. He looked down,
> saw a hole in his suit, and in a few minutes he was
> dead.

Pause for a moment and consider what happened. Try to determine what happened to John.

I have tried this example on many groups in a classroom setting. (You may want to try it on your work group, family, or dinner group.) The initial response of most people is that he was shot. When I push them for other possibilities, other answers come out: "He was stabbed," "He had a heart attack," "He wasn't watching and was hit by a bus," and so forth.

Then I ask why John was "walking along slowly."

They reason that perhaps he was very old or tired, or maybe he was being thoughtful.

Then I ask what kind of "suit" John was wearing. Many people are convinced John was wearing the kind of suit you wear with a shirt and tie—they accept this as a fact, when it is only a conclusion, or an opinion or assumption. My question usually triggers new thought processes: "Oh! It could be a spacesuit, or a swimming suit." This thinking leads to different conclusions and a search for additional data, which nearly always results in a more accurate determination of the truth.

In this incident, John is a deep-sea diver. Why is he walking slowly? Anyone who has tried to walk underwater knows why.

Avoiding the temptation to regard conclusions as facts is one of the skills that enhances your ability to be an effective truth teller. Improving this skill will help you be more accurate in determining the truth. Then, *telling* the truth is up to you.

Here is another example:

> In a cabin on top of a mountain are 20 dead bodies.

Again, pause a moment. What happened?

I usually hear answers like, "Twenty hunters froze to death," or "People became stranded and starved to death," or "Hikers were sleeping and were asphyxiated by a heater."

Then, someone usually says, "Oh, we have concluded that these are human bodies, but maybe they are mice, or rats, or flies." Just changing their conclusions and assumptions leads them to a search for more data to clarify the truth—a good skill for truth tellers. In this case, the bodies are human, but none of these explanations identify what happened.

Then I ask, "What kind of 'cabin' is it?" Until I ask this question, most people conclude that the cabin is a log structure up in the mountains. Again, just asking the question starts off new thought processes and a more thorough search for the truth: "Aha! It could be an airplane cabin—maybe it's a plane crash."

So I ask, "What conclusion have you made about the mountain?" Of course, a mountain in their minds is a great hunk of earth that rises up out of a plain to make a high peak. "Aha! There are mountains under the ocean. The cabin from a wrecked plane or boat could be resting there."

My point of these two exercises is that honest people must develop the skill to recognize that "conclusions" are not "facts." They acknowledge to themselves that other conclusions are possible, and they humbly admit to themselves, "My conclusion may not be right; I'd better search for more information." This acknowledgment leads them to exercise their skills of inquiry to obtain more data to identify the truth. Such an approach nearly always leads to a more accurate determination of the truth. This means that they better understand the position of the listener in hearing their version of a story and can anticipate, and often can correct, faulty conclusions before they are jumped to. Thus, the ability to envision alternate conclusions is one of the skills that raises us above the "Chopsticks" level of truth telling.

As I discussed in Chapter 3, the great persuaders in our society seem to have great difficulty with this skill. Although all of us are persuaders to one degree or another, for some professionals the ability to persuade others is the fundamental key to success or failure. For these people, the drive to win, make the sale, or achieve some other specific result is so important that they will use any and every available tool, especially the tool of exaggeration, to attain it. Rather than acknowledge a conclusion is only a conclusion, or even some subset such as an opinion or an assumption, they argue that their conclusion is a fact. And rather than exercise the humility required for the honest search for truth, they look only for ways to bolster their argument. In one sense, these people are not really vicious liars, they have just become so enamored with their goal of persuasion that the truth suffers from benign neglect. For them, truth is not the primary objective, so the skills needed to identify the truth never get developed or used.

Those who are at the "Chopsticks" level of truth telling tend to treat their conclusions as facts, which often leaves them far short of the truth. This often results in conveying falsehoods, even though they sincerely believe their words to be the truth.

To be a truly honest person, we must first develop the skills to identify the truth and separate "conclusions" from "facts." We must also be skilled in the art of inquiry to obtain as much useful data or information as possible.

Conveying the Truth

Second, honest people have a well-developed capacity to convey the truth once it has been identified. This skill involves all of the abilities and sensitivities of a good communicator. In this case, I am not talking about the ability to persuade, but *the ability to convey truth so that it is clearly and rightly understood by others*. It requires all the techniques of communicating: word selection, tone of voice, facial expression, body language, actions, silence, and so forth. Similarly, each of these skills can be used to deceive, mislead, and swindle, but in the context of truth telling, the goal is to clarify the truth, enlighten, and ensure that the receiver has clearly understood the message.

As we discussed in Chapter 2, skilled truth tellers are not just concerned with stating the facts, but also with conveying a true impression. The failure to convey a true impression comes either from the lack of truth telling skills or from the deliberate and clever misuse of these skills to convey meaning.

On the other hand, the lack of communication skills can result in conveying a false impression, even though the person intends to be truthful. Without the ability to articulate clearly, a person may select words that convey a different meaning than the one intended. Often, for want of an adequate vocabulary, people use words that sound right, or "close enough—you know what I mean," but they do not convey an exact or even adequate meaning.

Experiments have shown that when people see partial lines in a drawing, they usually connect the lines in their mind to make a complete picture. But, in the receiver's mind, the picture may be very different from what the artist intended. With word pictures, this can be even more complicated—even with highly educated people.

For example, I can remember having a conversation with the faculty supervisor of my doctoral thesis. I had used the word "peer" in my thesis, and he wanted me to clarify my meaning. He said, "Don't you really mean an 'equal' rather than a 'peer'?"

I responded, "That's exactly what I mean." But, somehow in his mind the word "peer" meant "superior" or "mentor," not an equal or someone at the same level. Words can mean different things to different people.

Also, the same words or phrases sometimes have different meanings depending on their context. For instance, if I voice the words "a part," do I mean a condition of separateness or togetherness? I may be speaking of unity, as in "I want to be *a part* of that group," or difference, as in "That is separate and *apart* from what I am talking about." Usually, the context will clarify the meaning, but not always. Skilled truth tellers are aware of this challenge and are skilled, willing, and able to make the extra effort needed to make sure that a true impression is conveyed.

The neophyte or unskilled truth teller will often become defensive: "I stated the situation clearly. It's not my fault if they don't understand English." Then they meticulously review each word to justify that it was not their fault they were misunderstood. On the other hand, people who are skilled in honesty are sensitive to recognize, either through body language, facial expressions, or verbal responses, that listeners may be getting the wrong impression. Then, they skillfully review and clarify until they are confident that recipients have received a true understanding.

People at the "Chopsticks" level only worry if they have made a defendable statement that they can use later to protect themselves from claims. They do not understand that the obligation of truly honest people is not only to make correct statements, but to test and make sure those statements are properly understood. *Skilled truth tellers are sensitive to what is being understood, not just what is being said.* So, the truth is often sacrificed because, even though people desire to be honest, they blunder due to the lack of skills to convey a true impression.

The Deliberate Misuse of Communication Skills

On the other hand, some people who possess the skills to convey a true impression deliberately misuse those skills. The great persuaders are frequently guilty of using these skills to mislead or to swindle rather than to convey a true impression. They are so eager to win a prize, make a sale, win an election, or win an argument that they become very skilled at abiding the letter of the law while still conveying a wrong impression. Clever wordsmiths, image makers, and advertisers are very skilled at this.

Years ago, I cut out a cartoon that showed a man driving his recently purchased used car back into the lot with a look of serious disappointment on his face. Above the entrance was a sign that read, "Guaranteed Used Cars." In the caption, the lot manager was explaining, "You misinterpreted the sign: We guarantee the cars to be used."[2] Often in our society, the skills for conveying a true impression are used cleverly to entrap.

People are often told to read the fine print before signing a contract. Why? What is there in the fine print? Why is it placed in fine print? The great persuaders know that people generally overlook the fine print; and even if they do read it, they generally don't understand it, or they conclude it must not be very important or else it would be in large print. The failure to convey the truth or the deliberate attempt to distort the truth occurs in oral communication as well as written.

Recently, over the radio, I have heard advertisements that encourage people to invest in commodities, which are generally regarded as high-risk investments. One of the advertised commodities is heating oil. During most of the 60-second advertisement the speaker paints a glowing picture of how you can leverage $5,000 into $20,000 in just a few short months. Other similar ads declare how you can earn 100 percent a month on your investment. In the last 5 or 10 seconds of these ads, the voice speaks so fast that it's almost impossible to hear, let alone understand what is being said. The voice mumbles quick phrases like, "This return is not guaranteed; you could lose all your investment," and other statements designed to meet the technical requirements of the law, but they certainly don't meet the requirements of being a skillful truth teller—they surely don't convey a true impression. In this case, the most important thing for investors to know is that these are very high-risk investments. But such fear-inducing aspects are skillfully downplayed and even subverted. The impression conveyed is that everyone will have great opportunities for quick wealth without any but a little risk. (At the end of one of the ads, one advertiser cynically comments, "Oh, the lawyers make us put this in . . ." Then quickly, as though it were unimportant, the qualifications and limitations are routinely stated like some monotone and pedantic bureaucratic poetry.)

For those who aspire to being honest, you must recognize that desire alone does not make a person honest. To be an effective truth teller, you must acquire and practice the proper skills. You must be able to distinguish what is true from what is false, and cultivate the skills to convey the truth so that it is properly understood by recipients.

CASE: *Sincere, but False*

For several days there had been talk around the factory floor that a larger company was planning to buy out Pacific Manufacturing Company. Pacific supplied parts to many large manufacturers and assemblers, and the company employed nearly 300 people.

The foreman of one of the departments began to be concerned about the rumors because of the implications they had for his job and also because of the effect they were having on employee morale. After listening to the rumors for several days, the foreman decided to get to the heart of the matter. The next afternoon, while things seemed to be going smoothly on the floor, he quietly slipped away to the superintendent's office on the second floor of the administrative section of the building. When the secretary ushered him into his boss's office, the foreman closed the door and sat down. After relating to the superintendent the talk he had been hearing on the factory floor, the foreman asked, "Is there any truth to these rumors? I just need to know."

The superintendent knew that negotiations had been underway for a possible buyout. And just that morning he had been in the president's office, where he had been given strict instructions to "keep this absolutely quiet. In the next two days we will be in very sensitive negotiations, so 'mum's' the word. Flatly deny that any talks are going on if you have to." So, according to his instructions and faithful to the trust the president had placed in him, the superintendent told the foreman, "There isn't going to be a buyout. You know that there will always be rumors going around in this industry. This is just more groundless talk."

The foreman returned to his crew, and, during a coffee break, he explained to them that he had investigated the rumors and there would be no buyout of Pacific Manufacturing Company.

Three days later it was publicly announced that "A successful merger has been negotiated between Pacific Manufacturing Company and General Systems, Inc. The owners and management of both companies are pleased with the arrangements. The Pacific Manufacturing plant will take on the name of the other company, but otherwise it is expected that company operations will continue as they have in the foreseeable future." Business as usual.

Questions:

1. If you were the foreman, how would you feel? What would you do?

2. Did the foreman tell a falsehood? If so, does that make him a liar?

3. Does the sincerity with which he spoke to his crew make him a truth teller?

4. Can a person be sincere and still be a liar?

5. Was the foreman a skilled truth teller? Should he have exercised more skill at finding out the truth? Should he have been more skillful at conveying his message to the crew?

Section Two

Dilemmas

Chapter 5

Is Lying Sometimes the Right Thing for an Honest Person to Do?

The True Man

Honor is something we all profess,
But most of us cheat—some more, some less—
An' the real test isn't the way we do
When there isn't a pinch in either shoe—
It's whether we're true to our best or not
When the right thing's certain to hurt a lot.

—Edgar A. Guest[1]

NOT LONG AGO, I attended a lunch for one of Rotary International's large clubs. While I was visiting with a senior executive of a large bank who was sitting at my right, the conversation turned to business ethics.

"Is lying sometimes the right thing for an honest person to do?" I asked him. Before he could answer, the CEO of a manufacturing company sitting on my left, who had not been involved in the conversation, blurted out, "Absolutely not!"

Turning in his direction I responded, "Why not?"

He said, "Lying is always wrong under any circumstance."

I asked him, "Do you have children?"

"Yes, we have five."

"And what did you tell them at Christmastime about Santa Claus?"

"Well . . ." he said in a subdued tone.

Then without waiting for an answer I asked the two men a series of questions: "Would you lie if it might save the life of a family member when confronted by a gunman? What if it would win a war? Would you lie to save your company from bankruptcy and preserve 1,500 jobs for the community? Would you lie to provide cash to meet Friday's payroll? Would you lie if you could preclude serious embarrassment for yourself or your company? Would you lie to avoid hurt-ing someone's feelings? Would you lie to help a child struggling with his or her self-image?"

The questions were followed by a pause, and then the CEO observed, "I guess I need to rethink this whole thing."

Indeed, the main object of this book is to help you and those around you rethink some of these things—or, in some cases, just get people to think.

Everyone Justifies Lying at Times

Assuming most people would admit that, yes, they would lie under most of these circumstances, it is fun to contemplate the ques-tion: When wouldn't we lie? Only when we would face no negative consequences?

By answering the question about whether lying is sometimes the right thing for an honest person to do with a "yes," we give rise to three main points, and both developing the skills to implement these points and managing the consequences of assuming that lying is occasionally justifiable and appropriate are critical for anyone who aspires to becoming a more honest person.

First: *We must recognize and acknowledge that we all justify lying and deception under certain conditions.* This point is an essential key to doing something about ethical behavior. As long as a manufactur-ing CEO thinks that people should always tell the truth but remains unaware that even he doesn't follow that guideline, he can do nothing to correct the situation. He will neither set for himself conscious guidelines that can give him direction as to when lying might be appropriate, nor will he police his own deceptions. We cannot correct unethical behavior if we are not even aware that we are engaging in it.

Second: *We must understand the implications of assuming that lying is sometimes justifiable and appropriate.* Once we acknowledge that under some circumstances lying is acceptable, even if those cir-cumstances are extremely rare, then arguing whether a person is hon-est or dishonest is a moot question, and further discussion of the issue is only wasted effort. If we admit that lying is sometimes okay, then claiming that we are honest people is a self-deception. The question that we should now discuss is "Under what circumstances is it per-missible to lie?"

To have an effective relationship with another person, having an understanding of the special circumstances in which that person will be dishonest will do much to maintain a healthy working relationship. For example, if I know that you think it's okay to lie about Santa Claus to your children, but I also know you would never mislead your employees about a decision to close a plant, then we can work together. Likewise, if I know that you consider it appropriate to be deceptive to avoid bankruptcy and then I assume that you would not mislead others to avoid personal embarrassment, when in fact you would, this could raise serious difficulties in our relationship.

For instance, computer whiz Michael Dell of Dell Computers started his highly successful business called PCs Limited by "purchasing IBM computers on the gray market. . . ."

> At the time, IBM did not allow dealers to sell PCs to anyone who would resell them. But unsold stock is every dealer's nightmare, so when Dell or his buyers knocked on back doors offering to buy up all the surplus stock at cost, retailers leapt at the chance. "I would go to, say a Computerland Store and tell the salesman I needed 10 or 20 computers. He would ask: 'Are these for resale?' And I'd say, 'No, I'm buying these for my fraternity brothers,' " says one of Dell's former buyers. Dell would then soup up the PCs with graphics cards and hard disks before reselling them.[2]

Knowing that Dell would engage in such deception with suppliers and competitors but not with employees or customers is the important thing to know. Since we have established that Dell and his staff are not honest in all circumstances, determining when he will be honest and when he will not is critical to a meaningful relationship. Otherwise, we can't rely on when Dell will deceive and when he won't.

Third: *Each person must establish deliberate and conscious guidelines for when lying is justified in business and when it isn't.* If such lines are not clearly and consciously drawn, then pressures rather than principles will dictate moral conduct. If there are no recognized guidelines, then no one can ever tell when a person is being honest or not. So, everyone would do better if they would stop mouthing the "always be honest" slogan and start talking about when it is okay and not okay to lie.

A good start is to discuss the questions listed previously in this chapter: Would I lie to avoid hurting someone's feelings? Would I lie to avoid serious embarrassment? Keep in mind the definition of truth as you go through such questions: "To tell the truth is not just to state the facts, but to convey a true impression."

When answering questions about when lying is justified and when it isn't, many people resort to the response, "Well, it depends upon the particular situation." They answer this way because they do not want to be tied to a rule or principle whenever truth telling would require them to pay a substantial price such as embarrassment, hurting someone's feelings, or losing an important contract that could jeopardize the company. Such a situational ethics approach, especially when combined with the motive to avoid being caught and cornered by some definite guideline, results in predictable consequences: People end up doing whatever the social or emotional pressures of the moment dictate. Rather than acting on the basis of ethical principles, they become reactors to or victims of the pressures of the moment. If people cannot make rational ethical decisions without the heat of crisis upon them, it is not likely they will make rational ethical decisions in the heat of battle.

Further, if people accept that lying may be appropriate in certain situations, then we have another important point to consider: the conflict between "what we say" and "what we do." For instance, if parents believe that certain circumstances would make some forms of deception appropriate, why do they teach their children to never tell a lie? Or, if employers acknowledge that certain lies are permissible, why do they demand strict honesty from their employees? Instead, shouldn't parents and employees raise their integrity and credibility by spending time with their children or employees to establish when deception is appropriate and when it isn't? By so doing, they can lift the level of integrity in the family or in the organization and come to some useful guidelines that everyone can agree upon. It seems that such a strategy would bring about a greater moral awareness.

The Noble Lie

One of the major traps that tends to draw aspiring honest people from the ethical path is the "noble lie." This trap is very similar to the "ends justifies the means" dilemma presented in Chapter 6. When someone feels that the goal is noble enough, any means including lying can be justified to attain it. The life and death struggle of war is one of the most obvious activities in which most people would feel that the nobility of the cause—victory—justifies the use of deception and lying in their grossest forms. Deliberately putting out absolutely false communiques about the locations of armaments or ships or intentionally leaking ostensibly secret false messages about troop movements are designed to lead the enemy to take actions that will assure "our" victory. In the meantime, the people back home are told about the "atrocities carried out by the enemy" which, in fact, never occurred, but the news garners public support for an overt attack on some group or country considered hostile. All of these actions are justified by the warring nations or factions as necessary to win in the "noble" cause of doing away with a "devil."

War is certainly a special case, but a fascinating irony is that corporate strategists often equate their economic battles with war, and they even begin to use war analogies and the language of war in their conversations and conferences. One company was known to hang pictures of a chief competitor's CEO on the company walls with the caption, "Don't forget who is the enemy." Employees often hear their bosses say things like, "Here is the battle plan," or, "We are really under attack from this competitor (or from the media)." All this war-like talk creates an atmosphere in which war tactics seem justified to win the "noble" prize. Deception, spreading unfavorable information about the opposition, leaking false rumors about company strategy, or engaging in industrial espionage now all seem legitimate. Thus, under "conditions of war" it appears to be okay to find out through surreptitious means what competitors are bidding on a contract so that a company can adjust its bid and win the contract.

In politics we often see candidates deviously demonized by their opponents through vicious rumors, dirty campaign tricks, false accusations, and the twisting of statements. All this is justified by the opponents in the "noble" cause of saving our country or government from destruction at the hands of the other party or candidate. Similarly, in business, those in power frequently engage in cover-ups and make misleading statements because they feel that it's important to preserve the administration's positive image and keep "less qualified people" from taking over.

We learned during the Iran-Contra scandal of the 1980s about a concept known as "plausible deniability." Apparently, some of President Ronald Reagan's underlings felt it was important to keep certain truths from him so he could stand in public and honestly deny he'd had any knowledge of certain acts. These people reasoned it was so noble to preserve the President's image of integrity—so important to the country—that the deliberate deceit of the President was justified.

Even in the medical profession, "Doctors need to lie sometimes," reported a study by the *Journal of the American Medical Association*:

> A team of physicians at Brown University in Providence, Rhode Island, surveyed 211 physicians to see whether they would lie in . . . hypothetical cases. . . .
>
> Physicians were asked if they would lie to an insurance company in order to help a patient obtain reimbursement for a routine mammogram, an x-ray used to detect early stages of breast cancer. [In the real world, a large number of health insurance plans do not cover the costs of preventive screening tests such as mammograms.]
>
> In the hypothetical case, a healthy 52-year-old woman goes to her doctor for a routine physical exam. Her insurance plan will not pay for a mammogram, [except] with one exception: If the doctor conducts the test because he thinks the patient might have breast cancer, the insurance company will cover the cost. Otherwise, the woman will have to pay $200 out of her own pocket.
>
> [The question asked was:] Put yourself in the doctor's shoes. You have absolutely no reason to think your patient has cancer. Should you lie and write down on the insurance claim that the mammogram was performed to "rule out cancer"? Or should you tell the woman that if she wants the mammogram as part of her physical, she will have to pay for it herself?
>
> Nearly 70 percent of the doctors surveyed said they would lie. . . . The duty to advocate in the interest of one's patient sometimes requires lying.[3]

Or, suppose a child is struggling with his self-image and has low self-confidence. He tries a significant new task, say a public performance, and does very poorly. Should you just be honestly frank? Or does the "noble" end of building self-confidence justify you in conveying an impression that the event wasn't as bad as it seemed to him? Should you select a minor good aspect of the experience and blow it up so that the child really feels that he did better than either of you actually think? What if you or someone else makes him feel good about the experience, and the boy decides to continue to try something that, had he been given your honest feedback, he gladly would have given up on? On the other hand, what if your blunt honesty causes the child to give up on something he wants with all his heart and could have developed as a talent had he continued?

A friend of mine, Cyril Figuerres, related to me a story of how his parents had done something similar to him by withholding information about his ethnic background to protect his positive self-image. According to his account:

> When I was a young boy growing up in Lahaina, Maui, I loved reading comic books, especially about GI Joe. From comic books, I soon learned that the American soldiers were always the "good guys" who wore nicely fitted uniforms. They were courageous, fought cleanly, and were always victorious. In contrast, the Japanese soldiers were always the "bad guys" who wore baggy, dingy uniforms. They were cowards who fought with dirty tactics and always suffered defeat. Even the acoustical property of their respective rifles differed. The American rifles had a rapid, crisp sound: "rat-tat-tat-tat-tat." But, the Japanese rifles had a slow, sluggish sound: "buddha-buddha-buddha." (Perhaps the comic book writer thought the great Buddha was reincarnated as a Japanese rifle!)
>
> My favorite pastime was to play GI Joe at the beach. My buddies and I would pretend we were attacking the beachhead, yelling, "Rat-tat-tat-tat-tat! Kill those dirty Japs!"
>
> Then came the day of reckoning. One day, an older boy disrupted one of our exciting beach attacks and said to me, "Why you shooting the Japs? You neva know you one Jap?" (Translation: "You never knew you were Japanese?")
>
> I protested, "No, I not one Jap!"
>
> "Yes, you one Jap!" he insisted.
>
> "No, I not!" I said. I absolutely refused to believe it.
>
> The next day, I asked my schoolteacher, and she confirmed what the awful boy had claimed. I felt devastated. I didn't want to be a "dirty Jap."[4]

Cyril felt betrayed by his parents who had never told him about his heritage: His father was Filipino and his mother Japanese, and he looked oriental. If you had been in his situation, would you have judged his parents as dishonest for withholding the truth about his ancestry? The way he tells the story, his parents had *intentionally and willingly* withheld the truth, which eventually resulted in devastating emotional consequences. Nevertheless, he knew their intent was pure and benevolent. They had spared him—and themselves—from dealing with one of the darkest periods of Japanese-American history during World War II, including overt Japanese aggression toward the United States, but which also involved America's betrayal of its Japanese-American citizens, the use of Japanese internment camps, and other atrocities. In this case, the cover-up backfired.

In a corporation, when someone does a foolish thing that could be publicly embarrassing—such as badly scarring the company's image or negatively affecting the stock price for thousands of stockholders—is a cover-up justified? If the media begins to suspect something and point fingers, is deliberately denying the accusation, although it is true, justified? Should the company simply hire a good public relations firm to put the best possible spin on the matter and minimize negative fallout? In such cases, how often do CEOs instruct their principal mouthpieces, "Now whatever you do, go out there and tell them the truth"? But are public relations firms hired to tell the truth? If telling the truth is what an organization wants to do, why should they need to hire a public relations firm?

The Little White Lie

Another major trap that haunts aspiring ethical people is the seductive "little white lie." The thinking seems to be that whenever we tell a small, insignificant, no-one-gets-hurt kind of a lie, then lying could be the right thing to do. Teaching children about a Santa Claus who lives at the North Pole with elves and reindeer could be one example. Handing out unjustified compliments or flattery may be another example. But what about lying about your age by only a year? What if a lie about age occurs on a driver's license application, and an underage driver hits the street in his father's souped-up Corvette?

President Dwight D. Eisenhower placed a great deal of emphasis on integrity in his career. He was a model of honesty, and that honesty was generally a key aspect of his public image. But Merle Miller, in his biography of him, gives clear evidence that Ike lied about his age on his application to West Point, but only by one year. He was aware that to get into the Naval Academy at Annapolis, he could not be older than 19, but he was 20 years old. And, thinking that the same rule applied to West Point, he wrote on his application a date that showed him to be 19 years old.[5]

Is this one of those deceptions that is so small and insignificant that it's okay? Besides, look at what his education and career enabled him to do in the service of his country and mankind. Does the promise of a good result or the hope of a better result justify the "little white lie"? In Eisenhower's case some may argue that he was justified. But, had he not been so successful, would we still feel that it was okay for him to lie? As it turned out, the age requirements at West Point were different. An honest answer about his age would not have kept him out. But does this fact make the lie less significant and perhaps even more justifiable? When a person intentionally lies, is it not just as morally wrong whether it would make any difference in the outcome or not? Eisenhower's fudging by one year on his age is perhaps not significant. But with the limited admissions at West Point, if his lying had allowed Ike to occupy a slot that perhaps would have left some other honest young man out, how significant was the lie? What if that person had been able to accomplish an even greater work? We'll never know.

According to one argument, even small lies are as morally corrupting as the big ones. The big ones may have far more devastating results, but the impact on society's moral fiber is no different.

So, Is Lying Sometimes the Right Thing?

So, is lying sometimes the right thing for an honest person to do? The answer is yes. In fact, nearly everyone lies periodically with "good justification." Now that this fundamental question is out of the way and you can get on with reading this book, what skills are necessary to manage this phenomenon without becoming a pathological liar?

The guideline that "I will never tell a lie," in light of what we have just discussed, is likely not possible. Even the skill of setting precise and useful guidelines is challenging. Here are two *examples* of such guidelines:

One person's guideline might be: "Lying is only justified under unusual and extraordinary circumstances." The few justifiable situations could be (1) when human life is in jeopardy, and (2) when a major institution, such as a church, university, or country is threatened. On the other hand, major embarrassments; loss of jobs, reputations, or contracts; sharp declines in stock value; and hurting people's feelings would generally not justify lying.

Another person's guideline might be: "In many circumstances lying may be appropriate." And this person's situations could be if the truth would hurt someone's feelings, cause the person to lose his or her job, cause great embarrassment to himself or herself or to the company, create a major loss of stockholders' money, disrupt the person's work group, or be seen as an act of disloyalty. In other words, whenever telling the truth would entail an economic or emotional cost, then lying is justified for that person, particularly when it is evident that the person will not get caught.

Anyone who aspires to being an ethical person must spend some conscientious effort in deciding when lying would be justified and then articulate meaningful and practical guidelines. I strongly suggest that you carefully consider the first example of guidelines given above—that lying is justified only in highly unusual and extenuating circumstances that involve the lives of close family members and associates. This more difficult path will help you avoid starting down a slippery slope of justification and rationalization that can lead to severe penalties. Start by making a list of specific situations that would definitely justify lying and another list of specific situations that definitely would not justify lying. Even if you or your group do not come up with a clear-cut, all-inclusive list, the exercise, in and of itself, will help you to gain greater awareness and enhance your skills to handle one of the major problems of honesty.

CASE: Birthday Shirt

Pam and Hal had not been married very long. Pam was so in love with Hal that she wanted to do something extra special for his upcoming birthday. The two were still students, and money was tight. Although she'd had very little experience in sewing, she decided that with time and concentration she could make a shirt for him, and the effort would show him how much she really cared. For six weeks she worked on the shirt secretly so that it would be a total surprise. She completed it just in time for his birthday.

Pam prepared a special dinner and had the meal all ready and the table set by the time Hal arrived home from his part-time job. After they ate dinner, Pam went to the bedroom and retrieved a handsomely wrapped box. Returning to the dinner table, she smiled, gave Hal a tender kiss and a hug, and wished him Happy Birthday.

Hal carefully removed the paper and opened the box while Pam watched with heightened anticipation. The style of collar and pattern of the cloth left Hal feeling that he would not want to be seen in public wearing the shirt. He had never worn a color like that, nor would he want to. And, when he held it up, he could tell right away that the sleeves would not fit.

At that moment Pam leaned forward, and, with excitement in her voice, asked, "How do you like the shirt, dear? I made it myself."

Questions:

1. If you were Hal, what would you say next?

2. Is this a time to be perfectly honest? Does this situation justify lying?

3. Keep in mind that "I really appreciate the effort you put into making it" really doesn't cut it, because Pam asked how Hal liked the shirt. So, if you were Hal and Pam prodded you for your answer, how would you respond to her now?

4. If you were Pam, how would you want Hal to respond?

Chapter 6

Noble Ends, Ignoble Means

"Lying, for instance, is not taboo but a necessary tool in battling Satan. Falsehoods help convert non-believers; they are therefore praised as 'heavenly deceptions.'"

—*Reverend Sun Myong Moon*[1]

WHEN ASKED IF the ends ever justify the means, most people, after a few moments of thought, will usually reply, "Yes." We can likely cite many examples in which otherwise unethical, immoral, and abhorrent behavior is justified when the ends are noble. For example, killing is generally considered wrong and even sinful and evil. Yet, when the object is lofty enough, very moral people engage in killing with little compunction, such as when a nation's freedom is threatened. Ethical and moral people voluntarily take up arms and march off in pursuit of the enemy and would threaten and willingly kill them. Or, when an individual is physically threatened, people often feel justified in killing one another "in self-defense."

The whole world of spying and espionage, CIA-style, with its deception, lying, double-dealing, cheating, duplicity, and subversive actions seems to be justified to the tune of several billions of dollars annually by respected, honorable Americans, especially when we feel we are being threatened by enemies or potential enemies. At times Americans apparently even feel that spying on their own allies is justifiable. Although spying on a friend doesn't seem ethical, in 1993 the CIA was found to be engaged in espionage against France.[2]

Although these incidents may seem far away from the lives of ordinary people, the same types of things arise in the lives of all people. Does the noble end of maintaining stockholder value justify coloring the facts or withholding potentially damaging information? Does preserving the reputation of an organization or an individual justify us in telling only part of the truth? Is avoiding hurting someone's feelings a noble enough end to justify questionable means—deceit?

Trust Is Critical for Bankers

Consider the case of one bank, with its depositors, stockholders, and employees. In 1984 Granite Savings & Loan (disguised name) was insured by the State Financial Insurance Agency. But, the agency was scheduled to go out of business in January of the following year. In the meantime, the trust company was earnestly trying to qualify for FDIC insurance, but so far had not been able to do so. In December, one month before the dissolution of the State Insurance Agency, a judicial court hearing considered the situation. The bank owners argued that if they had just three more months, they could qualify for FDIC insurance and thereby preserve the depositors' savings and stay in business. Granite was well-managed and profitable, and the depositors' savings were safe and secure.

However, one dangerous aspect of the case still loomed over the whole matter: If it were publicly announced that the bank's deposits were uninsured, most felt that the depositors would make a run on the bank to withdraw their funds, causing the savings and loan to close even though it was otherwise fiscally sound. That day, everyone in the courtroom—examiners, bank regulators, trust owners, lawyers, the judge, and local media representatives—agreed that in this case the ends were noble enough to justify the devious means of keeping depositors in the dark for a short time until other measures could be implemented. Their reasoning was that banks and trust companies operate on trust, and by maintaining that trust for a few months until the FDIC insurance came through, no one would be hurt and everyone would come out ahead.

So it was agreed. The media agreed that as long as no one else let the cat out of the bag they could keep quiet—but if anyone leaked any information, they would feel free to grab the scoop and report the whole story.

Through January and February, Granite managers worked diligently to gain the important right to claim, "Insured by the FDIC." They applied and received word back that their application had been "approved," but they would not be insured until three other conditions were met. By March, two of the three conditions had been fulfilled. The third one, "Increase financial capital," had not yet occurred. But everyone was working on the problem, and they anticipated gaining the needed capital within a couple of weeks.

So confident were the managers in their ability to achieve this final requirement that in March they erected a temporary sign on the front lawn of the bank's main office. Clearly visible to everyone who traveled along the busy thoroughfare nearby would be the words "This bank is FDIC approved." Technically, the statement was true because the trust had received a letter from the FDIC saying "Your application has been approved," but then the letter had listed the conditions that must be met before insurance would be issued.

Of course, the sign was a lie. In fact, a fundamental part of the whole banking operation was a lie. Why? What were the lies? First, most depositors had been led to believe that their deposits were insured unless they were told otherwise. The trust company allowed them to continue to believe that they were insured when, in fact, they were no longer insured. This lie was perpetrated by simply withholding information. Second, those who read the sign as they traveled the highway likely would not distinguish between "FDIC approved" and "FDIC insured"—thinking that they were one and the same. The clever use of language was a lie: Although it was technically correct, it gave the wrong impression, and "To tell the truth is not just to state the facts but to convey a true impression."

So it seems that those in charge of the trust company felt that the end—to avoid bank closure by precluding a run on the bank and maintaining trust—was noble enough to justify the means of ethically questionable and deliberately deceptive and dishonest behavior.

When Are Ignoble Means Justified?

If we are to suggest that the end justifies the means in certain instances but not all of the time, how can we distinguish between the cases in which we ethically would be justified and when we would not? It is not enough to say that your conscience will be your guide: In the savings and loan case, the bank managers were, and still are, considered "honorable" leaders in the community. But, at the same time, not being able to make the "right" decision under competitive pressure or when faced with the pressure to "save people's investments" has seduced many people across ethical and even legal lines in such cases.

Perhaps a useful, conceptual way of viewing the problem would help. Consider three general relationships between ends and means:

1. The ends are noble and great compared to the means, which are questionable or borderline ethical.

Ends—Noble   *Means—Borderline*

2. The ends and the means are balanced.

Ends—Moderately Good   *Means—Moderately Unethical*

3. The ends are only of minor value compared to the means.

Ends—Of Questionable Value   Means—Ignoble

Under these three scenarios, we can begin to set some reasonable guidelines about when questionable means may be justifiably employed to obtain some end:

    1. The ends may justify the means only when the ends are many times greater in value than questionable means.

    2. Whenever the ends and means are roughly the same weight of good and bad, the means are rarely justified, if ever.

    3. When the ends have little value compared to the gross wrong of the means, the means should never be justified.

In this thinking, it is not the absolute value of good or bad that matters, but the relative balance or imbalance between the two. That is, an end may have only moderate value, but if the means are only slightly over the line they may be justified in some cases.

Others may rightly argue that only the most noble of goals would justify unethical behavior. In other words, it should be a rare event. Before anyone decides to do something unethical to accomplish some goal, the merits of the goal should be tested to make sure they are so weighty as to be justified without question. Even though achieving a goal without ever resorting to unethical means may be difficult, embarrassing, and perhaps even cause significant loss, I believe that we should make sure that our cause is universally noble before we ever resort to unethical means.

Building Awareness

However, because it is such a widespread practice for the ends to justify the means even in small matters, I have emphasized the relationship between noble ends and ignoble means to encourage people to be more conscious of their decisions and their behavior rather than simply falling prey unconsciously to the seductions and pressures of stepping over the ethical line.

Again, as people become more aware of these issues, they will tend to make better informed and more ethical decisions rather than be trapped by the constant pressure to step over the line. I am not asking that everyone cease and desist with the practice of pursuing noble ends with questionable means; that would be unrealistic. But I hope that by raising the issues and stirring the debate, our decline in ethical standards can be slowed or even reversed. This could happen if each person, through conscious and deliberate effort, would refrain from giving in to the use of unethical means to obtain some end or marginal value. Begin by practicing in your games of Solitaire, in your local competitive sports, in your idle conversations with friends, peers, and associates. Then, work on how you pursue your financial and personal goals and career advancements. Before you know it, you will have "a reputation for integrity" to uphold, and you won't want to risk your new-found personal power by engaging in some shady and petty activity.

"The ends do not justify the means" should be the fundamental guideline. In real life, there may be some exceptions. But, in those exceptional cases, we should make sure and consciously decide that the questionable means really are justified and worth the potential risk to our character—the end should be so noble and worthy in relation to the unethical means necessary to attain it that everyone concerned would agree that it passes the test.

The Ends-Means Trap Is Subtle

However, the ends-means trap is more subtle than this, and for this reason I have dedicated a whole chapter to it. If we were to proceed based on what I've written up to this point, someone may be led to assume that when an ends versus means decision arises that (1) there will be an ethical decision involved, and (2) the person will clearly see, up front, what unethical means might be needed to carry it off. I wish it could be so clear-cut. But two things typically make things more difficult:

First, these conflicts often come to us in such a subtle manner that we generally don't know or recognize what we are getting ourselves into until it's difficult to back out—we're trapped. Initially, the end looms in front of us with such great value that the unethical behavior which is seemingly necessary to attain it is hidden from us or not fully understood. So, the ends appear to be of great and noble value compared to the apparently harmless unethical means.

Second, the "frog principle" comes into play, which we will discuss in Chapter 14. In the case of Granite Savings & Loan, the managers hoped and expected, when they put the deceptive sign on their lawn, that only a couple more weeks would be required to qualify for FDIC insurance. Instead, a couple of weeks lingered into several weeks, making it necessary to extend the lie, while the managers still figured that only one or two more weeks would do it. Then several weeks stretched into many weeks. When the bubble burst, the bank owners still expected that just a few more days would help them make everything right.

Was the Bank's Dishonesty Justified?

What finally happened? To recap, the original decision to keep the trust company's uninsured status a secret occurred in December. The State Financial Insurance Agency went out of business in January. All of the parties privy to the knowledge that the bank's depositors were uninsured kept their word. The FDIC insurance approval process dragged on through February, March, and into April. At that time, the judge called another hearing to evaluate the circumstances. Due to the state's open meeting law, a reporter from the community's leading television station was in attendance, and he felt it was about time that the withheld knowledge should become public knowledge. He wondered whether he should be a responsible citizen and inform the public of what he knew, or run the risk that some other reporter would get the scoop. He also felt that he would be derelict in his duty if he failed to report something as important to the community as the financial welfare of hundreds of depositors. Indeed, he reasoned, he had been wrong not to report the case last December.

The reporter decided to report the uninsured status of the trust company. When the bankers tried to persuade him otherwise, he refused their pleadings, but he agreed that he would not air the segment until after the close of business on Friday. The report was then seen by the public on the evening news. Bank owners, state regulators, federal officials, and executives from other banks worked frantically over the weekend to avert a crisis. The other bank executives knew that if one trust company failed, it could trigger an industry-wide chain reaction of bank depositors withdrawing their funds because of the violation of the perceived reliability and security of savings and loans.

Before the bank opened on Monday, arrangements had been made for the second largest savings and loan in the state to take over the trust company's assets and become the new owners of Granite Savings & Loan, effective immediately. The new owners were FDIC insured. The local presses and television stations were thorough in informing the public of the deal, so when the bank opened on Monday morning the smooth transition helped to avert a major crisis.

In this case, does the end justify the means? Discuss the case with your managers, employees, family, or your church group. An open discussion can help you determine where your group agrees on ethical standards and where it disagrees and establish guidelines for future ethical conduct in your group. At least a discussion will help you develop greater awareness of the real-world challenges of becoming an honest and ethical person.

Some of the questions you might wrestle with could be: Did the reporters, bankers, regulators, lawyers, and judge do the "right thing" by deciding to withhold information from the public in the first place? If the trust company had succeeded in obtaining FDIC insurance by the end of February would you still feel the same? Did the reporter do the "right thing" by making the issue public? Was he duty-bound as a reporter to do so? Was he acting as a responsible citizen? Even at the time Granite was acquired at the end of April, the bankers still were confident that just a few more days would have produced the necessary capital. Would you have recommended that the reporter and the others give the bank 10 more days? 15 more days? 21? Another "month or two"? If the reporter had not run the story in April, when would you have made the problem public? Whose responsibility was it to decide? When should it have been decided? Should a reporter decide the fate of a bank? Was anyone hurt by the deception at any time—depositors, bankers, reporters, regulators? If no one was hurt, was the deception ethical? Was it dishonest to put the sign "FDIC approved" in front of the bank, or was that action just a bit of sales "puffery"? If you had been an employee of the bank during the time it was uninsured and your parents had their life savings in the bank, would you have encouraged them to withdraw their money and deposit it in an insured bank? Would you have blown the whistle?

Whenever we consider using unethical means to attain some justifiable end, we become vulnerable to being seduced into a trap on the wrong side of the ethical line. If you want to be an ethical person, be prepared to pay the price at least some of the time.

CASE: Moving to Mexico

The Barton Textile Factory was a major employer in a small Midwestern town. Three hundred people were on the payroll. Although the jobs were not really high-paying, the typical $6 per hour wage helped many families to make ends meet in this rural part of the state.

Competition in the clothing industry was very intense, and margins were very tight, but the operation had always been profitable. Then, the owners learned that they could open a factory across the border in Mexico where they could hire as many employees as they needed for only $.60 per hour—significantly increasing profits for the company. This would eliminate the advantage that other manufacturers had who were already manufacturing offshore.

To keep from killing the morale of the employees, the announcement to the public was kept secret until just two months before the owners decided to shut down the factory. Two months later, the factory closed on schedule, and the operation moved to Mexico. The town was devastated, for no other local employers could take up the slack.

Questions:

1. Did the noble end—significantly enhanced profits—justify the ignoble means—leaving a town economically high and dry?

2. Were the owners ethically responsible?

3. Did the company owe the town anything? If so, what?

4. Should the owners have given the town a longer lead time, or at least let the employees know they were thinking about it? How early? Should they have given the town another month? More time?

5. Was management ethical to keep the move secret at all? Was it ethical to move the factory?

Chapter 7

Everybody Does It, or "When in Rome . . ."

"He who is ever brooding over results often loses nerve in the performance of duty. . . . He who broods over results is like a man given to objects of senses—he is ever distracted; he says goodbye to all scruples; everything is right in his estimation, and he therefore resorts to means fair and foul to attain his end."

—*Mahatma Gandhi[1]*

DURING THE SUMMER of 1968, Henry Rover, the young assistant to the president of a major life insurance company, found himself facing a minor crisis in carrying out one of his responsibilities. He was to administer the annual company-financed tour for all agents and their spouses who had attained their sales quota for the year. Each year the company sponsored an all-expense-paid trip to some exotic place such as the Caribbean or Hawaii. It was important that everything went smoothly so when the agents returned from the trip they would have pleasant memories that would serve as an incentive to work for a similar trip the following year. This year the vacation was to be two weeks in Europe. About 750 agents had won the trip, and, with their spouses, at least 1,500 people would be traveling.

Henry arranged for three planes to fly a total of 500 people every two weeks from the States to Europe, using the Madrid Airport in Spain as the European staging area. One Thursday morning in the middle of the effort, Henry was checking on a few last-minute details for Friday's logistical challenge: He would be supervising the unloading of 500 people from the three planes that were just arriving from the States, seeing them off to a happy start on their journey through Europe, boarding 500 others who were now in Madrid's hotels onto the plane for the trip home, and trying to be pleasant about the whole matter—he wanted to make this part of the trip a fitting climax to what likely had been an exciting two-week stay in Europe for the agents.

At 10:00 a.m. that same morning, Henry received word that a security scare had occurred at the airport. Since the airport was not equipped with modern x-ray or metal detecting equipment, this meant that the passengers' suitcases would be set out on the apron at the side of the plane with all passengers standing by while each suitcase was hand-searched by security guards. Obviously, it would be a tedious and inconvenient process, if not entirely irritating and potentially uncomfortable—hardly a fitting climax to a joyous vacation.

After some thought, Henry contacted the airport chief of security, Señor José Gonzales, and invited him and his staff to come to one of the finest hotels in Madrid that night for dinner. Señor Gonzales arrived with several of the members of his staff. As they sat down, with Henry's few assistants scattered among them, they noticed a small, nicely wrapped gift worth about $5 by the side of each plate. Next to the security chief's plate was a gift of slightly greater value, approximately $12.50.

After the dinner, Henry arose and tapped a spoon against his glass. Once he had everyone's attention he began:

> Señor Gonzales, we are pleased that you could be with us this evening. We are aware of the special demands placed upon you at this time because of the security scare, and so we feel honored that you could join us. You may wonder why we invited you here. Well, tomorrow morning at 11 a.m., we have 500 people to board onto three planes. And, knowing the security problem you face, we would like you to tell us how we can be of the most help in expediting that process so that our people can get away with as little inconvenience as possible and also minimize the extra burden of your responsibility. Señor Gonzales, please . . .

Henry gestured toward Señor Gonzales and sat down, and Señor Gonzales arose and said, "Señor Rover, this has been a most thoughtful gesture on your part and a very pleasant evening. Thank you so much for this wonderful dinner and for these splendid gifts that you have shared with each of us. If there is anything you can do, we will let you know." He smiled graciously and sat down.

The next morning, another American company arrived at the airport to board a plane at 7 a.m. It took the security team three hours to clear the baggage and load the plane. But, later that morning, Henry's three planes arrived on schedule at 10 a.m., were unloaded, and the passengers were taken efficiently to their hotels downtown. By 11 a.m., the planes were refueled and ready for loading. There was not a security guard in sight. The airline employees loaded the suitcases directly onto the planes from the agents' hands. Within 20 minutes, all 500 passengers were onboard the planes, and, in a very festive mood, they took off for home and arrived safely without delay or incident.

If you were the president of the insurance company and heard about this incident, would you: (1) promote Henry, (2) commend Henry, (3) do nothing, (4) reprimand Henry, or (5) fire Henry. Based on my experience, I believe that most executives would praise Henry for being such a good administrator who knows how to get things done, and they likely would not even inquire whether he had acted ethically or not. Results count, and Henry knew how to get results.

Two other questions are pertinent to our subject in this case: (1) Did Henry do anything wrong? (2) Will the president's reaction to the incident indicate how he feels about such behavior and set a standard of conduct for the people in the company? A discussion of these questions in your groups likely will reveal how concerned or unconcerned people are about such matters.

The Ethics of Management by Results

The modern-day, results-oriented philosophy of management, in many incidents, actually encourages unethical behavior among business managers, especially among middle and lower managers. The case just discussed identifies one of the causes that often encourages unethical conduct. The essence of management by results is that managers are judged on the economic results they produce, rather than on character or other qualities. The great emphasis placed by managers on results is one of the primary causes of unethical conduct and has to do with two powerful motivators: (1) the often intense pressure to obtain results, and (2) the system of rewards for those who attain them. Let's look at these two motivators in detail:

First, results-oriented management has a built-in value system that demands that results be the most important concern, if not the exclusive concern, of the organization. This pressure forces people to search constantly for ways to improve. And frequently, the place to look for such ways is in the borderline area of what is ethical or unethical. As competitive and managerial pressures mount, the temptation to step over the line—to stretch the truth, engage in questionable acts of bribery or "mordida," withhold information, etc.—becomes greater and greater until people succumb, especially when the few counter forces, if there are any, are weak in comparison to those pressures.

Second, the systems for rewarding people for results are another impetus for improper behavior. Usually when sales or other goals are met or new records are achieved, seldom does anyone ask if they were achieved ethically. When young managers accomplish a difficult task in record time, no one inquires if they cut any corners. On the contrary, they are acclaimed, rewarded, and held up as examples for others to follow, regardless of how they achieved the goal. Often, other people know about the questionable methods in which the champions indulge. These people see the recognition received and assume that the higher-ups must approve of such behavior, even though it is likely the higher-ups are not aware and usually don't bother to inquire. Too often in business, only the results count—inquiries about conduct are not made by top management unless someone complains. Oh yes, every company has its policy statements or memos about honesty and ethics, but from the employees' point of view, the standard is based on recognition of performance—action—and not on the employee handbook—mere words.

Our economic system continues to reinforce the rewarding of results while ignoring or avoiding any evaluation of the moral behavior that may have been used to attain the results. Over the past few decades, popular writing about business management has enshrined the concept of employee results, and generally *only* results, as the proper evaluation of a businessperson's behavior without giving any attention or concern to the standard of ethics of the person.

When I shared the example of Henry, in the case at the start of this chapter, with a highly successful insurance executive, he replied, "Well, I know what 95 percent of the other insurance presidents would do—they would commend and promote him." And when I asked him what *he* would do, he replied cautiously, "Well, I don't know, but Henry sure engaged in bribery."

Rewards Versus Policy

Results are so overwhelmingly important that when a company wins a big new contract, or if profits improve 75 percent, few bother to ask, "Was this accomplished in an ethical manner?" As a result of the failure to ask this question, several senior executives in large electric companies were indicted for price fixing. They pled "not guilty" to the charges, claiming that they didn't know what their subordinates were doing. However, with a few penetrating questions about ethical conduct, these executives could have turned up some suspicious activity. But, for the most part, no one asked, or else they only asked superficially. If people would search for unethical behavior with the same vigor that they search for unprofitable operations, most questionable acts could be revealed and purged or corrected.

In a more recent case, an airplane manufacturer was charged by the Justice Department for paying illegal sales commissions on its overseas sales. Company executives pointed out that the company has a printed policy against such activities, but, in conversations with the sales representatives, it became evident that the reward system for making sales outweighed the policy statements to the extent many reps maintained they were not even acquainted with the policy.

The problem of reward for results has its roots deeper than just company practices in the past three decades. It pervades our society. President Lyndon B. Johnson is one example of this. Surely, Johnson produced results, was successful in business, and finally attained the highest position of power and prestige the world had to offer. In his congressional district, as a representative, he produced more results for his constituents than probably any other congressman. His biographer writes that LBJ's ambition was "so fierce, so consuming, that no consideration of morality or ethics, no cost to himself—or anyone else—could stand before it." His genius was "for discerning a path to power, an utter ruthlessness in destroying obstacles in that path, and a seemingly bottomless capacity for deceit, deception, and betrayal in moving along it."[2]

We might say that Johnson's successful, results-oriented philosophy was already well-established at least three hundred years before Johnson. Baltasar Gracian, a Spanish Jesuit, wrote, "Win affection . . . learn how to be evasive . . . to enslave our natural superiors by the use of cunning is a novel kind of power, among the best that life can offer." He continues, "A victor needs no explanations. The majority do not look closely into circumstantial detail, but only at a successful or unsuccessful outcome; thus, one's reputation never suffers if one's object is attained."[3]

Surely, similar attributes and philosophies are found in other modern-day captains who know how to produce results. We might ask: Is it even possible, in a competitive and ruthless environment, to succeed in business (that is, become wealthy) without exercising some of these attributes at least in part?

This all suggests that if we in business really do have a sincere concern about honesty and ethics, we should consider more than just economic results when we select people for promotion or other recognition. Rewards establish and communicate what we mean by honesty and how much we care or do not care about it.

"Don't Ask, Don't Tell"

The story of a successful automobile dealership is another case in point. Consider the example of a man I will call Abner Sebald. Abner decided to leave his partnership in the retail office supplies world in the 1950s. He looked around for the best opportunity he could find to make it on his own, and he finally decided to acquire an auto dealership that was available for purchase in town. He knew little of the automobile business, but he was an excellent salesman and was well-known and well-liked in the community. One person said about him, "Anyone can trust Abner." So, Abner acquired the business, and over the next several years he became successful far beyond his dreams.

After almost 20 years of success in the automobile business, and after having become a man of influence in his home state, I called on him and found him to be in a rare solemn mood. As we sat on a bench in front of his business, he related to me an experience that was obviously troubling him.

He told about how, when he first purchased the dealership, he had recognized his ignorance of the business, so he had inquired of a few experienced auto dealers in the area, asking, "What are the keys to success in this business?" He soon got the message that dealerships are made or broken on the used car lot. Reselling the trade-ins was the key. So, he resolved to find a top manager for the used cars. He kept hearing about one man who had been managing a used car lot in a neighboring state. Eventually, he became acquainted with the man, Joe Steritt, and made him a very attractive offer to work for him. Joe lived up to his reputation; in a short time the business became highly profitable.

To increase used car sales, the company would occasionally send two or three employees to California to buy good used cars, drive them back, and refurbish them before selling them. The "ringer" cars often brought in customers just to see what was available, and sometimes those customers would make a purchase. So, the reputation of the dealership was improving.

Just a few days before our conversation, Abner explained, Joe (who was still the used car manager), another employee, and Abner's son Brad (who was home for the summer from graduate school in the East) had just returned from such a trip. Just after they arrived back at the shop, Brad approached his father and asked, "Dad, I want to know if you really believe all those things you taught me about honesty, or if it was just talk."

"What do you mean?" asked Abner, somewhat startled.

"Well, while we were driving back here, we were eating in a cafe. Joe was telling me how he markets these cars. He said he turns the odometers back on some of them. [This incident took place before federal laws prohibited this practice.] He says that on the Ford with 80,000 miles, he is going to make it 45,000."

After the conversation, Abner called Joe over to him and said, feebly, "Now Joe, we have talked before about turning back the odometers . . ."

"Yeah, I know," Joe interrupted. "But you want this part of the business to be profitable, right? And that car is a lot better car than the 80,000 miles showing on the dash."

In relating the incident, Abner told me that it immediately had become evident to his son that although Abner advocated high standards of honesty, he had tolerated something less on the used car side of the business. When it came down to it, Abner only checked the profitability of the lot, and he avoided making any inquiries about the day-to-day practices of "someone who knows how to manage a used car lot successfully." This incident, finally pointed out to him after over 20 years, was what had caused Abner's somber mood that day. Still, to this day, Abner is regarded as one of the two or three most honest businesspeople in the city. But it seemed to me that, at least for a while after this incident, he didn't feel that way.

"Everybody Is Doing It"

One of the entrapments for those who are earnestly pursuing results in a highly competitive society is the assumption or observation that "everyone is doing it." The feeling is that, in order to succeed in the face of aggressive competitors who are cutting ethical corners, you must do the same. If you are working in an industry, sport, or country where unethical behavior is frequently indulged in, those who try to stay above questionable behavior and stay in Arena A often lose and are working at a constant disadvantage.

For example, in a sport where others are taking steroids or other strength-enhancing supplements, those who strictly follow the rules are running against the odds and will likely lose. In a "non-contact" sport like basketball, those who try to avoid contact when their opponents willfully bump and run or push and shove are not likely to help win ballgames.

Or, in an industry where low-balling is common practice, or at least where key rivals engage in the practice, it's hard to succeed unless you do the same. The "everybody does it" line seems to make it all okay, right?

Low-Balling. We discussed low-balling in Chapter 3, but it has an interesting twist in the retail automobile industry. A friend of mine from Texas who had been very successful in the business explained it to me, and added that it was one of the reasons he got out of the industry—he felt increasingly uncomfortable with the practice. Low-balling, in this industry (and a few others from what I can gather), is the art of price quoting. When a potential buyer comes in and asks the price of a certain car, the sales agent quotes a price below what he knows the buyer will have to pay to get the car.

The justification runs something like this: The agent is aware that most buyers will take the information and go to the next dealer to get another quote. The first agent knows the second agent will low-ball the customer, too. So, in order to get the customer to come back a second time to talk seriously about purchasing, the first agent's original price must be low enough compared to the next agent to bring the customer back. Later, either dealer will have plenty of time to add on delivery costs, make-ready costs, options, warranties, etc. to make up the real price.

The whole process is much like a game of ping pong. The agents are professionals and hold the paddles. The customers are bounced from one side to the other, often with a clever spin of English added that causes them to react in unexpected ways. Agents who are experts in the game of low-balling have refined and perfected their skillful approaches many times over. They have developed the subtle psychological skills to high art.

In contrast, most customers seldom buy cars and are real neophytes. They rarely know when the agents are low-balling—let alone deal with them effectively. It's sort of like watching a professional tennis player take on a junior high school student as the professional tries to keep the game interesting.

"Favors." Speaking about my friend in Texas, another reason he left the retail automobile industry was because of the manufacturing

executives who came to visit each year. Nearly every winter the executives would hold a conference in his territory—El Paso. Among
other arrangements, he was expected to arrange for call girls to be
available for them. This really grated on his moral standards, "but, if
you want to keep in good with the big boys, you better go along. I
usually received extra favors from company executives because I
knew how to manage things," he explained.

Keeping Pace with the Competition

The feeling that to succeed you have to do what the competition
is doing is a common one. In the car rental business, for example, the
need to do what competitors do is widespread. A report in the *Wall
Street Journal* describes the plight a competitor would face if it did not
comply with industry practice, no matter how unethical. At that time
customers were reading advertisements about cars for rent at the unbelievable rate of $49.95 per week—it was not only unbelievable, it was
unrealistic. The quoted price seemed to have little or no relation to the
bill the customer would pay. With all the add-ons, customers would
end up paying about $175 per week. On the other hand, rental agen-
cies who tried to correct the practice were losing out to the companies
that were drawing customers in with apparently lower prices.

Frank Olson, then chairman of Hertz said, "Hertz had little choice
but to meet its smaller competitors such as Alamo, by doing some
unbundling of its own." The company first attempted to advertise
against the low-price come-ons but found that it continued to lose
ground against aggressive competitors, particularly in the Florida market, which he describes as the largest rental car market in the world.[4]

Unbundling. This "unbundling" technique, similar to low-
balling, is used in several industries. Unbundling is the practice of dis-
secting the actual costs of an item and then extracting some basic cost
for the purpose of advertising. Later, when the customer is ready to
pay, usually in advance, the company adds back all the other costs to
make up the total bill. In the case of car rentals, customers often must
pay extra for a 4-door rather than the advertised 2-door sedans that are,
strangely enough, not available; extra for the privilege of allowing
additional drivers to use the car; insurance costs that are often higher
than the per-day rental fee; airport access fees; astronomical gasoline
charges, and so on. An article in *Travel & Leisure* magazine shared the
experience of one fed-up reporter: "The quoted weekly rate of $159
for a Ford Taurus at Pensacola Airport came to $271.92."[5]

The same competitive urge that leads to low-balling and unbundling led one grocery store chain to advertise the wholesale price of its goods with a note in very small print at the bottom: "10 percent will be added on at the cash register." When compared to competitors' prices, the company's prices looked very favorable, until you arrived at the checkout counter and prepared to pay the inflated price. Still, the practice seemed to bring in good business, even though customers found it difficult to compare prices.

Insider Trading. The Wall Street scandal of 1986 is another example of the "everybody does it" philosophy. In this instance, the participants were using inside information illegally to make financial trades. I once served on an ethics panel discussion with one of the first men to be exposed and arrested in the fiasco. During an informal conversation I asked him, "What made you decide to turn yourself in and come clean?"

He replied, "Hell, I didn't turn myself in. They caught me red-handed."

"How did you get involved with this obvious wrongdoing?" I asked.

"You have to understand," he explained, "that environment was like a boiling cauldron—really high pressure. We didn't have the time or inclination to think about what was ethical or right. All you could think about is what it would take to win."

Apparently, his understanding of the rules of insider trading was not that it was illegal, which everyone understood, but that "everybody does it," and so they did. This thinking is backed up by a *Business Week*/Harris Poll conducted shortly after the scandal broke. Adults were asked, "How common do you think it is for people on Wall Street to engage in insider trading?" Sixty-three percent said very common or somewhat common. Then they were asked, "Suppose someone got a tip from a friend that the company he or she works for was going to be purchased for a lot more money than its current stock price. Would you, if you had the money, buy stock in that company or not?" Eighty-two percent said they would buy; only 14 percent said they wouldn't.[6] So, "Everybody does it" is widely used to justify unethical and illegal behavior.

"When in Rome . . ."

Bribery. Another example: In many countries, bribery is so appealing and commonplace that the corrupt practice is often justified by people who rationalize it to themselves and others by saying, "When in Rome, you must do as the Romans do." They explain that the practice is a part of their culture, and it will not go away. This is just the way you do business, they insist. It is accepted practice. They even argue that giving a bribe, "mordida," or "payola" is ethical. It's just the way the game is played in that country. So, if you're going to play, you'd better be willing to play by the same rules the others play by.

Some companies even plan and budget for the expenses and, in some cases, even base their international competitive strategies on the practice:

> A German corporation that pays bribes to do business abroad can legally claim tax deductions back home . . .
>
> A survey by the German Tax Line Service, which analyzes the impact of tax on business, has shown that as a strong mark makes exports more expensive, German companies try to compensate with higher bribes in standard international currency—the dollar. This only exacerbates the open-ended escalation of bribery costs. Indeed, the Japanese Economic Newswire has estimated that bribes worldwide cost businesses $45 billion last year; German companies alone reportedly pay $3.35 billion annually.[7]

Interestingly enough, in nearly every country under the sun, bribery and similar forms of political corruption are illegal. But, even in the face of these laws, bribery still seems to be the way of business in many countries. Without it, you won't get many contracts or permits. So, what should people do—go along with it or pay the ethical price? Tough call. And because many businesspeople are guided in these countries by the philosophy of "When in Rome . . ." their behavior feeds and nourishes the unethical and illegal practice rather than discouraging or stamping it out. They become part of the problem rather than part of the solution.

Such a practice can also backfire. Take Italy, for example, home of the "When in Rome . . ." argument. For years, Italy had the reputation as the place where bribery was always acceptable, and even legal. Well, it never was legal, but the people often acted as though it were. So pervasive was the practice that the head of the highly successful Olivetti Corporation, Carlo DeBenedetti, said, "Political kickbacks are the only way to keep a business alive in the corruption-filled Italian market." DeBenedetti also admitted in 1993 to paying more than $7 million to political parties.[8]

So commonly accepted had the practice become in Italy that even the politicians began to acknowledge their overt roles in it. Alfredo Vito of Naples, the most popular member of Parliament, was indicted for accepting bribes. He decided to give up his seat in Parliament and tell all: "I am the bribe collector for the Christian Democracy," he explained. "Bribery is a consequence of this system that I have decided to abandon forever. . . . People want honesty and transparency, and we are finished."[9] The cleanup has reached into other major Italian cities, too. According to *U.S. News & World Report*, "The dragnet now has reached the highest level of Milan's government, catching some 30 people so far including two former mayors and several top businessmen, who have acknowledged paying bribes to city contractors."[10] Thus, a major result of the new "clean hands" investigation has been that many powerful business executives and politicians have been arrested in Rome and other parts of Italy for following the practice, "When in Rome . . ."

In American business history, corporate executives have typically followed the same guidelines overseas until Congress and President Jimmy Carter passed the Foreign Corrupt Practices Act in 1977, making it a violation of federal law for Americans to bribe foreign government officials. Oh, but hold on a minute: This now creates a very real dilemma for American tourists and business managers who travel abroad. For tourists, if bribery is against the law, but it's the only way to stay out of trouble in most countries, what should a person do? Generally, people just go along with the simple practice of paying off police officers or other officials rather than exert the moral courage or suffer the consequences of doing the right thing. And, for American business managers, they now find themselves at a significant competitive disadvantage since the U.S. is the only country with such a policy. So, if bribery is the only way for managers to get new business contracts or pass inspections, what should they do? Many have already resorted to finding creative ways around the law, such as charging bribery costs to agents or partners in foreign companies or using other devices.

Whenever large profits, personal power, or easy access are at stake, the "When in Rome . . ." philosophy can be very seductive. It can quickly pull or push an ethical person over both the ethical and legal lines with relatively little struggle or self-justification; after all,

"Everybody's doing it." We should be very careful of such entice-ments, both for moral and economic reasons. As we see in Italy, although many may have reaped the benefits of bribery for years, some will now reap the punishment.

Maintaining the Image

The "everybody's doing it" trap is not exclusive to business or relations with foreign governments. In a luncheon meeting in 1996, a former legislative staffer shared his experience with me. I'll call him Derek.

During his six years in Washington, D.C., Derek served on the staff of a prominent senator and then on the staff of a congressman. While working for the senator, Derek explained that one of his pri-mary responsibilities was to open mail. He told how the senator received about 2,000 letters a month from his constituents and addi-tional mail from people who were not of his constituency but who wanted his attention for some cause or concern. The senator never saw most of the letters. Instead, the staff would open the mail and read it and then write a reply as though the senator, himself, was responding. Derek would use "the senator's personal signature stamp, stamp the letter in the appropriate place, and send it off." Neither the original letter nor the reply were ever seen by the senator.

"Sometimes," Derek continued, "someone who had received one of the letters would come to Washington and make an appointment to see the senator. When this happened, we would scurry around, find the letter and the reply, place them on the senator's desk, and then brief the senator on the issues just before the constituent came into his office." Once the constituent was in the senator's office, he or she usu-ally thanked him for his prompt reply to the letter. By now, the sena-tor was familiar with the correspondence, and so he never mentioned that he hadn't seen the correspondence until that day. The constituent would leave feeling very good about all the "personal" attention received. This reputation for giving personal attention to each person's correspondence was very valuable for the senator. "I actually have been in the offices and homes of some of the senator's constituents," said Derek, "who have the senator's 'personal' letters tacked to the wall or framed. They point to the signature with pride and tell me how they received a 'personal' letter from the senator."

One of the justifications Derek gave for this artifice was that "Everybody does it that way." Well, not quite. Maybe it would be more accurate to say that most people or perhaps only many in Washington answer mail that way. After all, Derek also told me about his experience in the congressman's office.

Derek explained that the congressman's office handled mail in much the same way as the senator's office had. However, one day a constituent came to the office, and the staff put the pertinent letter and reply on the congressman's desk. Later, when the constituent referred to the congressman's letter, the congressman immediately interrupted and said, "You need to know that I did not write this letter. These letters are all written by my staff. I seldom even see them. That's just the way the system works around here."

Are these congressional delegates honest? Does a person of integrity in public office deliberately lead constituents to believe that they have enjoyed the personal attention of a senator when no such thing happened? In some circles, claiming authorship for something written by another is called forgery or plagiarism.

This particular senator publicly rails against people who deliberately mislead, deceive, obfuscate, or lie. He preaches the importance of honesty and integrity. The congressman seems less willing to perpetrate the ruse when face to face with his constituents, but he still allows communications to go out over his signature when he is unaware of either the letter or the reply—a pretense that conveys a false impression.

If these elected officials want to be truthful, why don't they just be forthcoming about this policy and have their staff be honest and up front? In their letter writing, they could explain to the constituents how impossible it is for a senator or congressman to respond personally to such a large volume of mail, and so the responsibility to reply to the letter has been given to staff members. The staff member could then respond to the letter and sign it with his or her own signature and title, "Chief letter answerer for the senator."

If such forthrightness does not seem appropriate, then maybe we have found one of those rare cases in which lying is justified. We can then acknowledge that the practice of letter writing for someone else is deceptive, even dishonest, but it maintains a necessary image and reputation of giving personal attention to people that is critical for a politician's effectiveness. In other words, the effectiveness of a powerful person is more important than honesty in this case. In any case, we can at least be honest with ourselves.

The Danger of Slogans

An important part of managing this aspect of ethics is to realize that the phrase, "When in Rome . . ." and "Everybody's doing it" are attractive but deceptive slogans. Like all slogans, they become thought stoppers: We no longer have to think about what we are doing; the slogan accomplishes this for us, and we feel justified. Once someone comes up with an attractive slogan that people accept and recite, all critical analysis generally stops. Beware of slogans.

We boldly should question those who use slogans to justify their actions. Silence about unethical practices—deliberate or inadvertent—signals that slogans have become acceptable guidelines for individual behavior in an organization. Some may conclude that managers do not need to ask about ethical issues because the employees already know that ethics are important. But, in a highly competitive environment where "Everybody's doing it," such logic just won't do. It's like saying that employees already know that profits are important, so managers shouldn't have to mention them or check up on progress. What would happen if results were not continually monitored and the managers held responsible? Such is the seductiveness of the "When in Rome . . ." philosophy. If we do not consistently raise these issues to the forefront of management as matters of concern, they will ensnare even the most sincere and well-intentioned people.

CASE: The Hartford Interview[11]

During his senior year of college, George Hall was interviewed by the representatives of several business firms. The interviewer from one of the firms, an insurance company, asked George to visit the head office in Hartford, Connecticut, during spring break for another interview there. The company would gladly pay his travel expenses.

George lived in Boston, and he discovered that a business acquaintance of his father's was planning to drive to Hartford for Easter and would be pleased to have company on the trip. The interview in Hartford went well, and the company informed George that he would be notified shortly whether his application had been accepted. He felt confident that the decision would be favorable.

Shortly after he returned home and before he returned to school, George received a letter from the interviewer requesting him to prepare an invoice of his expenses on the trip so that the company could reimburse him. Although his travel had cost him nothing, George included in his statement a charge of $.26 per mile for travel, reasoning that if he could arrange a free ride to Hartford, that was his business and the result of his own initiative. He felt that he had no obligation to pass the savings on to the company, since the company didn't need the money anyway.

Questions:

1. Was George's reasoning right or wrong? Why?

2. If you were the employer and knew of this incident, would you hire George? Why or why not?

3. Surely, George has all the markings of a good entrepreneur—finding inexpensive travel and figuring out how to make money by it—would this not be valuable for any company? Is this a case in which ingenuity should be rewarded rather than penalized?

Chapter 8

None Dare Call It Bribery:
The Law of Obligation

"A decent man is not responsible for the vice or absurdity of his profession, and he ought not, on that account, refuse to pursue it. It is the custom of the country. There is money to be got by it. A man must live in the world and make the best of it, such as it is."

—*Montaigne*

PEOPLE OFTEN THINK of bribery primarily as one of those problems associated with businesses that operate in foreign countries. But the problem is large scale right here in "River City, USA." Most people are reluctant to actually call it "bribery."

A man I will call Harper Kellog, an executive of a very large corporation, has the responsibility for deciding who should receive the large contracts his organization lets out at regular intervals, and these contracts vary in size from a few thousand dollars to $5 million. Usually, the amount is somewhere between $100,000 and $1 million. Kellog was answering questions after a lecture to an MBA marketing class when the following exchange took place:

"Mr. Kellog," one student asked, "I am interested to know, if I were representing a company that was bidding for a contract from your organization, what could I do to influence your decision? Is your decision based solely on cost?"

"Cost is always a major factor in contract letting in our business," he replied. "But you must keep in mind that in this business the product and service we are looking for is complicated and often one of a kind. Therefore, we also must make significant judgments about many intangibles like a contractor's reliability, the competence of management and engineering staff, financial stability, and other factors."

"Then," continued the student, "can an effective sales representative make a difference in a decision?"

"Well yes, but only so far as he is able to give us evidence of the contractor's capacity with regard to the intangibles I just mentioned," responded Kellog.

Another student asked, "Mr. Kellog, I am aware that one of your contractors keeps a hunting and fishing lodge in Minnesota where the company regularly entertains potential clients. Is this kind of entertaining an effective tool to influence contract decisions?"

"No, I can honestly say it does not," Kellog responded quickly and assertively. "We must make judgments based on the facts. On one occasion the contractor you refer to took my wife and me to the lodge for a 10-day hunting vacation, and we had a marvelous time. But I can honestly say that the trip had absolutely no influence on any decisions I have to make when choosing contractors."

Some executives make such defensive statements knowing that they are not being honest, but others make similar statements and honestly think that what they are saying is so. We should beware of both groups: People in the first group are not to be trusted, and those in the second group have questionable competence, for they are naive if not just plain ignorant about the nature of *obligation*. This ignorance and the resulting public statements contribute greatly to the public's distrust and skepticism of executives' and politicians' public declarations and overall credibility.

In a time when business executives as a group are concerned about credibility and trust in the eyes of the public, Kellog's statement only adds to the credibility problem. National politicians make similar statements, admitting that they receive significant favors from certain business and labor interests, while at the same time maintaining that the favors have no influence on their decisions or positions.

Better awareness of the subtle nature of obligation would help businesspeople, especially those who have been trapped in a web of obligation, to (1) avoid stepping unwittingly into compromising situations and (2) shun statements and gifts that are patently unbelievable, and thereby prevent further damage to their credibility problem.

I assert that *no one can accept a favor or gift of kindness, no matter how small, from another person without incurring an obligation.* Or, to state it another way, every time we accept a favor or gift from another person, we incur an obligation. This is the law of obligation.

We can better understand and clarify this law of obligation by considering three questions: (1) What is an obligation? (2) How are obligations incurred, and how do they arise? and (3) Is it wrong to incur obligations?

What Is an Obligation?

An obligation, according to the dictionary, is "any duty imposed by law, promise or contract, social relations, etc." The last part of this definition, "social relations," is often either overlooked or its import goes unnoticed, but it can have great significance for business executives. The definition of "duty," which is a synonym for "obligation," may help highlight the implications of obligations. "Duty" means: "That which a person is *bound to do*, or not do, as a responsible person; the compulsion felt to meet such obligation" [emphasis added].[1] Most normal people instinctively and subconsciously sense that they are "bound to do" something when they receive a gift or favor, but they often feel uncomfortable about it. Nevertheless, even though a duty or obligation may cause discomfort or risk, any responsible person is, by definition, bound to do that which is expected by the obligation, as long as the expectation is commensurate with the degree of obligation.

Rolf Mengele, son of the infamous Dr. Josef Mengele who caused the death of thousands of people in the German concentration camps of World War II, couldn't bring himself to report his father to the authorities during the years of search following the war. In 1985, the year Dr. Mengele's bones were discovered (six years after his death in Brazil), Rolf was asked why he had never turned his father in. He explained that he couldn't turn in his father. Then, even after his father had died, Rolf kept the information to himself because he felt an obligation to protect those who had sheltered his father.[2] Obligations can bind people in ways that cause them to be unethical and even break the law.

Most people understand that there can be many degrees of obligation. A person may be bound, depending on the nature of the particular obligation or how it was incurred, to return a major favor or perhaps only a minor one. Usually the amount of obligation is commensurate with the favor that first created the social contract.

The law of obligation can be very simple and subtle, but it is still real. For example, when you go to another person's home and allow the host or hostess to hang your coat in the closet, this simple act obligates you to stay longer than if you had kept your coat on or held it in your lap. You have to stay long enough to justify the effort and to complete the social contract implied in allowing the person to go to that much bother. So, if you leave too early, the host or hostess has the right to feel, "Well, if that's all the time you were going to stay, then why did you allow me to put your coat away?"

Big Favor, Big Obligation

The North Carolina Council of Churches once wrestled mightily with the law of obligation. In 1984, it was about to publish a study on the moral conflicts of tobacco. One of the ministers explained, "We insist there's a moral problem when you're producing a product that causes death to a large number of people." Yet the report began to cause a great deal of anxiety even before it was published. Although council members felt a strong urgency to take a moral stand about the harmful effects of tobacco, the council's long-established obligations to companies in the tobacco industry made the situation difficult and complex, even perilous:

> "It would be pretty difficult for a local church pastor to go on a crusade against tobacco when there are large numbers of people in his congregation whose livelihoods depend on it," says Dennis Campbell, dean of Duke University's Divinity School.
>
> When one committee member is asked if he would raise the morality issue in his church, he says, "I'm not sure I dare." And with good reason: "If a preacher were to start something, he wouldn't be here long. We'd ship him out," says Gil Richardson . . .[3]

But, how did the obligation get to be so strong that it could *bind* these ministers so they couldn't speak out on issues of life and death? Simple: Over the years they had accepted great gifts and favors that bound them greatly. For example, Duke University was called Trinity College until 1924, when it was given $6 million by James B. Duke, a tobacco magnate. The Duke Endowment (from tobacco money) continues to provide funds for rural Methodist churches and a small pension to all retired Methodist ministers in North Carolina.

Accepting such favors or gifts does, indeed, incur an obligation. In the case of some churches, it has made them beholden to the tobacco industry. An oft-repeated cliché from our childhood conditions us to honor these obligations: "Don't bite the hand that feeds you."

One of the interesting things about obligations is that generally, when a duty is first contracted, both parties understand what specific or general thing the other party is bound to do. For example, for a legislator to accept a large donation or favor from a labor organization at the time certain legislation is pending obligates the politician to take a position that might even be opposite to what his or her position would have been had the favor been accepted from, say a business management group. The size of the originating favor also determines the extent of an expected obligation. In the legislative example, a small favor may only require the lawmaker to speak for the proposition, but a large favor would require significant campaigning and arm twisting for the organization's cause on the part of the legislator, along with his guaranteed vote.

Dangerous Obligations

Frequently, obligations are open-ended, much like a blank check. When a person accepts a gift or favor, usually it is left open as to when the corresponding duty will be fulfilled and exactly what might be required. The undated, undesignated check is placed in the drawer for some future need and isn't cashed in until the person granting the gift or favor has needs or desires arise that would merit it. The obligation may range from a simple introduction to a helpful contact or the sharing of useful information, all the way up to providing major support for a desired cause. So, this kind of open-ended obligation, without knowing at the time what form of payment could be requested, is the most dangerous of obligations. It often entraps the unwitting and binds them to do things that they otherwise would not do.

So, for our purposes here, an obligation is "that which a person is bound to do because of social relations." Innate in almost everyone is the feeling that we can't turn our backs on people who have done us a favor or who have been of help. When someone requests our assistance, we are generally inwardly compelled, because of some past gift or favor, to respond with help, even if we never asked for the original favor but it was given voluntarily. We often hear businesspeople, particularly executives, say, "He owes me one," when they are trying to decide who they should ask for help. Likewise, whenever an organization is seeking the cooperation or contribution of some other person or company, the "right" person is sent to make the request. That person is often the one to whom the "debtor" is socially bound or obligated because of past favors or gifts. It would be difficult, in such a situation, to turn down the "collector" without an extremely good reason.

How Are Obligations Incurred?

How, then, are obligations incurred? When are these social contracts made? And, how do the circumstances arise?

One of the most subtle obligations arises when a "receiver" asks for no favor, but something is given to him or her voluntarily. For instance, suppose a piece of property is coming up for sale adjacent to a receiver's property, which he would like very much to own. But, before he or the public can learn about it, an "obligator" or "giver" learns of it and says, "Say, I just heard that land next door to you is coming up for sale. An announcement will be made in about a week. If you want to do something before then, I suggest you contact Mike Riggs. He's handling it. If you don't know him, I'll be happy to introduce you—just thought you'd like to know."

If the man acts on this information, he automatically incurs an obligation. If he agrees to be introduced, a greater obligation is incurred. Even if he does not act on the tip, he also may incur a slight obligation just because the giver offered to be helpful.

Some may protest, "No way—nothing happened." They try to show that the two had no agreement, and so no one is obligated for anything. But such a response either is self-deceiving or comes from ignorance or naivete about social relations. Remember, any accepted favor incurs an obligation.

The story of the Godfather is the principle of obligations at work in its clearest form: The Godfather sees a man who does not have the money to pay for a proper burial for his wife, so he steps forward and offers the man money to cover the funeral costs.

"No," says the man, "I can't accept your offer because I could not repay it."

"Don't worry," says the Godfather. "I just want to do something nice for you. It's just a gift."

Later, when the Godfather returns and asks for a favor that seems highly suspect and unethical, the receiver realizes that he is bound to a contract made some time ago when he didn't realize it. But it is now difficult or impossible to turn his back on the request.[4]

When Are Obligations Incurred?

Consider what happens when a salesman calls your home and says, "Your name has been selected by our company to receive a free gift. May I deliver it to your home tomorrow night? There is no obligation."

You say, "Yes, I guess that would be okay."

Then, the following night, he rings the doorbell and says, "Here is your gift," and he hands you a small calculator or a deluxe pen set. "Would you mind signing this form to indicate that I delivered your gift?" While you are signing the paper, he continues, "By the way, our company has just come out with a new life insurance policy. Could I take just a few minutes of your time to explain how valuable it could be for you?"

Do you have any obligation to let him in for "a few minutes"? Surely, after the salesman has gone to all that bother and has driven all that way to deliver your "free gift," he reasons, you are obligated to listen for at least five to ten minutes. Now, you are not obligated to buy, because that would mean a repayment larger than the obligation, but only the most crass would turn away the salesman flatly without at least some twinge of conscience.

But, when did you incur the obligation? When did you "sign the contract"? When you said, "Yes, I guess that would be okay," after he asked if he could come deliver the gift.

In fact, the insurance company is fully aware of the psychological obligation and has deliberately designed its sales approach to take advantage of that principle. When the salesman told you there was no obligation, that was a lie. He conveyed a false impression if he did not expect you at least to listen to his pitch.

When a person asks for a gift or favor from another person and the person grants it, the obligation is more binding and usually requires a greater return on demand than if the favor had been volunteered.

Suppose an executive has ambitions of becoming the president of a business organization. He approaches the president of the local chamber of commerce, knowing that the president has a strong influence with the chairman of the organization's selection committee. He tells him that he would like to become president of the organization and asks, "Would you mind putting in a good word for me?" The president obliges and makes a considerable effort to influence the board on behalf of the executive. Later, when the chamber president comes around to ask the new president to purchase supplies from one of his own companies or a friend's company the president may be obligated to purchase from that company even if another supplier has a better offer. Thus, manipulating the principle of obligation is a form of bribery.

Attempting to preclude the negative effects of obligations, some companies establish what may seem to be rather rigid policies. One company does not allow any of its employees to go to lunch with suppliers or potential suppliers unless the employees pay for their own meals. Ten-day hunting excursions, weekend entertainment packages, and basketball tickets are definitely out. In fact, any supplier who maintains an entertainment account would be suspect of attempting to incur obligations.

Although we must exercise great caution when making generalized statements, we must nonetheless admit that no area of human interaction—professional, religious, private, or otherwise—is free from the challenges created by the law of obligation. Here are a few examples of how the law of obligation affects certain industries:

Medicine. One day I attended a seminar meeting with the staff of a medical school and the representatives of a large pharmaceutical company. The meeting was conducted by a medical doctor who was designated as the medical school's "ethicist." The discussion centered around the free dinners sponsored once a week for the school hospital's resident interns by the pharmaceutical company: Once a week, all of the medical students interning at the hospital were expected to attend a meeting with the medical staff to review the students' experiences. The meetings were generally held in conjunction with a dinner, sponsored by the pharmaceutical company, which seemed to work much better for the students than if no dinner was served. In fact, when the meetings were held without dinners, attendance dropped significantly. So the hospital invited the company to return and again sponsor the meals.

However, other pharmaceutical companies began to voice concerns that the dinners gave the sponsoring company an unfair advantage. For example, students at the dinners were reminded of the company's generosity in sponsoring the meal, and at each meal the company had the opportunity to introduce one or two new products. The pharmaceutical company reasoned that the expense was justified because, by associating this act of generosity with the company's products during the students' formative professional years, the students would be enthusiastic about recommending or prescribing company products to patients in their individual practices. On the other hand, the medical school and hospital had no budget money allocated for the dinners, and the company had provided a helpful boost to the school in improving the learning process.

Some faculty members questioned the ethics of the practice. Those who felt that the practice posed some serious ethical problems felt that the dinners incurred for the students some very real obligations that may or may not be in the best interests of some patients in the future. Also, the practice seemed to be incurring certain obligations for the medical school. Still, the faculty felt that student attendance at the dinner meetings was very important, and many students, faculty members, and businesses saw nothing wrong with the practice. They argued, as do many people who engage in such practices, that the school's and students' professional judgments would not be swayed by accepting such favors.

During the same discussion, the doctors and the pharmaceutical company representatives discussed the practice of pharmaceutical salespeople providing doctors with free samples of new product. Did such a practice incur questionable obligations for the doctors? A company representative volunteered, "We would love to get rid of the practice of providing free samples."

One of the doctors asked, "Well, then why do you keep doing it?"

"Every time we limit or cut off free samples our sales drop significantly. We can't afford to stop the practice," he replied.

During the discussion, I recalled that I had recently gone to see my doctor for a checkup. He was a young, new physician, and had not been practicing very long. He asked me, "Are you taking any medications?"

"Occasionally I take [a brand-name, over-the-counter antacid] that my former doctor recommended for upset stomach," I replied.

"Well," he said, "we don't know yet, but there may be some negative side effects with that medication." He opened a cabinet that displayed an ample supply of prescription medication. He handed me a small supply of "free" capsules and said, "Here, take these, and I'll write you a prescription so you can have a supply on hand."

I followed his instructions because I have confidence in the medical profession. But, when I went to get the prescription filled, I found that the new drug cost many times more than what I had been using. Since then I reflected, "If he had some doubt about the drug I was using, why didn't he recommend some other over-the-counter medication or perhaps a generic brand of the prescription?"

I told this story in the meeting at the medical school, but not one doctor present came to the defense of my physician's actions.

In this same meeting, another doctor volunteered that he and his wife had been invited recently to go to Palm Springs for a three-day seminar sponsored by a drug manufacturer, with all expenses paid by the sponsor. He estimated the total cost of the trip would have been about $5,000. He explained that the three days were filled with vacation activities, including golf, sight-seeing, fine dinners, and so forth. The only obligation he had was to attend a one-hour "educational session on pharmaceuticals" at some time during the three days. No one in the meeting spoke out saying that was wrong. It seems that they felt it was common practice and acceptable for companies to sponsor such trips.

Around the time of the meeting at the medical school, the *New England Journal of Medicine* reported:

> We must recognize that these enticements [gifts, trips, honorariums, etc.] are not entirely free because they add to costs that are passed on to consumers—our patients. As Rawlins noted in 1984, "Few doctors accept that they, themselves, have been corrupted. Most doctors believe that they are quite untouched by the seductive ways of industry's marketing men . . . that they can enjoy a company's 'generosity' in the form of gifts and hospitality without prescribing product. The degree to which the profession, mainly composed of honorable and decent people, can practice such self-deceit is quite extraordinary."[5]

Some are trying to buck the practice:

> "Students get textbooks, almost everyone gets stethoscopes, and I've heard there's even free pizzas the third and fourth year," says Joshua Sharfstein, a first year medical student at Harvard University, who shuns such favors as unethical. Last fall, he organized a drive to return free medical dictionaries and textbooks on cranial nerves emblazoned with the name of the pharmaceutical benefactor . . . "Only about ten percent of first year students," says Sharfstein, "sent their books back."[6]

Do these practices—free samples, retreats, etc.—influence doctors? Do they influence the quality or expense of the care that patients receive from their doctors? Should the practices be discontinued? Legislated? Moderated?

Politics. The problems with bribery and the law of obligation in politics have had widespread attention in the media. One senator's experience, as described in the *Wall Street Journal*, seems to be replicated over and over again by other elected officials.

According to the article, lobbyists seem to have targeted the senator's two most pressing concerns: (1) getting reelected and (2) supplementing his income sufficiently to help him keep his children in top schools. The lobbyists employed two main devices to help him resolve those concerns: They contributed substantial campaign funds to him and arranged for speaking engagements around the country with honoraria. One prominent lobbyist remarked, "We don't just want to give money to people. We want to get involved in dialogue. The only way to get a favorable hearing is to deal with [the senator's] problems [money for reelection and family expenses]." To the lobbyist, these favors at least obligate the senator to allow access to him. Surely, by accepting the assistance, the politician has incurred some obligation to the lobbyist's cause.

But the senator's reaction to concerns about his capitalizing on the favors was interesting:

> Boy, I'd have taken money from anybody in that campaign, that was my attitude. . . . Maybe in the first couple of years I would have said that [perhaps there is a better way to finance campaigns], maybe even through the campaign. But now there's probably a sense of realism that comes with one re-election that says—that's the way it is. Bad as though it may seem, it's still better than second place. . . . I don't feel sleazy. . . . Having to ask some people that are lobbying out here, and all that sort of thing for money, that doesn't bother me. . . . I'm really not for sale; I can't be bought.[7]

Bob Dole, former chairman of the Senate Finance Committee, once jokingly remarked, "Some of us are uncomfortable taking honoraria. I am uncomfortable taking campaign contributions. So, I compromised: I decided to take both." Many people seriously question whether politicians either don't understand or simply choose to ignore the law of obligation.

And the practice of influence peddling and favor exchanges is not likely to change as a time-honored American tradition. After all, it gives many American companies who are good at it an advantage over foreign competition. In 1994, Lord Young, the former British Minister of Trade and Industry, explained, "Without kickbacks, British entrepreneurs would be unable to compete abroad. Some foreign businesses say they have difficulty competing in the U.S. market because of the ability of American firms to gain influence through political contributions."[8]

Food Inspection. Meat inspectors also wrestle with the law of obligation. The USDA, it seems, "feels obliged, like all public agencies, to maintain the myth that all rules are rigidly enforced." Yet, within the industry it is commonplace, "that if all meat inspection regulations were enforced to the letter, no meat processor in America would be open for business." The inspector has significant discretion: ". . . he is not expected to enforce every rule, but rather to decide which rules are worth enforcing at all."

In such an environment, where significant judgmental decisions are made, inspectors are subject to some subtle influences controlled by the packer, including gifts or favors such as office supplies, freezer coats, and "cumshaw" (a gift of meat). Every day packers throw away hundreds of pounds of edible meat for one reason or another. According to old-timers at one plant, "It isn't a good inspector who pays for his Sunday dinner." The unwritten code says, "Don't accept more than your family can use," "Don't solicit meat from the packer," and "Don't let cumshaw influence how you do your job." Apparently, these ground rules form an accepted distinction for the industry between a customary gratuity and bribery. Most packers and inspectors feel that the practice facilitates both the working relationship between inspectors and packers and the production process without any negative effects.

"Sure, I accept bundles of meat to take home for my family," says one inspector, echoing many others. "But that doesn't affect my decisions in the plant one iota, and the packer knows that. The fact of the matter is that if you get on a high horse and refuse to take a bundle, it makes it much more difficult to get the job done."[9]

Does this mean, in this case, that the law of obligation does not apply? Or do we see some self-deception here?

Journalism. The writers and editors of automotive magazines often serve as advisors and consultants to automakers and frequently accept such freebies as airline tickets, rooms at resort hotels, clocks, briefcases, and free use of some of the hottest cars on the market. But one such writer, formerly with *Car and Driver* magazine, claims his writings are "untainted because of his own integrity," and that of the magazine's editors. "I'm not afraid to bite the hand that somewhat feeds me," he insists. But, at the same time, these "buff magazines rake in huge amounts by producing 'special issues' that are magazine-length promotions paid by a single manufacturer. . . . But they look just like regular issues."

"I think it's a scandal," says Stephen Isaacs, a professor at Columbia University's School of Journalism. "How can you believe any word in a publication that allows such practices?"[10]

Financial Planning. "Yes, there are certainly frauds out there," says Robert A. Hewitt, chairman of the International Association of Financial Planners. But, "in spite of some of the sensational headlines, most fraud and abuse is perpetrated not by financial planners, but by frauds posing as financial planners."

So, how do these crooked planners accomplish their dire deeds? "Crooks use the same marketing and sales techniques that legitimate financial planning professionals use, which is why they're so camouflaged," says Scott Stapf of North American Securities Administrators Association. "Crooked planners will work through community organizations, unions, and church groups, and will make presentations. Afterwards, they get lists of members and move in with sales pitches. It's a very effective way to set up people, because they trust the planner, and *feel guilty about having gotten the free advice*" [emphasis added].[11]

Here is another blatant example of salespeople who deliberately manipulate their prospects using the law of obligation to make a sale.

Real Estate. According to a report in the *Wall Street Journal* the law of obligation in the form of an incentive program can affect the price of a house:

> Home buyers, beware. In many of the nation's real estate markets there is a price on your head. In New York, home sellers are offering $5,000 bonuses to real estate agents who bring them live buyers. In Phoenix, a real estate firm is pooling $250 from each of 40 home sellers for a $10,000 door prize for one of the agents who sells their homes. In Southern California, sellers are offering cars to agents who find buyers willing to pay their asking price.[12]

In markets where agents ostensibly attempt to represent both buyers and sellers, buyers would be wise to be aware of the obligations that agents have to sellers, who often pay sales commissions out of the purchase price. That obligation, or incentive, can seriously affect how open and truthful agents will be with buyers, and it can affect agents' statements about what kinds of offers the buyers may or may not accept.

Professional Tennis. According to Michael Mewshaw in his book, *Short Circuit*, under-the-table payments for special appearances may create obligations that cause some players to agree ahead of time to rig lucrative exhibition matches. But, some argue, "inducements to top players simply reflect their proven ability to draw crowds." But others argue that the rules against undisclosed appearance fees should either be enforced—which virtually everyone in tennis admits would be next to impossible—or repealed, allowing the whole subject of payments to be brought into the open.[13]

No, bribery—or in these cases, our euphemism for it: the questionable use of the law of obligation—is not just a problem associated with doing business in foreign countries. It exists right here in "River City, USA" on a big scale, even though many people are reluctant to recognize it for what it is. It also seems that the practice of bribery by manipulation of the law of obligation is universal. Again, whenever anyone accepts a favor, whether asked for or volunteered, an obligation is incurred, and an invisible signature is attached to a very real contract.

Is It Wrong to Incur Obligations?

In the normal course of business and social relationships it is practically impossible to avoid incurring obligations. The question becomes: Which obligations should be accepted, and which should be rejected? Managers must become astute enough to avoid contracting obligations unwittingly—such are often the worst kind.

Be aware that by accepting any favor or gift, you are creating a contract of obligation—a duty to repay. Avoid becoming obligated whenever the "payment" of an obligation might conceivably come in conflict with your own interests or with the interests of those to whom you owe a first or greater obligation. Particularly be cautious about the people and organizations with whom you knowingly enter such contracts by accepting their gifts or favors. The unaware may find themselves bound to do the will of unsavory people who demand payment contrary to your interests or the interests of your organization. In its ugliest form, this is known as blackmail. In milder forms you may find yourself in a situation that causes some embarrassment to you, your boss, or your organization.

Avoid accepting favors or gifts that might influence you later to claim that you felt no obligation or thought the gift or favor would have no influence on you or your decisions. Such claims are the start of a cover-up to avoid embarrassment and only add lying and deceit to indiscretion. Be willing to recognize, if not openly acknowledge, that every obligation has the power to modify, distort, or even destroy objectivity.

On the other hand some obligations enable us to bind our work groups and partnerships more closely together for better morale and greater cohesiveness, and create a spirit of loyalty and unity. And certainly gifts and favors are part and parcel of family life and true friendship. Often, an attitude of helpfulness can develop in work groups because of the constant stream of favors given between people working together. In one example, one of the women in a work group so often volunteered to help others with their jobs that when she came down with an extended illness, the other members of the team felt they owed it to her to preserve her job by working extra hours, without extra pay, so someone else would not be brought in to replace her.

Further, lasting friendships and true love are based on both partners' mutual adherence to the principle of obligation. Acquaintances ripen into friendships as two people strongly feel the need to live up to the obligations that thoughtful deeds and considerations impose upon them. A bond of trust is the result of favors accepted and repaid over time when neither party has failed to repay or at least recognize and express gratitude for the gestures. The reluctance or failure to live up to such obligations can breed distrust.

Before we begin to work with another supplier, we should make sure that we are not still obligated in some way to previous suppliers. And, before we begin to deal with potential new customers, we should immediately find out if they are already obligated to other suppliers for the kind of business we would like to do, and to what extent. This same reasoning applies equally to circumstances and influences that demand the time and attention of prospective suppliers, as well as contractual obligations. This awareness allows us to assess exactly whose interests should be first in mind and then respect those commitments to the proper extent.

For example, one insurance company manager encouraged his new recruits to buy a new house with a large monthly mortgage payment. According to him, this served as a daily reminder for the recruits to get out and sell enough insurance to meet their payments at the end of each month. But, if I were a prospective customer to such an agent, I would have good reason to question whether he or she really had my interests at heart or whether the obligation overpowered all my concerns in the effort to get my business and earn the commission.

This principle is so subtle and so real to me that I prefer to do all my shopping at stores where the clerks and managers know me personally, rather than at stores where I am a stranger, because those who know me have a greater obligation to be more forthright with me because of our personal friendship.

So, to answer the question—is it wrong to incur obligations?—obligations are like fire: When they are misused or get out of control they can warp and destroy, but when appropriately applied in the right human relationships, they can warm and empower.

How do we know when the law of obligation is being misused? This is what the study of ethics is all about. Ethics are applied morality and society's guide to differentiating the appropriate uses of such things from the inappropriate uses. This is why we must improve our awareness and search for definitions that are clear enough to serve as useful guidelines for future behavior.

Some companies have already gone through this exercise and have crafted enforceable policies for their employees. Here are a few examples: "It is unethical for any employee to accept any gifts, lunches, or tickets for entertainment from anyone who supplies or contracts with the company." "It is unethical for employees involved in purchasing or contracting decisions to pursue negotiations with potential suppliers who employ or routinely subcontract to a close relative of the employees. Such negotiations are to be handled by another employee of the company." "It is unethical for employees to be involved in making decisions that benefit another company if they have a vested interest in the other company," and so on.

Selective Perception

One principle of human behavior often causes or leads people who are obligated to others to indulge in self-deception. This is called "selective perception." Selective perception causes us to (1) select from each experience only the things that are satisfying or that reassure us we are right, and (2) deliberately ignore, or even psychologically "blank out," the things that suggest we are wrong or things that may be mildly disturbing. When questions or evidences arise that would suggest that, in being true to our obligations, we are not being objective, fair, or honest, we tend to blank out the evidence or refuse to answer the question. This relieves us of the mental anguish that would come from recognizing the problem.

For instance, someone may make a less-than-honest statement in order to be true to an obligation. And, since most people see themselves as trustworthy in their obligations and friendships and also honest in their speech, when these principles come into conflict with each other, as they often do, the mind "blanks out" the idea that "perhaps I have made a false statement" in order to eliminate the internal conflict.

According to ethics writer David Cherrington, if I sincerely believe that I am basically honest all the time, but my words or behavior begin to conflict with this belief, psychologically it will be much easier for me to redefine "honesty"—and, by so doing, keep my record of honesty perfect—than to admit to dishonesty and then try to correct all my errors by confronting family, peers, bosses, customers, suppliers, the public, and so forth. This tendency to rationalize and justify, rather than correct and modify, leads to an interesting phenomenon: Many people in prisons, who have been caught red-handed in acts of fraud or embezzlement, still claim from the depths of their jail cells, in all sincerity, "I am basically an honest person," or "I got a bad rap." Similarly, senior executives perched high atop their luxury office suites built on the backs of their defrauded and often powerless past business associates, still insist, "This company values the highest standards of integrity and good character." Such is the power of selective perception.[14]

So strong is the principle of obligation and so real is the principle of selective perception that, in convenient combination, they lead to the honest but nonetheless real self-deceptions by the likes of executives such as Harper Kellog mentioned at the beginning of this chapter.

None Dare Call It Bribery

Many businesspeople grapple with deciding where acceptable influence ends and bribery begins. Where is the line—lunch? entertainment? holiday gifts? Considering the dictionary's definition of bribery, we find that many people in today's business world would be faced with some fascinating challenges, even in common practices: "Bribery" is "money or a favor given or promised to a person in a position of trust to influence his or her judgment or conduct—something that serves to induce or influence."[15]

If we take this definition of bribery at face value, and if we begin with the premise that bribery is unethical, we soon begin to raise some very serious questions about the morality of many widely used sales practices. After all, most lunches, free trips, tickets to entertainment events, and other gifts are employed basically to *induce or influence* someone's judgment or conduct. If salespeople and purchasers did not influence others in ways that bring the desired results—increased sales or reduced operating expenses—they would be hard-pressed to justify such expenditures to stockholders.

If businesspeople feel that this definition of bribery is not appropriate, then we must begin the search for a new definition that distinguishes between gifts and favors that are bribery and those that are not. Or, as we discussed with certain kinds of lies, we could identify gifts and favors that are "acceptable bribery" and "unacceptable bribery." Regardless of our approach, the status quo gives us nothing but a slippery slope to negotiate. At the top are acceptable acts of giving favors for acceptable levels of influence, with blatant bribery somewhere near the bottom—with no identifying marks, signs, nets, flags, or guardrails indicating where "acceptable bribery" ends and "unacceptable bribery" begins. This lack of definition, combined with the pressure for results and our own self-interests, tends to guide our business conduct right down the slope with no counter forces to alert our consciences that we are approaching or have crossed the line.

Bribery and the Pressure of Results

When the pressure for results gets high enough, even individuals and organizations known for their honorable reputations have been found to engage in acts that are, by definition, bribery. Interestingly, such details of bribery are often kept from the public spotlight, and those involved seem to engage in self-justification by rationalizing, "The action was justified because the results were so very important."

Such was the case when a large regional retailer announced that it would be opening a new store in a city where it previously had no outlet. Initially, the chain's management favored a newly developing area on the edge of the city for the location, and expressed its intention to city planners. But the mayor and others were concerned about the city's deteriorating downtown area. Regardless of the chain's decision, the retailer was of such outstanding caliber that it would not only attract customers to the new location, but other retailers would desire to be located nearby. So, the city planners reasoned, if the retailer located the new store on the outskirts of town, the downtown area would lose its existing customer traffic and further precipitate its demise as other retailers relocated to capture the flow of traffic.

After several weeks of intense behind-the-scenes activity and an occasional news report or editorial on the matter, the retailer announced that it would build its new store in the city center. Everyone involved seemed to express satisfaction and confidence in the city's booming downtown renewal project.

Later, after the new construction was underway, I had the opportunity to meet with the mayor. I congratulated him on such an outstanding achievement of getting the highly reputable retailer to lead the way in rejuvenating the downtown area. I then asked, "How were you able to swing this one?"

This man, who many regarded as having high ethical standards and personal principles of conduct, replied with evident embarrassment, "Do you know what it took to get that decision? It took $80,000 under the table."

When I asked him what he meant, he was unwilling to go into detail. He mentioned a few vaguely worded items such as waiving normal utilities fees, deferring taxes, and "other items."

Under the definition of bribery cited above, were the city's actions in influencing the retailer's decision bribery? It certainly appears so. But, in our society, such efforts and inducements to get prominent businesses to locate in certain areas, make a sale, or conclude a contract seem to have become commonly accepted practices, suggesting either that certain forms of bribery are approved in a competitive business setting or that it's time to identify a more appropriate definition of bribery. In the meantime, no one dares call it bribery. After all, the term "bribery" seems so harsh for what we commonly accept as good, old-fashioned business savvy—the ability to get the job done, "whatever it takes." Again, until we are willing to call a spade a spade, the game continues without rules or guidelines, with each player deciding the rules as he or she feels appropriate.

CASE: The Pay-Off [16]

A building contractor explained how he used the law of obligation to his advantage:

> In the course of my work I regularly pay off town council members, though not in money. Contracting depends on time. If you need a subdivision approved or a section rezoned, you simply can't wait around until your case reaches the town meeting in the ordinary course of events. With a little help the case can

be put on the next meeting's agenda and voted on quickly. This help consists in offering, say, a brick-laying job to one of the council members who is in the business. That person gets the case on the agenda and uses his or her influence to follow up and see that the decision is favorable. Then I send Christmas presents to the council member to let the person know that I remember the favor with gratitude. Council members are always looking for such jobs and gifts.

There really isn't anything dishonest in this practice. I never ask for anything unreasonable in the approval of subdivisions or the rezoning of sections, and I do not harm the town in that respect. And the council member's work in laying bricks, or whatever the job happens to be, must be up to par, or the person's business reputation will be ruined. I have never had to complain about the quality of work that I have given out to a council member, and I have never heard any complaints about the council's decisions in my favor, except from those who stood to gain by impeding civic progress. All I do is buy time—to everyone's benefit.

Questions:

1. Is this a case of bribery? How?

2. Are the council members obligated to the contractor because of his favors? If so, in what way?

3. From the council members' point of view, do such favors constitute conflicts of interest?

4. What should the contractor do? What should the council members do? Why?

5. If you were a citizen in this community and knew about such practices, what would you do about it?

Chapter 9

Play by Which Rules?
Personal Ethics Versus Gaming Ethics

"To hold up a standard of applying, in any literal sense to work-a-day life, the teaching of the Judeo-Christian tradition [the Golden Rule] is to put an impractical, if not impossible, burden upon management. It is tantamount to no less than projecting the executive group into a situation of perpetual sinfulness."

—*Benjamin Selekman*[1]

RICHARD B. HAWS, president of Multi-Products Inc., was speaking with his friend and lamenting how "the average young man today has no concept of how to beat a competitor and how to squeeze money out of every dollar." Picking up his office copy of *Who's Who*, Haws showed his friend that he had attended college for three years, worked as a salesman in a local business for another five, and then moved to New York in 1929 to sell for the Lawton Machinery Company:

> We were living in a nice apartment and had all our money in the market when the crash came. I went to our landlord and asked him to let me break the lease, but he pointed out that he needed money more than ever now, and refused. I went home to think about it, and then returned and pleaded with him to let us move to one of his cheaper apartments. Finally, he agreed. He moved us the next day and that night brought up a new lease for me to sign. I looked him in the eye and said, "Oh, no. When you moved us out of that first apartment, you broke the lease. We're moving out of here tomorrow." That's the sort of sharp thinking—in that case born out of financial necessity—that young men don't seem to use today. They certainly don't learn it in business schools.[2]

Is this just "sharp thinking" as Haws claims, or is this dishonest behavior born of deceitful practice? This question often evokes animated controversy—some defending Haws' position, and some attacking Haws' actions as unethical. Some argue that Haws is playing by the rules: He broke no law; he just took advantage of the law. The other side argues that he did not play by the rules because he deliberately deceived the landlord.

Who is right? That depends upon which set of rules you apply to the situation. One of the fundamental ethical problems in our society is that everyone carries around two different, distinct, and legitimate sets of ethical standards. When we say two sets of standards, I don't mean a good one and a bad one, but two valid and morally defensible, commonly accepted standards. The problem arises when one party believes the "x" set of rules is appropriate in a given situation, and the other party believes the "y" set of rules is what should apply to the same circumstances. And, because most people fail to recognize that everyone employs two distinct sets of rules in their daily lives, we never can deal with the problem effectively. This leads to frustration and heated accusations of unethical behavior by one side toward the other.

A Double Standard?

At this point, you may feel like scolding me with, "You may use two standards, but I certainly don't. I have one standard, which is my measure in every facet of my life." But let's test this declaration:

I still claim that everyone lives by two standards of ethics. So, you ask, "How do I abide by or tolerate two standards?"

First, everyone I know has one standard that I call "personal ethics" or "religious ethics." Under this set of rules, most of us generally would agree that it's wrong to deliberately mislead or deceive another person, or to steal. We also would agree that it's wrong to identify another person's weakness and then deliberately design a scheme to take advantage of that weakness for personal gain. In other words, under this set of ethics we literally live the Golden Rule.

So, why do we so often deliberately mislead others, or consciously deceive people and intentionally take advantage of their weaknesses for our own personal gain, and even steal—all the time thinking that we have done nothing against the Golden Rule?

"I would never do such a thing," you say.

"Oh, yes you do, and you either do it or approve of it all the time," I insist.

"When would I ever deliberately do such a thing?" you ask.

I am glad you asked.

Did you ever play a game of tennis? Did you ever deliberately lead your opponent to believe that you were going to return the ball cross court, when all along you knew you were going to send it right down the alley? Or, when playing poker, did you ever try to lead the other players—through your facial expressions—to believe that you had a poor hand, when all along you held a Royal Flush? Or, in a game of chess, have you ever caused your opponent to change his or her mind because you grinned openly as the person considered moving a key piece to a new position, when all along you didn't have the faintest idea what you could do to stop your devastating losses? Have you ever watched a champion athlete such as a basketball player, football quarterback, or volleyball spiker who was unskilled in the art of deception—head fakes, double pumps, quick steps, hidden-ball tricks, intimidation, etc.? Have you ever cheered with joy when the opponent of your favorite team drops the ball or gets penalized so that your team wins the game?

"Ah," you say. "Those are games, and there are different rules for competitive games!"

Very good. You are getting the picture.

In competitive games, the rules or ethics are different than in personal life. I call this second set of rules "gaming ethics" or "sporting ethics." In gaming ethics, deliberately misleading and deceiving others is not only allowed, it's an essential skill for winning. To take advantage of another's weakness is not only allowed, it's expected of good players. If, in a competitive game of tennis, you discover that your opponent has a weak backhand, it is ethical to drill the ball to that backhand as much as possible. In football, quarterbacks are expected to identify any weaknesses in the defense and then intentionally throw or run the ball in that direction—all for their own gain. In baseball, stealing bases is a good strategy for baserunners; in football and basketball, stealing the ball is one of the objects of defense. When playing chess or monopoly, if your opponent inadvertently makes a poor move or choice, if you are playing seriously you are expected to take advantage of the situation before the person recognizes the mistake. Under gaming ethics, we take advantage of all that the laws or rules allow.

So we agree that there are two sets of ethical standards: "personal ethics," in which we never deliberately mislead or deceive other people or intentionally take advantage of their weaknesses for personal gain; and "gaming ethics," in which purposely misleading or deceiving other people, or stealing, is not only allowed, but encouraged, practiced, and perfected, and taking advantage of another's weakness for personal gain is the best way to play the game.

Most people try to govern their personal lives by personal ethics, and in competitive games they apply gaming ethics. I think that most people understand this behavioral switch, and few are upset by it.

Which Rules Are Appropriate?

"So, what's the problem?" you ask.

The problem is which set of rules to live by in the competitive business world: Is business a competitive game, so that gaming ethics are appropriate? Or is it an extension of our personal life, so that we ought to govern our business by the higher standard of personal ethics?

I first learned about the problem of two conflicting sets of ethical standards in 1968 when I read an article by Albert Carr in the *Harvard Business Review*. Carr wrote, "If an executive allows himself to be torn between a decision based on business consideration [gaming ethics] and one based on his private ethical code [personal ethics], he exposes himself to a grave psychological strain."[3]

It appears that both Carr and Selekman (at the head of this chapter) suggest that business is a competitive game. Hence, gaming ethics may be appropriate, even unavoidable, when conducting business. If a football quarterback tries to avoid all deception, he will win very few games. Also, in business, executives who attempt to avoid all deception will have trouble building a successful business, and if they fail to take advantage of competitors' weaknesses in products, services, contacts, or information, they will lose out on business to their competitors who practice gaming ethics.

In 1986, the best-selling author of a real estate book was a guest on an early morning national talk show, discussing his new book. The interviewer asked him, "What is the essence of your book?"

He responded, "The key is to find someone who has a great desire to sell, so you can get property for a very good price."

A panel member quickly reacted, "I believe it's ethically wrong to take advantage of someone else's economic misfortune."

The author's defense was, "Look, this is the best-selling book ever on real estate."

In his book, the author talks about searching for "don't wanters"—people who don't want their property. In the real estate world, of course, the term is a euphemism for people who are desperate to sell. Exploiting another's economic desperation for our own personal gain does not seem like an ethical principle that most of us would advocate as part of our personal code. However, many people have little or no compunction about acting this way in a business setting.

The two panelists are examples of the two different philosophies. The panelist was advocating personal ethics. So, even though it is legal and profitable to do what the author was advocating, the recommendation violated the panelist's ethical code, which says that you do not exploit the desperation of another person to your own advantage. The author, on the other hand, saw gaming ethics as appropriate to the situation, much like a poker game, and that the key to success in the competitive world is to take advantage of all the law or rules will allow.

Now let's take another look at Mr. Haws described at the beginning of the chapter. Is he ethical or unethical? Clearly, if we apply personal ethics to the world of business, he behaved unethically, for he deliberately deceived the landlord. But if we believe that business is a competitive game, then gaming ethics are appropriate, and Mr. Haws has been as upright and ethical as any football quarterback.

When businesspeople fail to distinguish between the two sets of rules, confusion, frustration, and accusations abound—especially when one person thinks personal ethics are the best standard for the situation and another thinks gaming ethics are the way to go.

Business Ethics

Besides these two major sets of ethics, businesspeople may want to consider one more set of ethical standards, "business ethics." This set can also be called "ethics for profit" or "amoral ethics." The well-known economist Milton Friedman hinted at this set of rules when he said that the primary responsibility of business is to increase its profits, suggesting that the rules are actually "amoral," not immoral.[4] According to the dictionary, "amoral" is defined as "outside the sphere of morality, non-moral."[5]

Basically, this position suggests that businesses should abide the laws of the land, but beyond that they should not be held to a typical moral code. Instead, they should be held responsible for making a profit—period. This responsibility requires businesses to abide by economic rules, not moral standards, and has little or nothing to do with morals at all. If projecting the image of high moral standards helps the bottom line, that strategy is legitimate. Nevertheless, in business ethics, management follows a standard of personal ethics because it produces economic results, not because it's the right thing to do.

Management may give to charities because the act of charity enhances the company's image, which results in winning more customers and improving profits, not because management has a moral obligation to do so. And, when the profits are passed on to shareholders, they have a personal responsibility to do morally appropriate things with their money based on personal ethics. But, business ethics are amoral, and businesses should not be governed by a moral code except to make a profit.

Facing Up to the Consequences of Your Choice

Now we understand that at least three sets of rules govern people at work. Businesspeople would do well to establish which set of rules they will follow at which times, and then discuss their philosophy with others to increase agreement and awareness. Then, they should abide by their belief system, applying the different rules to the appropriate situations as they have agreed, in both word and deed. Otherwise, confusion will continue to reign supreme, and accusations of unethical behavior will increase as the gulf widens between the two main camps and as fewer people understand or accept the concept of business ethics.

Additional confusion often arises when executives advocate personal ethics in their public speeches and statements, but then they deliberately practice gaming ethics. We frequently hear top executives proclaim that they strictly stand by truth and honesty, but in the pressure of the "business game," they indulge in a highly refined practice of deception. For example, how often do senior executives stress truthfulness and high moral standards in their talk, but then they spend hours with their managers huddling over the annual report to stockholders, trying to manipulate the words so that bad financial news does not show or appears to be unimportant? Or, how often do corporations restate their gift-receiving policies at Christmastime— "We remind all employees that it is strictly against company policy for any employee to accept gifts from suppliers, either at work or at home"—while, at the same time, the sales department is updating its list of important clients to whom will be sent impressive gifts "to show our thanks for your business"?

One CEO I know warned his executive team, "If I catch any one of you so much as accepting a free lunch from a supplier or potential supplier, you will be fired." Yet, this same CEO continues to supply his salespeople with generous expense accounts to buy lunches and entertainment tickets for customers and potential customers.

This duplicity sends conflicting messages to employees: We practice personal ethics when dealing with our suppliers—lest we find ourselves obligated in some way—while we practice gaming ethics with our customers—making sure they make the "right" decision. Wouldn't it show more integrity to just openly acknowledge that business is a game and that gaming ethics is the proper way to play? Let's at least be honest with ourselves.

On the other hand, what would happen if your organization decides to operate within the realm of personal ethics while all the other companies in your industry choose to play by gaming ethics or an amoral set of business ethics? You place yourself at a serious competitive disadvantage as others take advantage of all the law or rules will allow. Or, back the other way, wouldn't you be placing yourself at risk by choosing to play by gaming ethics when others are living by personal ethics? You could be left wide open to charges of stepping over the ethical line, and you or your employees may occasionally cross over the legal line, too, and may get caught.

And what if you decide to do what others in your industry are doing? If that means personal ethics, wonderful; we're all in heaven, and we're all rich, too, right? But if everyone is playing by gaming ethics, and especially if we get to be "good at it," we subject ourselves to the weak moral stance of "Everybody's doing it," and risk jumping or being pushed across the legal lines right into jail or heavy penalties. After all, even sports teams and their key players get suspended, fined, ejected, heavily penalized, etc. Isn't that more damaging to careers and livelihoods in the business world?

Play by Which Rules?

So what should we do?

   1. Acknowledge to yourself that at least two sets of ethical standards, both accepted and legitimate, govern people's actions in the world of business. You may even consider the third set, an amoral variety of "business ethics."

2. After thinking through the implications of embracing each one, make a tentative decision about which set generally applies to your organization and industry.

3. Discuss the concepts with others. Make sure everyone understands the different options independent of your beliefs. Then, share opinions and explore together the implications of pursuing each path. See if you can reach a group agreement on a common approach.

4. Implement the decision.

5. Periodically review your group's progress in establishing the chosen set of rules. Explore the problems, barriers, difficulties, and rewards that surface as a result of choosing this particular set of rules to play by.

CASE: *The Entrepreneur*

Rex had been a top accounting student at the university he attended, and he received several outstanding job offers before he graduated. He accepted a position with a nationally recognized financial firm and soon began to impress his employer. He was highly regarded by the clients he served, and his employer gave him some unprecedented opportunities and advancements faster than most people who worked at the firm.

However, for some time, Rex had considered going out on his own and becoming his own boss. After four years with the firm, he decided it was time to make his move. He had gained a great deal of valuable experience, had established a solid reputation in the business community, and now had many valuable contacts. After laying his plans out carefully, he gave his firm two weeks notice and then set out on his own. The risks of his entrepreneurial venture were soon moderated when he found that several of the firm's clients were willing to switch to him for their financial services. Financially, his first year on his own was much more successful than he had expected.

Questions:

1. Did Rex act ethically? Wherein did he? In what ways did he not?

2. Is "stealing clients" simply a matter of competitive gaming ethics, or is it unethical?

3. Does it make a difference whether Rex enticed the firm's clients to switch or the clients volunteered?

4. Should Rex have let his firm know about his plans when he began to think about going out on his own, or is withholding such information just another part of the competitive game?

5. How would an ethical, honest person handle such a situation?

Chapter 10

There Are No Gray Areas:
Principles in Conflict

*"Many good qualities are not sufficient to balance a
single want—the want of money."*

—*Zimmerman*

IN 1974, IN the NATO Defense Organization, a major decision was
being made about which fighter plane would be used by the military
organization. Analysis and debate mainly centered around two new
American-designed planes: Northrop's F-17 and General Dynamics'
F-16. The French-built Mirage F-1 was also in the running. After all
the performance tests, and taking into account the cost of manufacture
and the cost of operation, most people involved felt the F-16 was significantly better. The French, however, still held out for their machine.

One member of the decision team was Paul Stehlin, a high-rank-
ing French Air Force officer who had been commander of the Air
Force under Charles de Gaulle. When a reporter asked him for his
opinion about the best choice, Stehlin said that in his honest judgment, the American-made F-16 was superior. After he made the public statement, the French Air Force promptly retired him from the
reserve for his "unpatriotic" remarks.[1]

This example shows one of the fundamental causes of dishonesty
for many members of organizations. Senior executives and the public
frequently criticize front-line employees and mid-level managers for
being dishonest, but when the employees are honest they often are
punished much like the French officer was. This apparent hypocrisy,
of advocating honesty but rewarding dishonesty, arises because people
fail to recognize the intense dilemmas inherent in complete honesty.

Right Versus Wrong?
Dilemmas of this kind constantly plague businesspeople.
Benjamin Selekman writes that to expect business executives to live

the Judeo-Christian ethic places them in a state of perpetual sinfulness—or, that it's impossible to expect managers to obey all the principles of the Judeo-Christian ethic and still keep their jobs.[2]

Most people believe that ethics are simply a matter of choosing between right and wrong or between good and bad. Actually, for most people, day-to-day decision making is not that simple. Some decisions create severe stress, not from choosing between right and wrong, but from being forced to choose between two right principles. This is what I call the "conflict of principles." A conflict of principles occurs whenever two right principles come into conflict in such a way that when we choose to obey one principle, we violate the other principle. Abiding both principles to their fullest extent in such an instance is usually impossible.

For example, a common and frustrating conflict for many people is between honesty and loyalty. The Judeo-Christian ethic teaches that people should be honest, but it also teaches that they should be loyal and obedient. In the case of the French general, he faced a conflict between honesty—or loyalty to his own conscience—and loyalty to his country. He could have been loyal to his country and argued in favor of the French plane, and this might have protected him from the wrath of his fellow citizens and even won their praise, but he would have been forced to live with a conscience that reminded him he did not tell the truth.

Also, sometimes people face a conflict between loyalty to one person and loyalty to another. In the same example, it could be said that the general faced a conflict between loyalty to his country and loyalty to NATO. Again, he could have been loyal to his country and recommended the French plane, but perhaps he recognized a design flaw in the French plane and by recommending it he may have jeopardized the safety and maneuverability of NATO pilots in the future, all by not giving his honest judgment or opinion when asked for it. And, if he did know of such a flaw in the French plane, then we can even argue that he was loyal to the French Air Force by not pointing out the flaw to the public, quietly recommending the F-16 instead.

Loyalty Versus Honesty

Loyalty and honesty are frequently in conflict when people are asked to express their judgments about others, particularly when one person is the other person's boss or subordinate.

For example, Adam Collins had worked for the Nary Company for several years. For the past six years, he had been a superintendent under Mike Hannah, the vice president of production. During that time, they had worked together closely, and Adam felt that he knew Mike very well, and he liked him very much on a personal level. However, he felt that Mike had become obsolete as a leader.

In the past, Mike had demonstrated technical competence, but he had never been a leader. In fact, Adam felt that if it weren't for the experienced superintendents under Mike, and their technical abilities, the company would be having serious difficulty. But, as it was, the company was holding its own, but it was not nearly as strong as its resources and potential suggested it could be.

One day, as Adam was waiting at the corner for the light to change so he could cross Main Street, George Owen, the vice chairman of Nary Company's board, arrived at the corner alongside him. Adam knew Mr. Owen reasonably well through other contacts in the community. After a casual exchange of greetings, Mr. Owen asked, "Adam, I've been wondering about our management team. In your opinion, just how good of a manager do you think Mike Hannah is? Is he giving us the leadership the company needs?" As the light changed, both men began to walk across the street together, and Adam needed to choose between loyalty and honesty.

If you were Adam, with strong desires to be honest, but at the same you wanted to be loyal to Mike Hannah, what would you say to Mr. Owen? Is there a way to answer the question that is both honest and loyal? Remember, "To tell the truth is not just to state the facts, but to convey a true impression."

In such an instance, many people would put on their "political" cap and try to come up with something that is "technically" truthful, or that skirts around the issue but is essentially misleading or disloyal. They would avoid the question by saying, "I'm not sure that's an appropriate question to ask me," or "How do *you* think he is working out?" or "I really like him personally," or change the subject by saying, "Oh, watch out for that car." These are messages of subtle criticism and would not be loyal—"Nothing is as damning as faint praise."

In fact, anything short of an enthusiastic endorsement of Mike Hannah would convey a message of criticism. Also, George Owen knows Adam—that he is honest, and if he thinks highly of his boss, he won't hesitate to say so. So, any hesitation or attempt to maneuver around the question would be understood by Mike as a form of disloyalty if he had been present in the conversation or if he had found out about it later.

On the other hand, if Adam decides to react to the question with real loyalty by giving Mike a strong endorsement, would he be dishonest? Such conflicts are relatively common and affect everyone.

Another similar incident that shows the intense pressure for people to be loyal to their bosses occurred in the public spotlight and involved people who were both respected for their reputations of honesty and loyalty. During the Vietnam War, General William Westmoreland was in command of the American forces under President Lyndon B. Johnson. Johnson was under pressure from Congress and the American public either to show that the conflict was leading to an American victory or to pull out the troops. He asked General Westmoreland to give evidence of American success. But, when Westmoreland asked Colonel Gains Hawkins to produce numbers to back him up, the numbers were never enough to satisfy Johnson that he could convince Congress, let alone the public. After repeatedly revising the numbers, Gains finally could no longer live with his role in the deception:

> [General Westmoreland] was trained from the start in accepting and obeying commands. He remained loyal to his own vision, and his definition of loyalty. Therefore when his intelligence officers showed him estimates that reflected the darker reality, he rejected those estimates and demanded that the enemy's troop level be lowered. He did this, I suspect, without even realizing what he was doing.
>
> In 1967, [Colonel Gains] Hawkins was caught between the conflict of two loyalties—the first to the truth as he saw it, and the second to orders from a superior that forced him to doctor his work during time of war. He had followed the traditional loyalty, gone along with his superiors, and in the process he had begun to feel that he had been untrue to himself.
>
> The true figures he came up with then reflected a lack of American progress. Yet that would be a difficult problem for a President facing a reelection campaign. The first time he brought in the figures, they were rejected so he made them a few percentage points more acceptable . . . and the second time he brought them in they were rejected.

> He [Colonel Hawkins] had lost the one thing he
> prided himself on—his own honesty.
>
> Someone asked what he thought about
> Westmoreland, and he [Hawkins] said, more in sad-
> ness than anger, "He left his honor in the same damn
> place I left my integrity."[3]

Many people debate whether anyone really ever faces such a situation. "It never should have been that way," they demand. They
believe that if we can just be a bit more patient and calm, we can
always find a way to be both loyal and honest if we so desire. Indeed,
we would all like to have it both ways. But life is not that way.
Conflicts of principles do exist, and we should stop trying to avoid
this reality. Recognizing that conflicts of principles can, and often do,
exist is the first step in handling one of the major root causes of dishonesty. This kind of conflict is exactly what induces or traps people
into lying—people rarely make an outright decision to lie.

Which Principle Comes First?

When faced with a conflict of principles, people must decide
which principle to obey and which to violate. Too often, the decision
is made in the pressure of the moment, rather than based on the
thoughtful adherence to principle. Those who are trying to "get
ahead," especially young people, decide whether to be honest or loyal
based on which path would better further their careers.

For many, their first urge is to say, "Well, I will be both honest
and loyal." But, again, in many situations, it would be impossible to
do both. Recognizing this reality is important in dealing "honestly
with honesty." In the case at the start of this chapter, telling the French
general that he can be both honest and loyal in speaking to the
reporter is a grand delusion, which does not help him deal forthright-
ly with the problem.

So, what should we do when faced with such conflicts? How do
we decide which principle to abide by and which to violate? Should
we be honest or loyal? How do we decide which person or group we
should be loyal to, if honesty is not the question? To answer these
questions, we must establish a hierarchy of principles. The principles
must be ranked in order of importance or priority.

Now, most people recognize that some things are more important
than others. For instance, I think that most people believe it's more
important to preserve a person's life than to avoid a lie, if they were

forced to choose between the two. And, for many, it's more important to be kind than to be completely honest. But, between honesty and loyalty, which is the higher principle? Once the higher one is identified, then of course that's the one we will obey and the other we will reluctantly violate.

A hierarchy of principles can be established in one of two ways: either because of our personal convictions or as a result of adopting the hierarchy established by an organization, whether it is explicitly stated in policy or expressed in its reward and punishment system. Hopefully, for our peace of mind, these two will be the same. However, whenever this occurs it generally means that honesty comes in second for the organization. Most organizations, and society in general, prefer loyalty over honesty and give it the greater reward.

One successful businessman recalled in his autobiography how he learned the hierarchy of priorities. When he was a young man just starting his career, during an interview with his mentor, the company owner who had already established his own successful business, the owner asked, "What is the most important characteristic to be successful in business?"

Immediately the young man responded, "Integrity."

"No, it's not," replied the employer. "Loyalty is the most important and always comes first." He later added that integrity was also important. But, regardless of which principle is actually more important, by making the statement he firmly established which principle was at the top of the hierarchy for him, and he emphatically announced that whenever the two came into conflict the young man was to choose loyalty.

This same order of priorities is constantly reinforced in the organizational setting. Only at the peril of their careers will aspiring young employees ignore this basic hierarchy when making decisions between the conflicting principles. Even when they would be speaking out to expose an act of gross wrongdoing, loyalty will still invoke a greater reward.

Speaking the Truth Can Be Disloyal

One young junior manager of a large retail chain learned this generally unwritten rule the hard way. Alex Sanderson had just been promoted from head clerk to assistant supervisor and had been relocated from Pennsylvania to a new assignment in Massachusetts. Each of the chain's stores included a management team that consisted of a manager, a supervisor, an assistant supervisor, and a head clerk. Managers, in addition to their salary, were paid a percentage of store profits, determined after each semiannual physical inventory. And, since variations in inventory could impact profits, some managers faced a temptation to "stretch" the rules of inventory to show a greater profit and so increase their bonuses and opportunities for advancement.

After he had been in Massachusetts for several weeks, Alex observed that the store's inventory books were inaccurate and violated company inventory management rules. But, when he called this to the manager's attention, the manager told him, "Don't worry, nearly everybody does it this way." But violating company rules weighed upon Alex's mind, and he felt that the manager was being dishonest. The second time he raised his concern, the manager said, "Take care of your own business; I know how to run this store."

Several weeks passed, and Alex began to worry about the dishonest practices of the store manager. Finally, in desperation he contacted an officer of the company and exposed the store's dishonest inventory methods. After a thorough investigation, the company officer verified Alex's story, and he disciplined the manager.

However, the other members of the store's management team soon found out who had reported the violations, and they began to alienate Alex from them. In addition, Alex felt guilty for having been disloyal to the store, until he finally resigned. In the meantime, the officers of the company at headquarters were anxious to retain him, for he was a competent person with good management potential and unusually high standards of honesty. Rather than allow him to resign, the company offered him three months of paid leave so that he could consider a new assignment.

After several weeks, one of the company officers began to inquire to see if any of the chain's stores would accept Alex as an assistant manager. But, the company grapevine had already become acquainted with the incident, and, as Alex already sensed, no one wanted to take him on because they could not trust his loyalty. Reluctantly, the company let the promising young manager go to pursue his career elsewhere. Ironically, the dishonest manager, though he was disciplined, retained his position as manager (likely because he had the reputation of being a "profitable manager"), while the honest young man with potential was now unemployed.

Loyalty Rewarded over Honesty

Telling the truth to expose the wrongdoing of a superior is certainly a perilous step. An excellent book called *Whistle Blowing,* a compilation of famous incidents in which people have exposed gross fraud, shows that time and again, society does not reward the "tattletale."[4] Such people find out that no one wants them around because of their questionable loyalty. In our society it is worse to be a "squealer" than to be dishonest.

Part of the problem is that honesty is rarely rewarded when it is chosen over loyalty. In fact, it is generally punished either formally or in subtle ways. To reduce the personal conflict for people who are not psychologically prepared to suppress their honest opinions, perhaps we should reassure them that being "less than honest," when loyalty to the boss or the company is at stake, is acceptable. Then, at least, we could acknowledge the practice and allow it to continue in the open.

On the other hand, this raises the question, under what circumstances is dishonesty in the cause of loyalty acceptable? When the company is profitable and growing? When times are tough? When we would avoid embarrassment to the company? When we would lose too many customers? When we want to keep information about our internal difficulties from competitors? When it would precipitate too much new legislation in the industry or force the company to conform to more rigid standards?

In another public incident, Martin Feldstein, chairman of the President's Council of Economic Advisors, realized the consequences of straying from the administration's official line about the consequences of the federal deficit and other budget concerns, although he was not attempting to expose any wrongdoing. He found out publicly that the administration preferred that he be loyal instead of honestly expressing his professional opinions:

> President Reagan's chief economist still had a job yesterday, but his hold on it appeared to be tenuous.
>
> Martin Feldstein, chairman of Reagan's Council of Economic Advisors, was publicly rebuked by White House officials, who are upset that he has strayed from the official line on such sensitive issues as the budget deficit, tax increases, and defense spending. Larry Peakes, Reagan's chief spokesman, said, "Obviously, the President and Secretary of Treasury don't agree with Mr. Feldstein, and are

> unhappy that the economist has been voicing his dif-
> ferences in a series of recent speeches."
>
> Further, another aide said the economist's public
> statements have tainted him with disloyalty and
> shown him to be "not a team player"—a major sin
> within any administration.[5]

Some argue that Feldstein's voicing his disagreement in a public speech was his sin, even though he was honest. But, what should Feldstein have answered if a reporter had asked for his opinion? Should he be dishonest and cover up any disagreements he might be having with the President? Should he simply say, "No comment," and assume that no one will take such a response as a subtle statement of disloyalty? Or, should he simply voice his opinion? As the reporter indicated, the greater sin in the eyes of society is to be disloyal.

Too often, in my opinion, honesty takes a back seat to loyalty. Expressions of candid thinking, particularly when they are at variance with those in authority, is construed as a lack of loyalty or a display of questionable support, or somehow conveys that the person is not a team player. By this, it seems most managers feel that the best team players are the ones who can comfortably suppress their true feelings, conflicting ideas, and candid observations that would not correspond with those of the people in authority. When these people are asked, "Do you agree?" they can say "yes," even if they don't agree, and not for a moment feel dishonest about it. Consequently, in situations when the boss asks, "Let me have your honest opinion," unless our opinions are similar to the chief's, we don't often take the invitation too literally. As a result, businesses do not embrace creative new ideas or challenge their own thinking in an effort to improve themselves. Diversity of thought is subordinated to orthodoxy as interpreted by the boss.

Conflicting Loyalties

Sometimes loyalty problems center around the problems of choosing who to be loyal to and then how to handle the situation, particularly if the choice will require a shifting of loyalties. One senior manager, the executive vice president of a large organization who had kept his position under a succession of several presidents, advised aspiring young subordinates, "Never get involved in controversial matters if you can possibly avoid them." Then, he demonstrated his philosophy a short time later:

When the new president accused a mid-level manager of having made a foolish decision, one of the manager's peers, another mid-level manager, reassured the president that the person's actions had been carried out under the direction and approval of the former president. He also explained that the executive vice president had been in on the decision and could verify the fact. But, when the manager's peer turned to the executive vice president for confirmation, the executive vice president remained silent. Of course, this disturbed both mid-level managers.

After the meeting, the executive vice president put his arm around the manager who had attempted to defend his colleague and said, "You must remember, we have a new president—a new pharaoh is in the land. The things that went on before are no longer valid."

When the junior executive protested, "At least you could have verified the truth of the matter," the executive vice president simply patted the junior manager on the shoulder, restated, "There's a new pharaoh in the land," and walked away. After all, he knew that the manager under attack was unpopular with the new president, and to have defended him or to have admitted that he "made a foolish decision" in such a tense situation would only diminish his own standing in the eyes of the new president.

Would you say that the executive vice president was honest? Loyal? In the man's defense, many try to show that he never said anything dishonest. But, is silence or withholding information being honest? On the contrary, in contract law if someone is discovered to have withheld pertinent information the contract is nullified, and the person can be taken to court for the deception. In social relations, withholding information is often the cause of broken friendships, marriage annulments, and violations of trust—even if it is done in an attempt to be loyal.

Once when I was working as a consultant with a large firm, occasionally I sat in on informal daily "coffee-break" sessions with the company's top executives. The company's chairman seemed, in my mind, to fit the mold of an authoritarian. One day, the company's communication problems became the topic of discussion. After the session broke up, I was cornered by one of the key executives, who had been with the company for thirty years and had survived all the comings and goings of people. He was among the executives who were held in the highest regard by the boss. He asked, "How would you evaluate the openness of the communication of this group?" After he listened to my candid response—that communication was much less than open—he volunteered, with a twinge of confession and acquiescence, "Yes, I have been sitting around this table for over twenty years. Everybody sits on their own ideas until they learn what the boss has on his mind, and then you have never seen such enthusiastic outspokenness supporting the chief's ideas."

In most organizations, when the principles of loyalty and honesty come in conflict, loyalty is the most prudent path to survival.

The So-Called "Gray Areas"

Besides loyalty and honesty, other principles also create conflicts: time with family versus time at work and career success; honesty versus effectiveness in producing results; doing what's best for yourself versus doing what's best for the organization; honesty about fiscal matters versus maintaining stockholder value. When these conflicts arise, many are prone to label them "gray areas," and business carries on as usual without any real growth and learning taking place.

But, labeling a situation a "gray area" is not only wrong, it also can be harmful. It fails to resolve the dilemma in a rational or helpful way. Calling a situation a "gray area" suggests that the situation is clouded, or that it's hard to see what the problem is, or that it's impossible to resolve logically, or that no right or wrong answers exist. Therefore, whatever decision is made is okay, "As long as it doesn't hurt me." But the truth is, situations can be made clear, even though they may require extensive thought and difficult decisions. By labeling a conflict of principles just another gray area, we avoid having to face up to the unpleasant task of choosing between two conflicting principles.

Rather than call these dilemmas "gray areas," we should recognize them as conflicts of principles. This recognition can lead to establishing a constructive process for dealing with such conditions deliberately and rationally by: (1) identifying the conflicting principles, (2) stating the conflicts and the consequences of each option clearly, (3) determining the hierarchy of principles that should apply and why, (4) recognizing and regrettably admitting that the other principle must be broken for now—not because the principle is wrong or would not apply, but because it has been subordinated to a higher law or purpose by logic that is morally sound. Such an approach would also enable us to explain our reasoning to a critical audience: "Let the consequences come; we understand and agree to them."

Handling Conflicts of Principles

Most managers with any degree of sensitivity have experienced conflicts of principles. But, what is the best way to deal with them? Although there are perhaps no simple solutions, here are a few steps that can help you cope with such dilemmas:

1. *Recognize that insolvable conflicts between loyalty and honesty occur.* Do not try to go through verbal or mental gymnastics. Simply recognize and admit the reality of the dilemma. If others see the dilemma but we deny it, we only raise questions about our credibility or competence. To deny that a conflict exists, when it does exist, is probably one of the worst deceptions of all.

2. *Establish a hierarchy of values.* If loyalty comes first, then say so and then live with the results. Many managers claim that honesty comes first, but then they reward loyalty more. This can be very confusing for newcomers to the organization, but those who survive will do so by giving little heed to what managers say and by following what the system rewards.

3. *Do not get upset if you find that someone has been dishonest to maintain loyalty.* Even "honest" people indulge occasionally in dishonesty to avoid being disloyal to friends.

4. If you are the boss, *be careful how you excuse subordinates in front of others if they are found to engage in a little dishonesty or deception in defending a management decision or action you made.* Generally when this occurs, most managers would feel good about the integrity of the person who is loyal, but they give no thought to the deception passed on to the other party, and so tacitly approve of the dishonesty. In such cases, leaders would do well to deliberately communicate under what conditions dishonesty is allowed or expected and where it is not. Sweeping general statements such as, "We believe in being honest" will not do in these cases.

5. If you truly want to establish honesty as your high-priority principle, then *be willing to accept what appear to be acts of disloyalty.* You must give greater rewards for honesty than for loyalty.

CASE: The New Purchase

Several months after her husband's death, Maria decided to use some of the proceeds from the life insurance policy to buy a new car. In all their married life, they had never owned a new car. She was now 68 years old and had never been involved with the purchase of a car, new or used.

Maria went to a car dealer that sold the make of car her friend told her was good. She looked around the lot, noted sticker prices on the windows of a few cars, and asked the salesman some questions about the cars just before he was called in to the office to take a call. She knew nothing about the customary bargaining for a price and was unaware that practically no one paid the "sticker price." Not finding any reason to be concerned, she decided to purchase a dark green, four-door sedan.

She walked in to the salesman, who was now off the phone, and said, "I'll take that green one that costs $14,995" (the sticker price). She took out her checkbook from her purse and asked, "Do you add sales tax to that amount? If so, what's the total amount I should write this check for?"

The salesman was taken aback for a moment. He seldom had customers who paid with a check, and he had never found a customer willing to pay the "sticker price." For a few moments, he pondered the problem: Should he just take her money or tell her that, if she requested it, she could get a lower price? Finally, he resolved simply to take the price she offered. He reasoned that it would result in a little higher commission for him, and also: What would the owner think if he found out that he had turned down the full price when it was offered? Besides, it was her choice, not his. He had done nothing to pressure her to buy the car, and he hadn't even talked price with her.

Questions:

1. If you were the salesman, would you take her money as she has offered? Is that ethical? Why or why not?

2. Would you offer her a lower price? If so, how much? The deepest discount possible? Half the best discount? How would you justify your final price to yourself and to the owner of the dealership?

3. What is the best thing to do for you? For her? For the owner of the dealership? What is the right thing to do?

4. What would the Golden Rule dictate in this situation? What does business dictate?

5. What would demonstrate the salesman's loyalty to the dealership? To the customer?

Chapter 11

"Don't Be a Tattletale": The Whistle-Blower's Dilemma

"No man can tell whether he is rich or poor by turning to his ledger. He is rich according to what he is, not according to what he has."

—Henry Ward Beecher

SHORTLY AFTER THE Challenger space shuttle disaster, I was teaching a business ethics class at a major university. I had heard that a nationally known company that supplied equipment and materials to the U.S. Department of Defense had introduced a new program on ethical behavior. Since I knew the person who had started the new program, I invited him to speak to my class to explain how the program worked and what results the company was experiencing. I hoped that, in a time when business managers and politicians were being fired upon with accusations of unethical behavior, this lecturer could engender a healthy respect for the moral integrity of most people in the "real world" in the minds of my students.

The man explained the details of the company's ethics program and the philosophy behind it. One of the key elements of the program was to encourage employees to behave more honestly by providing incentives for those who report the unethical behavior of others. For example, the company wanted to discourage the illegal practice of employees punching each other's time cards. Whenever employees knew they would be coming in late or wanted to get away from work early, they could ask fellow workers to punch their time cards at the regular time. So, by fudging by an hour or so, they could still receive a full paycheck. Reciprocity in this practice was common, and over time, this practice generated a system of mutual obligation.

The company expected that by rewarding those who reported such practices, and others such as receiving gifts or favors from suppliers or taking bogus sick days, it could stop or minimize them and create a climate of a higher standard of moral behavior. However, he explained that the training was just under way, and it was hard to tell how it was working.

In his discussion with the students, he was asked by one of them, "So, I guess you must be recruiting that engineer from Thiokol?" The student was referring to an engineer with Morton Thiokol who, during the investigation after the Challenger disaster, explained that he had warned Thiokol's management that the shuttle's O-rings could fail in low temperatures, but that his supervisors had ignored his warnings and told him to keep quiet. Then, after he had been candid and honest in reporting the experience to investigators, management tried to fire him.

The student felt that this man would certainly fit in with the lecturer's company since it employed many engineers in the defense industry, and he seemed to fit with the company philosophy of reporting wrongdoing. But, the students were surprised by my friend's reply to the suggestion: "No! We wouldn't hire him. That engineer went about reporting the incident in the wrong way."

Bucking the System

The new ethics program my friend's company was trying to implement seemed to have at least two flaws: First, the program was bucking against human nature and the deeply ingrained value our culture instills in us at a very young age and reinforces throughout our lives: "Don't Be a Tattletale!" We teach our children from an early age not to tell on other people's misbehavior—we don't want them to become "squealers" or "snitches." But, after all of that culture is ingrained in them, we still expect them to violate that mandate in certain circumstances, such as when we want them to help us root out unethical behavior in our employees or when the police are investigating a suspected criminal act.

In many instances, the government also has difficulty enticing people to report illegal practices. For example, in Utah the state government gets frustrated by people who license their vehicles in other states, but who then drive them illegally in Utah. Utah law requires that after you have taken up residence in the state you have 90 days to register your car and obtain Utah license plates. But some drivers license their cars in Oregon, for instance, because the registration costs less than in Utah. Then, by using a former address or by claiming a parent's home in Oregon as their address, they continue to retain Oregon licenses and registrations even though they live in Utah and are not students or temporary residents.

Finding that many vehicle owners engaged in this practice, one Utah sheriff appealed to the members of his community to report suspected violations in their neighborhoods or places of work. He asked people to report vehicles with out-of-state license plates that parked in their neighborhoods over extended periods of time, such as two years. He promised that they could remain completely anonymous—just give the location, description, and license number, and the sheriff's deputies would handle the rest. He gave several good, rational arguments for the local citizens to report the cars: Their tax dollars were subsidizing these "scroungers" who refuse to pay their fair share to keep up state roads and provide for police protection; they would not have to pay any social price because no one would know who reported the cars, and they could take pride and satisfaction in helping to secure law and order in the community. But, even with all the logical arguments, very few people in the community volunteered to help the sheriff by anonymously blowing the whistle on their neighbors.

The deeply ingrained cultural commandment, "Don't be a tattletale," creates such an environment of guilt for going against it that even logic and rational thinking cannot surmount it. What's my evidence? At the time of the Utah license plate problem, I asked the 40 students in my university class, "How many of you would help the sheriff if you knew a vehicle in your neighborhood was in violation of the law?" Hesitantly, one hand went up. I have found similar results in discussing other cases of whistle-blowing.

Over the years I have tried to find out whether people were hesitant to point out wrongdoing simply because the consequences for the person reported were minor or petty. I reasoned that maybe people felt they were being nice by not inflicting their associates with compliance to burdensome regulations, or perhaps they felt hypocritical by reporting someone else's misdeeds when they, themselves, wouldn't obey such rules. But, I find that even when someone has committed a gross criminal act, people still are extremely hesitant to report it. The dilemma is simply another example of conflict of principle: wanting to be loyal versus wanting to correct wrongdoing. For most people, loyalty wins out—even in cases of gross misbehavior.

However, even though whistle-blowing occurs infrequently and with unusual agony, it does occur. The case of the "Unabomber" is an interesting example. For 18 years someone regularly had been sending deadly bombs through the mail. The anonymous mail bombs had caused the death of three people and had injured 23 others. For years, authorities had tracked every lead to no avail. In the early part of 1996, the published reports of the bombings began to catch the interest of David Kaczymnski, who picked up a few of the clues and began to suspect his brother, Theodore Kaczymnski. After a lengthy analysis of his own, he became convinced that his brother was the Unabomber, and he reported Theodore to the authorities. An FBI agent investigating the case commented, "He [David] was as torn as anyone would be, between doing what is socially right and loyalty to his brother."[1] As heinous as the crime was, it took considerable internal debate and agonizing for David to come forward and "do the right thing."

David didn't see himself as a hero—far from it. In fact, he became angry when news leaked to the press that he had "squealed" on his brother. Many people empathized with his difficulty and asked themselves, "Would I turn someone in?"—especially if the person was a family member. Many were grateful for David's action, but found it difficult to call him a hero. For the same reason, most organizations, professional societies, trade associations, churches, and governments find it difficult, if not impossible, to police themselves.

Once when I was serving on the athletic committee of a well-known university, a competing university was caught violating NCAA regulations and was suspended from play. In our next committee meeting, the discussion centered on finding out if our university was guilty of similar behavior. We also wondered how the rival university had been caught. One of the coaches gave an interesting insight: He said the NCAA has no police to enforce the rules. The only way the association can find an occasional violator is if a rival school files a report. So, he explained, the reason violations seldom surface is "because we are all doing something that is not appropriate, so we feel hypocritical about reporting someone else." Such a system makes self-policing difficult, if not impossible.

Similar difficulties in reporting are found in the medical profession. Most doctors hate the idea of serving as witnesses against a fellow professional, especially one they know on a personal basis. If you add to that the threat that the accused person might file a lawsuit against a witness or accuser for slander, libel, or character assassination, then only the most grossly unethical conduct will ever get reported.

Whistle-Blowing Can Be Dangerous

A second problem with my friend's ethics program is that whistle-blowing can be dangerous. For example, an April 1996 evening news report announced that two airplane mechanics testified in a Senate subcommittee investigative hearing about unethical inspection practices and safety violations in the airline industry. The mechanics, along with the senators who were questioning them, felt that because their testimony would be incriminating to airline companies, their lives would be in danger. So, to reduce the potential threat, their names were withheld from the public, their faces were shielded from the cameras, and their voices were disguised. This incident further demonstrates the depth of our cultural bias against whistle-blowers.

Intuitively, you would think that in a society preaching morality and leaders who "insist" on high standards of ethical integrity, the people who point out miscreant conduct would be held up as heroes and role models to be emulated, or that companies would reward such people as the epitome of loyalty. But counter-intuitively, reporting wrongdoings is not only a social no-no, it can be dangerous to your career and possibly even your life.

Additionally, whistle-blowers cannot be protected from the backlash that may result as a consequence of their reports, which largely emanates from our "don't ask, don't tell" society. Although many organizations, especially police forces, go to great lengths to protect whistle-blowers, it is still difficult, in fact almost impossible, to keep back the forces that oppose them—just ask anyone who has blown a whistle. Even managers who admire whistle-blowers for their courage in exposing fraud, or cheating, or embezzlement in other organizations would hesitate to hire such people into their own organizations because they question the loyalty of such people. So, whistle-blowers who are known to have reported their past employers' unethical behavior—no matter how justified their actions—find it difficult to find other jobs regardless of their skills.

When Trusted Lieutenants Blow the Whistle

A letter to the editor of *CFO* magazine describes one such case in which a chief financial officer, Mr. Nazeley, didn't even blow the whistle—he just took exception to the company's president. Imagine what might have happened if he had chosen to go public with his problem:

> No one really can discuss ethics unless he has been asked to do something that is unethical. Ethics has a different meaning to each of us. *And I have never met anyone who didn't believe that he or she had high morals before an ethical issue forced a certain decision.*

Faced with such a dilemma, you must weigh loyalty to family against loss of employment and income. You must also deal with the frustration and stress of the situation, as well as eventually face the day of the dreaded decision. Being a CFO does not spare you this anguish. CFOs have to care for the needs of themselves, their families, their employers and professional responsibilities just like everyone else. This is a very stressful situation and a constant balancing act.

What compounds everything is that we live in a world of financial survival. Without money, no one can exist. . . . Everyone has financial problems. If you quit, you could be out of work for years. The employer will not give you a favorable reference, and who is going to hire a CFO without references? You could tell a prospective employer your dilemma, but most people don't want to hire problems. If you quit without a reason, you will not collect unemployment. If you collect unemployment, the employer knows you quit for a reason and generally will not give you a good reference. Your friends will tell you to sue for breach of employment ethics and hope you get a settlement. But what lawyer will take this case on contingency?

Once you have been through this type of ethical dilemma, you become more understanding of the motivating factors. I am a white knight who did the right thing and was out of work for 18 months, losing my self-respect in the process. Was it worth it? That is a personal question that I don't have the answer to. But please, God, don't offer me this choice again [emphasis added].[2]

Mr. Nazeley describes the pain, misery, and suffering that can arise simply for resigning based on refusing to participate in unethical actions. He didn't even blow the whistle or accuse anyone of wrongdoing, but look at the personal price he paid. If resigning in such an instance could cause such a cost, imagine the price he and his family would have paid if he had chosen to blow the whistle and expose the unethical behavior.

In another letter to the editor in the same magazine, the writer already had been tried and was serving a jail sentence but still requested that his or her name be withheld.

After reading "A Question of Ethics," it seemed as if you had published my story. I was CFO of a company in Savannah, Georgia, during 1989. Everything was going fine until the owner decided to expand and, in the process, hire people under the Federal Job Training Partnership Act (JTPA).

At the beginning, it seemed that through the JTPA the company would be helping people train for good jobs. But as the program progressed and the City of Savannah began to pay the fees for training new employees, I noticed that the workers were never available when I tried to check on their progress and personally supervise the program. I should add, however, that when it came time for these people to sign their time sheets, they were always present.

After several months, telephone calls from the JTPA office started coming in, and the owner was the only one allowed to field them. My instincts told me that something was very wrong, and when I started asking questions, I found out that the owner was not paying the JTPA employees as he was supposed to. Instead, he was keeping the money for his personal use.

My response to this information was to quit, and for nearly two years I had no contact with my ex-employer. Then, one day a Labor Department investigator showed up at my house asking about my employment. In time, there was court action, and I had to relay what I knew of the JTPA incident and my reasons for quitting. But that was not enough. According to the government officials, I should have reported the suspected problems to the JTPA office. *I was charged with conspiracy to commit fraud.*

Right now, I have five months to serve, five months of home confinement, and three years probation for not knowing what the owner was doing. The sentence is not the worst part. My career has been destroyed because I tried to do the job I was being paid to do. I learned the hard way that a CFO has no witnesses or friends, and that owners will not back you up when things go wrong. The way I see it, there is more risk working at the top of management than at the bottom of the ladder [emphasis added].[3]

If whistle-blowing is required by law (and it appears that it is), it can place people in impossible circumstances. Such people will pay a very high price, regardless of whether they blow the whistle or not. If they speak out, they become social outcasts and are suspected of disloyalty, but if they don't, if their consciences don't take their toll, the law may.

In another letter, the person also asked that the magazine withhold the name, even though the writer doesn't identify any wrongdoing. Apparently, just discussing the possibility of blowing the whistle was so threatening that the person didn't want to be identified. Perhaps the person worried that if his or her employer learned of these feelings, the person would be suspected of disloyalty.

> Professor Leo V. Ryan writes that integrity is the most important quality of a CFO. But the truth is that loyalty and allegiance to the business owner of a closely held company are what's essential.
>
> Management positions, particularly in the areas of accounting and finance, require walking the fine line between right and wrong as well as crossing that line when the owners demand it. My responsibility as a CFO is to inform owners of the consequences of that action, then move forward, realizing I am placing myself in a tenuous position at the same time.
>
> Ethics, personal and professional, are important to me. And there may be a time when I, in good conscience, cannot cross that line. If that time comes, I will properly advise the owners and pray that they take my advice. If they won't I will resign.[4]

Other than the fact that this person's name was withheld, two other aspects about this letter are interesting: (1) Apparently, on one or more occasions, this person had already crossed the ethical line "in good conscience," but the person felt that if the time came when crossing the line would violate conscience then he or she would resign. It's curious: What would allow this person to be unethical "in good conscience" in one instance and not in another? Is it a matter of degree or how much such an action might cost? Is it whether or not "everyone is doing it"? (2) This person explains that, if asked to do something that would force him or her to cross the line and not "in good conscience," the person would definitely resign, but blowing the whistle isn't even an alternative. This suggests the person's acute awareness of the devastating effects of whistle-blowing.

On the surface it seems that our society would be better off if we had more willing whistle-blowers. After all, if more people were willing to report wrongdoing, we could establish greater awareness and elevate the moral standard. If everyone worked to enforce higher standards of ethical conduct rather than leave it all to the police, we would be better off, wouldn't we? Surely the police can't do it all. We all must do our part to help establish, and influence people to live up to, higher standards of ethics by creating a culture that rewards ethical behavior instead of punishing it.

When Whistle-Blowing Is Socially Acceptable

In some areas, whistle-blowing seems to have gained some acceptance. For example, cellular phone owners on the highways of large cities are often encouraged to report suspected drunk drivers by calling 911. Apparently, law enforcement officials have been receiving many useful tips from cellular owners who are helping to curb the problem. What about this arrangement gives people the impetus to violate the "don't be a tattletale" rule, and how can we apply this example to other cases in which we need more willing whistle-blowers?

First, *the targeted behavior is widely accepted as wrong*. Drunk driving, with its gruesome tales of traffic accidents, personal tragedies, and family and community suffering, is almost universally condemned. Messages are widely publicized for people to designate drivers, call taxis, and to not let friends drive drunk. It seems that only defense attorneys are willing to stick up for drunk drivers these days.

Second, *people understand how the "wrong behavior" directly affects them*. Most sober drivers can see how a drunk driver could affect them here and now. Also, many people are personally acquainted with families who have been devastated by drunk drivers, or even by alcoholism alone.

Third, *reporting illegal behavior can lead immediately to positive results*. Reporting a suspected drunk driver will direct a police officer to the scene within minutes and, hopefully, get the drunk driver off the road before any physical harm is done.

Fourth, *it's simple and anonymous*. With a phone at the ready and many cellular phones on the highway, callers can be confident that no one will ever find out who reported the incident.

Fifth, *reporting total strangers who are posing a threat to others seems easier than reporting a friend or boss.* It's more like filing a report than "tattling" on a person; reporting an event instead of confronting someone. It always seems easier to take action against a "thing" than a person you know.

Applying these five rules to other cases where we need more willing whistle-blowers can help us reduce the social pressure on whistle-blowing.

What should a corporation, or an institution, or a school or a family do?

1. Discuss the impact of unchecked unethical behavior in the workplace and the impact of a whistle-blowing culture. Be prepared to deal with the fallout of the discussion if you are in a "don't ask, don't tell" environment.

2. Determine if establishing a culture of whistle-blowing will help your situation and discuss the idea with your group. Educate the group about the need for such a culture and the implications both of establishing and not establishing a culture of whistle-blowing. Discuss the pros and cons of how a whistle-blowing program would affect the group and the individuals in it. Make a group decision to work together on the plan that will work best.

3. Identify the specific steps that are needed to establish whistle-blowing as a socially acceptable part of your group's culture. A single memo will not change a culture. Instead, plan a sustained effort over an extended period of time to implement the program and to get feedback from participants. Use the feedback to improve or change the program.

4. When you get started, select only one or two aspects of your group's activities to work on. Do not try to encourage everyone to report every kind of suspected behavior at once.

5. If you are a leader and want to develop a culture that permits or encourages whistle-blowing, be prepared to become the target of whistle-blowers.

CASE: Ronald MacNeil[5]

At the end of his junior year of high school, Ronald MacNeil was looking around his home town for a summer job. After about a week, he heard that an electrical supply warehouse was moving to another town nearly 30 miles away and was looking for temporary help to accomplish the move. Ronald applied and was hired at minimum wage for the duration of the moving job. He found himself working with four other young men, three of whom he already knew fairly well. The five estimated that the job would probably last about three weeks.

The boys worked well together and did their job to the satisfaction of their employer. They kept careful count of their hours worked, but they were surprised when their first week's pay was noticeably less than what they had expected. When they brought the matter to their employer's attention, he blandly informed them that they could hardly expect to be paid for the time they spent riding in the truck from one town to the other. He also reminded them that summer employment was not easy for high school students to find that year.

Ronald and the others were furious, and they were convinced that the owner was cheating them. Next week, the other four boys started slipping wire, switches, and other supplies into their pockets and urged Ronald to do the same. Although he agreed that they had been treated unfairly, Ronald refused to join them in pilfering supplies and threatened to report them if they continued the practice. When they threatened to "get him" if he gave them away, Ronald decided to remain silent, but he still did not participate in taking supplies.

Questions:

1. Was the employer justified in refusing to pay for travel time?

2. If not, were the boys right in making up their wages by taking supplies?

3. If they were not, was Ronald justified in keeping silent about the matter?

Chapter 12

A Promise Is a Promise?
When Is My Word My Bond?

"To be trusted is a greater compliment than to be loved."

—*David O. McKay[1]*

ONE OF THE MOST frequent complaints about others in business is that people cannot be trusted: "He doesn't keep his commitments," "She won't honor our contract," "That company never lives up to its end of the deal, but it won't pay you unless you live up to your end." Much of business advertising affirms this problem: "We give honest value," "A name you can trust," "You can depend on us," "If you don't need new brakes, we'll tell you so," "With us, the price you see is the price you get."

All of these ads play on the widespread concern that you can't always trust what a company says. Good advertisers and salespeople identify common customer concerns, and then capitalize on them in advertising and sales pitches. If skepticism about trust was not such a pervasive concern for customers, advertisers would be foolish to use it as leverage.

What Is Your Word Worth?

I once served on the membership committee of a service club. One day the name of a prominent businessman was proposed for membership. As usual with other applicants, the name was circulated among members for their reaction. More than one member protested. When the members were invited to explain their concerns, one detailed his experience as a supplier to the man's business. Among other grievances, he cited specific examples in which he had contracted with the man to deliver services for a specified price. Then, after providing the services, the businessman would respond, "That service wasn't that valuable to us after all. So, here is what we will pay." Then he would remit a check for a smaller amount.

When asked why he continued to do business with the man, he replied, "Well, his company does a lot of business with us, and we just have to put up with it." Later, other members of the committee spoke up about how honest they considered the man to be, and they placed his name on the ballot for membership. When the votes were tallied, he had received more negative votes than anyone else had in years, but not enough to defeat his membership, so he was admitted to the club.

What do people mean when they say, "My word is my bond," or when someone says, "She is someone who keeps her commitments"? Is it like what Oliver North said during his campaign for the U.S. Senate? He admitted to reporters, "I acknowledged in an informal, off-the-record meeting with a handful of members of one committee and some staff that I had not told them everything they wanted to know." He confessed to "misleading" Congress, but insists he never lied.[2] In a later press conference, when asked what he would do about the lack of honesty in Washington, D.C., particularly in light of his behavior in the Iran-Contra hearings, he reportedly said, "I was not under oath. I would require everyone who testifies before Congress to do so under oath."

Is my word my bond only when I am under oath or contract? Is my "word," in testimony or promise, only valid if I raise my arm to the square and swear on the Bible or if I "cross my heart"? What if I cross my fingers as I speak? If I sign a contract, is it only binding if a staff of lawyers can't figure a legal way out of it or around it? Or, have I given my word when I lead someone to believe I will do something? If we have a verbal understanding, when does it become my "word"—after we nod our heads and say "yes" or "okay"? After we shake hands? After our attorneys draft a legal document and we both sign it? When the judge and jury say so?

When Is a Promise a Promise?

Early in 1993, most people believed that a very sought-after basketball player would return to his university for "one more year" before turning professional. No one expected the budding superstar to stay till graduation, but many believed he wasn't ready for "the big time." Also, it appeared that he had indicated he would return.

Then, in the spring, he announced he would go professional rather than return to the university. The discussion swirled widely. Many expressed disappointment, but understood that, with talk of a possible salary cap on professional basketball teams, he could lose out on several million dollars if he waited one more year. Others argued that, even though he originally may have indicated he would return, when circumstances change you must allow the new circumstances to enter into the decision and possibly change his mind, especially when the new circumstances amount to that much money.

Others declared that his decision was simply indicative of our greedy society, that trust is too easily given short shrift when a better deal comes along. One person remarked, "In a greedy world where politicians won't keep their promises, where corporations hire teams of lawyers to find loopholes in contracts when agreements no longer look favorable, what a lesson this young man could have conveyed to the youth and adults of the world if he had stood before the world press and said, 'This may cost me a few million dollars, but my word and honor is worth more than that.'"

For those who may know to whom I am referring, I do not cite this example to criticize him or assign blame, but to demonstrate that the problems surrounding changing circumstances are common to many who are about to make a decision. Indeed, most of my friends have told me that if they had been in the same position they would have done the same thing. So, perhaps this young man's actions depict how many of us would act when it comes to keeping our word under changing circumstances.

Contrast this example with another professional young man, an accountant whom I will call Hank. His father was a prominent businessperson in the community. One day, as I was walking I met up with Hank's father, with whom I am acquainted. After an initial greeting, he said:

> Do you know what Hank did? He upset his wife and the rest of us last week: He phoned a bank to get information about refinancing the mortgage on his house, and he obtained information about interest rates, closing costs, and other things. Then, when he finished his conversation with the banker, he said, "I'll be there in the morning."
>
> So, when I heard about it, I told him to go see a banker friend of mine. He did, and he found out he could save $400 in closing costs. But he refused to do business with my friend and save the $400. He said to me, "I told the other bank I would be there in

the morning, and I must keep my word." Hell, that
was only a casual comment, not a promise.

Whenever I relate this incident to others, I get mixed reactions.
Some say, "He'll never make a successful businessman. You have to
take advantage of every financial opportunity," or, "That's foolish—
he never made a promise or signed an agreement." Others say, "That's
great, but too ideal to thrive in this competitive world." Only a few
say things like, "That's just what we need to change our world: people who are willing to pay the price to keep their word and be worthy
of trust."

The answer depends on where you draw the line about promise
making. What does it mean to give your word or make a promise?
When is a promise a promise, and how do you know when you've
made one? Keep in mind that if you believe giving your word only
happens under oath or when you sign a contract with two witnesses,
then that leaves people open to change their minds—sometimes at
your expense. On the other hand, if you believe that you give your
word when you lead someone to believe or do something, then you
must keep that word—even if a better opportunity comes along. In
my opinion, the value of someone's word as a dependable promise
rests upon a continuum, depending on the person's belief about the
nature of verbal contracts:

My word is my bond:

Only when I am under oath   *When I lead someone to believe*

In order to elevate the level of trust in our society, I believe we
should place ourselves toward the right side of this continuum. Often,
problems arise in business when one side says, "They promised me,"
and the other side says, "We made no promises." Sometimes, in these
cases, one side believes a promise was made, but the other side never
intended to make a promise. Other times, clever businesspeople
manipulate language and implications that entice people to believe
one thing, and even close the sale, but later they reveal that nothing
was ever promised, or that technically, the implied things only apply
to certain circumstances that wouldn't apply to this customer.

The Skill of Promise Keeping

People skilled in honesty and ethics don't hang onto the technical meanings of individual words. Instead, they sense or try to find out what the other party is understanding or concluding from a given exchange because they understand how selective perception influences how "promises" come to be. After all, as discussed in Chapter 9, selective perception determines how people interpret a message—meaning that sincere people can intend to make no promise while the recipient sincerely believes a promise has been made.

For example, if a manager talks to a discouraged employee he or she may say something like, "I'd really like to see you get a large bonus at the end of the year if our sales increase, assuming we can keep our costs down—especially if we can get that new product finished and you continue to demonstrate how you have added value to the company." And, assuming the employee has a great need for increased income, selective perception may cause the person to conclude, "The boss promised me a significant bonus." All the ifs, assumptions, and uncertainties mentioned by the boss may be ignored or "blanked out" because they make the bonus uncertain.

Managers who are skilled in ethical behavior can sense how others could interpret such messages. In this case, they would go to extra lengths to correct any misunderstandings and make sure the employee recognizes up front that the bonus is not a promise but a desired result. Managers who are unskilled in ethical behavior will assume that the employee understood the message just as it was delivered—with many contingencies. Later, they must cope with the employee's accusations of broken promises.

People who have questionable integrity often are glib about making promises versus making inferences. Without serious thought or commitment, they are quick to say, "Oh yes, we can do that," or "Oh yes, I'll do that." Then later, they find it difficult to keep their commitments, or they back out. Sometimes they make casual comments that imply a promise but have no intent of fulfilling it.

On the other hand, people who have genuine integrity are reluctant to make promises or even imply them. They think through what it would take to fulfill a pledge before they make it—or at least consider whether it is within their power to keep the promise and whether they are willing to put forth the effort to complete the obligation. They consider it abhorrent for people to make casual or glib promises or commitments when there is no serious intent of following through. They consider their word a sacred treasure that they do not give out lightly or without thought. Such people of integrity, more often than not, carefully estimate their promises with regard to scheduling and financial forecasts, and then try to fulfill their promises early and under budget if they can—giving lengthy apologies, occasional concessions, and plenty of advance notice if they find they can't. They often go to great lengths to keep their word, even when others consider the promises inconsequential.

When Circumstances Change

One of the most vexing challenges for people who want to keep their word is to determine what to do when circumstances change. Sometimes we make commitments to do certain things, but then something unexpected comes up making it difficult, if not impossible, to keep the original promises.

For instance, suppose Robert says he will attend a meeting on Friday, but on Wednesday he is admitted to the hospital after a serious stroke. Most of us would acknowledge that this would justify his failure to keep the commitment. We would not criticize him at all for not appearing at the meeting. But suppose Rebecca, from Chicago, agrees to make a public presentation at 8:30 a.m. on the morning of the 14th of next month in Kansas City. She arrives at the airport on the evening of the 13th and finds that her flight has been cancelled and no other flight is going to Kansas City that night nor early enough for the meeting the next morning. Is she excused from missing the meeting, and if so, would she still be considered a person of her word? Probably most would say yes. After all, she did the best she could, and she had no way of knowing the flight would be canceled, right?

But Rebecca herself would disagree. For her, a promise is a promise. She asks the travel agent to check the availability of all flights into Kansas City from other cities that she could connect with from Chicago tonight. Still no luck. Then she checks the price of a private jet, but it's too expensive for her and the group to which she will be making the presentation. The bus and train are available, but she fears they would make too many stops and not arrive in time. Finally, she decides that if she leaves now, she could drive overnight and arrive in time to get two hours of sleep before the presentation. So, to keep her commitment, she drives the whole way and, on two hours of sleep, makes her presentation at considerable personal cost, effort, and sacrifice.

Was Rebecca's effort beyond the call of duty? Did she exert more than she needed to keep her promise? Couldn't she simply call and cancel the presentation? Could someone who wanted to keep his or her word do less? What would Abraham Lincoln do? If you were part of the group that was to hear Rebecca's presentation, how would you feel about dealing with her in the future? Is she silly, or is she just doing what she said she would do?

By acknowledging that some circumstances would justify our failure to keep a promise, we maintain a certain level of sanity and comfort. We can even maintain that we are people of our word, and that our word is our bond. But how large a price must we pay or how much personal sacrifice must we endure to honestly claim that we did our very best to keep a commitment? What circumstances would allow you to justifiably change your mind, back out of an agreement, or go back on your word? When circumstances change, are you justified in changing your mind, or is that a violation of your promise? What if a million dollars or more is involved? What if it can be done legally? Should you keep your word or fulfill a contract only when it doesn't cost anything more than you first expected? Or should you keep your word at all costs?

A good measure of the value of a person's word is how much he or she is willing to give up to keep a promise or commitment. Would everyone be willing to break their word if given the right price? Can money really buy anything, including someone's honor, promise, or word? Just as beliefs about the nature of verbal contracts relate to the value of a person's word, beliefs about when it is acceptable to allow circumstances to change an agreement or promise impact the strength, and also the value, of a person's word as a dependable promise:

If circumstances relating to my commitment change, I am willing to change my mind:

|————————————————————————————————|

Frequently, when it's to my advantage   *Never, no matter what the cost*

Again, the further right on the continuum we tend to place our marks, the more trust people can place in our words. However, moving closer to the right also implies having much greater amounts of information at hand when we make our commitments. How far people are willing to go and how much they are willing to sacrifice to carry out a promise are good indicators of how much they believe in the phrase, "My word is my bond."

What Price Honor?

Peter is a reputable drywall taper. In the construction of a home or building, when the frame has been put up and the electricity, plumbing, and ventilation ducts have been installed, a drywall crew comes to attach sheets of drywall to the inside walls. Then, a taper smooths the walls by filling in cracks and holes and shaping corners with drywall tape and spackle. Peter is so good that when he is done most people would not be able to detect where the joints are. Over the years several contractors had employed Peter to finish off drywall jobs.

Peter loved to talk about a man named Larry, who was the best drywall contractor he had ever worked for. According to Peter:

> Larry has never missed a payroll in 20 years. Even when he hasn't been paid on time, Larry will go to the bank and borrow money rather than be late with a paycheck. In this business, it's common to have your pay delayed because a contractor hasn't been paid yet or some other excuse. But not with Larry: With him you know your pay will be there when scheduled or before. Larry is a man of his word.

When I was in my teens, I had a job driving a truck. One evening, when a half dozen of us truck drivers stopped to eat at a cafe, the group began to tell some stories about truck driving. One driver, Ed, told how he had purchased a large wrench from Sears-Roebuck. "They told me it was guaranteed," he said:

> "If anything goes wrong with it, just bring it back, and we'll replace it," they told me. Well, one day I was trying to remove a flat tire from my rig, and one of the lug nuts was stuck. I put that big wrench on it, and it still wouldn't budge. Finally, I found about a four-foot piece of heavy pipe and attached it to the wrench handle to get some leverage. I laid it out just about horizontal. Then, with all my 215 pounds, I jumped on the end of the pipe and something gave way. I went over to the wheel to check the lug nut, but it was still in place—the wrench had broken. I should have known that much leverage could break anything.

Well, I remember them saying I could bring it back. Somehow I knew they wouldn't replace it because of the unreasonable abuse I had put it through. But I couldn't afford another wrench, so I thought it would be worth a try to see just how good their promise was. Well, I took that dang wrench in. They just looked at it and said, "Well, that won't do you any good." They never asked me any questions, just handed me a new wrench. It's hard to believe they meant exactly what they said.

Similarly, in 1995, an evening news story reported how a lumber company in Maine had promised a charitable organization that it would donate the materials, valued at about $33,000, for the organization to build a log cabin. The charity then could auction off the cabin to raise funds or use it for events as it saw fit. But, shortly after the company made the promise, the lumber company's plant burned to the ground. The financial losses were so great that the company would likely go under. The reporter, who was aware of the company's promise to the charity, prodded, "I guess this means the charity will lose a major donation. That's too bad."

"No," responded the company owner. "They will still get their building materials just as we promised."

Getting Around a Promise

Contrast this with the attitude of a young and successful entrepreneur I once knew. One day I was in his apartment, waiting for him to conclude a telephone conversation, and I could hear his side of the conversation. He was speaking with a banker trying to arrange for a multimillion-dollar loan to help him conclude a business deal with a group in Japan. The young man proposed an idea that the banker apparently didn't like, and the banker must have said something like, "That would be illegal," to which my friend responded, "Look, there's no law that we can't find some way around it."

Another businessman who felt that way was a man I will call Bjorn Sedgewick, who owned a successful silver mine. Another man, whom I will call Ian Belz, made a mining claim on a piece of land adjacent to Sedgewick. Apparently, Sedgewick's mine began to extend into land claimed by Belz, and Belz pointed it out. Sedgewick then proposed, "I will put up the money for extending the mine into your property if you will operate the venture, and we will each hold a 50 percent interest in the mine." Belz agreed, and the venture got underway. Each subsequent day showed that the venture would be profitable for years to come.

After some time passed, Sedgewick came up with another idea. He told Belz:

> I've located a mining engineer in the East who could really be helpful in our mining operation. I believe I can get him to join us for a portion of ownership in the mine. If you will give me 2 percent of your 50 percent, I would put it with 2 percent of my part and offer it to him. That would give him 4 percent ownership, and we would each retain 48 percent.

Belz agreed and signed over 2 percent of his ownership to Sedgewick to make the offer. Time went by, and when no engineer appeared Belz confronted his partner about the arrangement. Sedgewick admitted that there never was an engineer, but he had used the ruse to gain control of the mine—he now owned 52 percent of the stock and the controlling interest in the mine.

According to the attorney who represented Belz in a subsequent lawsuit, when Belz challenged Sedgewick in court, Sedgewick responded, "Unless you are willing to do that to your own mother you won't succeed in business."

People who take this approach to the law and to their business partners are only focused on producing results. When it comes to keeping promises, gaming ethics are the favorite tool. For them, abandoning a promise or pulling out of a deal not only is appropriate when money is at stake, but whenever they can gain an advantage by doing so.

Till Death Do Us Part

From time to time everyone faces the challenge of deciding how far to go to keep a promise. In the past, a person's honor was determined by his or her ability to keep a promise. For example, we hear stories about how Abraham Lincoln walked many miles just to return a book or to pay a small debt he owed on time. But the changing social climate about the value of a person's word is no better depicted than in the strength of today's marriage vows.

When people are married, they make solemn vows at the altar in front of a priest, rabbi, or officer of the public court. The bride and groom generally exchange vows that include the phrase, "To honor and cherish till death do us part," or something similar, that binds them to each other for as long as they live. But, today's divorce rate suggests that these promises simply are not taken seriously, or if they are, people find easy justification for breaking those vows.

First of all, the marriage ceremony, regardless of religious or civil authority, clearly establishes that a contractual promise is being made between two people. The ceremony is typically performed in public, in front of witnesses, and in a solemn setting. The marriage contract explicitly states that each partner must vow total allegiance to the other from now on—"till death do us part," or "for as long as they both shall live"—through both good times and bad, in sickness and in health. By law, such a bond cannot be formed with anyone else while the contract is in place.

But, in spite of all the solemnity and specificity, large numbers of people—by some counts as much as 50 to 60 percent—walk out on these promises. Why? Perhaps many were not serious about the promise to begin with. Or perhaps expectations were too high. Still, people who want to be worthy of trust must be careful about giving their word or bond, even in marriage.

Second, things change. Perhaps this is why people are so willing to break their vows. People age and start to look different to each other. They get annoyed by petty behavioral quirks and never deal with them correctly. They want more variety. Responsibility becomes a great burden. These people reason, "Well, things have changed, and morally I must be allowed to get out of a bad or hastily made promise." But, what changing circumstances would justify a person violating such solemn and heartfelt promises? Surely we can think of some, such as adultery, physical abuse, or gross negligence, but I think most of us agree that very few circumstances would justify breaking off such a vow. On the other hand, we likely can document many cases in which people kept their marriage promises despite abuse, excessive drinking, infidelity, or lack of support. Are these people honorable? Some say yes—keep a marriage alive no matter what the cost; others say no—when circumstances change for the worse, get out, don't suffer.

Regardless of how we feel about individual cases, our general attitude about marriage and divorce likely reflects our moral commitment to keeping our word. Excuses such as "I'm no longer in love," "I found a more beautiful woman," "I found a man with more money," "Our relationship has lost its zing, and I want more out of life," "I just want to be free," or "I fell in love with someone else"—are indicative of our casual approach to solemn promises and contracts and reflect the actual value of our word in other, less important matters, too.

When It Hurts a Lot

For those who want to be worthy of trust, they should think twice about how quickly they would forego marriage vows. They should ask themselves, "How large a price am I willing to pay to earn someone's trust? How much am I willing to show that I can be trusted to keep my word?" Marriage is a good place to start; the world of business is another good place.

We live in a selfish world: "I" want to be happy. "I" want money. "I" want to be president. "I" want to be free. For many, anything that will get them closer to getting "me" what "I" want justifies the breaking of almost any promise—or a lawyer can help them get around the law. These are not people of honor. Their word is not their bond. They cannot be trusted. How far someone will go and what price someone will pay to carry out a promise is the best measure of integrity and honor.

In such a selfish society, it is refreshing and reassuring to find people who truly believe "my word is my bond." We all have dealt with people who make promises—maybe they will keep them, and maybe they won't. Big deal, right? "Don't trust anyone," we say. They have a good excuse, but we can't count on them.

But, in contrast, what if we knew people who, no matter how seemingly insignificant the promise or how much it will cost them, will do what they say? They go to every effort to keep their pledge. If they believe there might be a chance they won't fulfill, they tell you honestly about it up front. If they do not tell you up front, you know it will be done—seldom if ever giving an excuse. These are people of real integrity. They try to meet your expectations even when they forewarn you that they might not do it. They make that extra effort—even when there's nothing to gain or when others think such a small promise doesn't require such a large effort—because "my word is my bond," and it is highly important and valuable for them to do so.

CASE: A Better Offer

During the month of February, in the last term of his MBA program, Greg was interviewing with various companies and looking for a good opportunity to launch his career. He was offered a good position with a prominent Dallas company that had an international reputation for producing high quality products—probably the highest quality in the industry.

Greg and his wife traveled to Dallas at the company's expense to meet with company officers and take a look around. After he returned to school, Greg told the interviewer over the phone that he had decided to accept the company's offer and would move to Dallas as soon as he finished his degree at the end of June. At this point he had not signed anything or written an acceptance letter. The company was delighted to have Greg on its team since he was a bright and highly motivated young man, and began to make preparations for his arrival.

A little over two weeks later, another company made an offer. Greg had visited the other company in Atlanta before his trip to Dallas, but he thought the company had lost interest. Although the money was about the same as the Dallas position, the Atlanta assignment would be better for Greg's career goals, offering him the kind of experience he would need to pursue his career path. After considerable deliberation and consultation with friends and a few of his favorite professors, Greg decided to accept the new offer and notified the Atlanta company of his decision in a letter. He then penned a note to the interviewer in Dallas to tell him that he had changed his mind and would not be accepting the position there.

Questions:

1. Did Greg do the right thing?

2. When is a promise a promise? Did Greg make a promise?

3. Is Greg a man of his word?

4. How far should a person go, or how much should a person sacrifice just to keep a promise?

5. When is it appropriate to go back on your word or change your mind?

6. In business, is it acceptable to follow whatever is the best course for you personally? If you don't look out for yourself, who else will?

Section Three

What to Do

Chapter 13

Living the Golden Rule in Business

"As a principle of universal application, competition defeats itself; it can be justified at all only on the notion that the success of the winners, who are few, equals the disappointment of the losers, who are many . . . it leaves the group worse off than it would be without it, always assuming that disappointment is as bitter as triumph is sweet."

—*Learned Hand[1]*

W HEN YOU WERE a youngster, how often did you hear another child cry out, "That's not fair!"? It seems that children are particularly sensitive about what is unfair. Sometimes they complain about other children who have violated the understood rules of a game—and frequently follow the complaint with the whine, "I'm telling." Other times they use the complaint to demand something they want when their parents have told them they can't have it—a new toy, more candy, or five more minutes of television at bedtime.

Many times, the charge of "unfair" clearly is legitimate: Generally, someone has violated a well-established rule or has been inconsistent in its application. For example, in soccer, touching the ball with your hands—unless you are a goalkeeper or you are putting the ball in play from out of bounds—is against the rules, and if a referee does not make the call when it happens, the opposing team will insist that it's unfair, even if it was accidental—especially if they have been called on it and the other team hasn't. The rule is very explicit and should be consistently applied.

Other times, the rules are not as explicitly stated or formally established, but people who are placed at a disadvantage because of a behavior develop a keen sense about its fairness. For example, it seems unfair if a bigger child pushes or bullies a smaller boy, or if an older child takes advantage of a younger child in bargaining for things with trickery, or if one child gets to stay up later than another child.

193

Equality seems to be integrally important to fairness—each child should get the same size piece of cake, or a toy of similar perceived value, or the same amount of time with the controls to the video game.

Sometimes discrepancies are not weighed so carefully. For instance, in basketball, it is not unfair for one player to be consistently taller or more talented than another—as long as the teams are in the same league—even though height and talent give an advantage in competition.

In the adult world, people are often stumped by what is fair or unfair. Rules and laws can be complex, inconsistently applied, or even unknown, unwritten, or nonexistent. But, generally, ethical people are considered "fair," and unethical people are "unfair"—though they will always insist upon how fair they are, too. The term is frequently invoked with much unclarity.

Terms such as "fair play," "level playing field," and "equal opportunity" are frequently invoked by people in the world of business. For example, many American companies have complained that Japanese businesses are unfair because they sell their goods in the United States for less than American companies can produce them. And, when Americans have sued or lobbied Congress for trade barriers, Japanese companies have called the American businesses unfair for forcing customers to pay higher prices for Japanese-made products that are made at a cheaper cost than American products. In other situations, employees often complain about "unfair" labor and hiring practices that favor or discriminate against certain groups. Or, companies in the same industry accuse other companies of sneaky marketing and advertising practices, price fixing, or other unfair competitive tactics.

Everyone seems to have a strong sense of what is "fair" and what is "unfair" from their own perspective, but there seem to be very few commonly accepted standards for measuring fairness.

What Is Fair?

Whenever I think about the celebrated Bible story of David and Goliath, I consider how unfair it must have seemed for such a giant and heavily armored man to go up against such a young and apparently unarmed boy. But, I wonder if Goliath and the Philistines wouldn't have had a legitimate complaint that David didn't fight fairly: He didn't fight in the traditional manner, face to face with a sword and shield. Instead, he was sneaky, catching Goliath off-guard by remaining far away and hurling rocks at him with a sling—an instrument not generally used in battle and probably never in hand-to-hand combat. But, since the Philistines are not around to raise the issue, we in the twentieth century view David as a clever Israelite hero.

Fairness can be divided into two general categories: first, instances when specific and well-established rules and understandings exist, and second, when no rules or precedents exist. In the business world we find many practices that are governed by long established codes, such as: Competitors must not collude with each other in setting prices or to engage in "insider trading." When people are found engaging in these practices, they can be prosecuted. The people who are caught in these practices generally know what they were doing and knew it was wrong, or at least they knew going in that, if caught, a penalty would result, and they understood the risks. In basketball, for instance, a player might deliberately commit a foul to stop another player from shooting a game-winning basket late in the game, but knows that the foul likely will be called by a referee. It's simply a strategic move, though ethically questionable.

However, things get tricky when no guidelines exist or the application of them becomes inconsistent. In these cases, people are often accused of unfair practices when the practices are uncommon or not understood. We probably cannot expect to rid ourselves of such controversies because we will always have standards or rules that are not agreed upon or not applied universally. For example, as discussed in Chapter 9, some businesspeople see business as a competitive game, while others feel that the higher standard of "personal ethics" should apply.

Does the Golden Rule Solve the Problem?

Whenever businesspeople debate what's fair and what's unfair—usually to an unsuccessful standoff—someone inevitably will invoke the Golden Rule as the best clear-cut solution to the matter: "Just live the Golden Rule: 'Do unto others as you would have them do unto you,'" they say.[2] In their minds, that statement solves the problem and should put an end to the discussion. Often, listeners nod their heads in agreement and the discussion ends. Business goes on as usual, but with nothing resolved—no better understanding of fairness or what would constitute "right behavior" is reached.

Often, these people not only believe that simply invoking the Golden Rule will put matters to rest, but they also believe that their organizations live it—that they actually follow the Golden Rule. In my opinion, this is a grand delusion for most people. In reality, living the Golden Rule in today's rough-and-tumble corporate world can be stressful, if not impossible.

The devil is in the detail. Implementing such a sweeping policy reminds me of the story of the wise old owl and the centipede: In the forest, a centipede began to complain about his sore feet. Indeed, 100 sore feet can pose a serious problem. His forest friends could not help with the problem until one suggested, "Go consult the wise old owl."

The centipede limped up the forest trail to a large tree where the wise old owl was seated on a sturdy branch. The centipede called to the owl, "I have 100 sore feet. My friends tell me you can solve my problem."

Looking from side to side, the wise old owl contemplated the perplexity for a few moments, and then responded, "I think you ought to turn into a fish."

The centipede immediately began to envision himself floating around in the water—no sticks or stones to stumble over, no feet to coordinate. "Thank you, wise owl," he said. "I'm sure that will solve my problem." And he happily limped away down the trail till he came to the bend in the road. He stopped, thought for a few moments, turned around, and limped back up the trail to the tree. He called out, "Thank you again, wise owl, for solving my problem. But I have just one question: How do I turn into a fish?"

Turning his head from side to side, the wise old owl responded, "Don't ask me. I only make policy decisions."

Certainly, "Just live the Golden Rule" is great moral advice for anyone on any occasion. It's the essence of human goodness and the foundation of trust. But, living in a competitive world is the reality most of us face and remains one of the greatest challenges to our Judeo-Christian belief system. Under the Golden Rule, "a good [ethical] person is concerned with and responsible for the well-being of others."[3] So, for people in business, living the Golden Rule is like turning into a fish—virtually impossible. Just consider the question for a moment: How can we be concerned about and accept responsibility for the well-being of others when our individual success is so often driven by how we *compare* with others: competitors, co-workers, etc.—and when the motto of the entire business community is either "look out for yourself" (translated: "make myself money") or "enhance stockholder value" (translated: "make a profit for the company"). This conflict of interests prevents anyone who is serious about both business and the treatment of others to successfully fill both roles.

In a competitive system, those who feel compelled to look out for the welfare of others face an almost impossible task in becoming successful in business, and the people who place self-interest first most often claim the gold. The Golden Rule is distorted in this context: "Whoever has the gold makes the rules." Most of today's success literature will confirm that to accomplish whatever you want, you must remain totally focused on your goal—which, by definition, means that you cannot allow yourself to be distracted by what others might want. Good business means finding a competitive advantage (or "niche," "customer segment," or whatever you want to call it) and exploiting that advantage to make money. Those who use their resources to worry about, feel responsible for, or help their competitors will seldom reap the benefit, at least not financially.

On the other hand, self-interest can lead to excellence. The obsession to be the best can focus you and refine your skills to help you win a prize or make money. Living the Golden Rule, on the other hand—thinking of others first—doesn't usually win gold medals or large amounts of money. The Golden Rule is about winning other things: It can be the symbol of a truly great and moral human being, one known as "an honest person." But such people will not likely rise to the top of profit- or performance-oriented organizations.

The Golden Rule Neurosis

Facing up to the conflict created by the desire to live the Golden Rule and the reality of our competitive system is useful for those who want to improve their morality or associate themselves with a more ethical group. But the frustration about wanting to succeed in business while, at the same time, living the Golden Rule is enough to make a person neurotic.

Someone once explained "neurotic" to me by comparing it to schizophrenia. According to his reasoning, a schizophrenic person believes $2 + 2 = 5$, while a neurotic knows that $2 + 2 = 4$, but hates the idea. Similarly, reconciling competition with the Golden Rule leads to neurosis. At least I feel neurotic about it: I recognize that the two principles do violence to each other, and I very much dislike the situation.

Still, many people believe that competition and the Golden Rule are compatible. These people may want to do some rethinking: If the object of competition is to beat someone else, or be better, or to put someone else down, is this the Golden Rule? In sports, at least we can say, "It's just a game," but when we're talking about someone's reputation, career, workforce, and family standard of living, we can't be so casual or flippant.

Once while I was eating breakfast with the CEO of a *Fortune* 500 company, I asked him how he was able to reconcile the competitive world with the Golden Rule. Without hesitation he said, "I don't." I admire that answer. At least he is honest with himself instead of trying to deceive himself and others that taking customers from a competitor is, somehow, living the Golden Rule. By recognizing that the two are not compatible in a business setting, he is not adding hypocrisy to the list of immoral behaviors among executives. (I chuckled to myself in thinking that his position gives him a *competitive edge* and a moral leg up on those who deny or fail to recognize the problem.)

Fair Price

Let's look at fairness in light of two fundamental activities that affect nearly everyone: prices and wages. It seems we are always hearing talk about "unfair prices" or "unfair wages."

What is a fair price? In the business world, pricing gets a greater share of criticism as being "unfair" than perhaps any other activity. Companies often question the techniques of their competitors in setting prices that appear to be lower than cost or lower than is feasible for them. Consumers often feel unfairly charged for goods and services.

In the spring of 1996 gasoline prices went up dramatically almost overnight. Everyone was complaining—people at the office water cooler, clerks at the grocery store, newspapers, radio and television talk shows, all the way up to the White House and Congress—about the "fairness" of the gasoline prices, even to the point of demanding formal investigations into the matter.

Many people believe there is such a thing as price gouging or unfair pricing. The logic of "simple economics" fails to pacify their frustration. For instance, they feel that for retailers to double or triple the price of bottled water immediately after an earthquake, or for hoteliers to double the price of rooms during "peak seasons," would be unfair. Again we must ask the question, what is a fair price?

Let's look at the matter with a hypothetical case. Suppose you discovered a real cure for AIDS—something like what the Salk vaccine did to polio, except that this cure could be effective even after someone has contracted the disease—like what penicillin did to infections. After you calculate the costs of producing and distributing the medication, you figure that your total cost per cure would be about $1,000. And, because you know the market for the treatment will be large and immediate—the number of people with HIV and AIDS—you would spread out the costs of development and advertising over the number you expect to sell by building it into the price. So, all of your expenses would be covered by the $1,000 cost per cure. What would you charge each patient for the treatment? What would be "fair"?

People who want to be fair would start out by setting some "fair" relationship of the price to the cost. For example, grocery stores often mark up their most popular items only three or four percent over cost—sometimes less. That would suggest a price of $1,040 for the AIDS cure. Is that fair? In another example, many furniture retailers often mark up their items 100 percent or more over wholesale costs. That would mean a price of $2,000. Is that fair? In the computer software industry, resellers often charge as much as 500 percent over cost. That would place the AIDS cure at $5,000 per treatment. Is that fair? Keep in mind that the market can probably bear these prices—or at least insurance companies can. Does this fact influence your reasoning?

Finally, let's consider the pharmaceutical industry—the industry that would be working with you to promote and distribute the medication. According to one report, a pharmaceutical distributor sold a potassium supplement to hospitals at $2.03 for 100 tablets, but retail pharmacies were charged $27.31—a 1,245 percent markup. And, assuming the manufacturer marked up the cost before selling the product to the distributor, the amount could be 1,700 percent or more over cost.[4] Keep in mind that the customer hasn't seen the bill yet—the pharmacy doesn't care as long as it gets its percent, right? Now the customer is paying perhaps $40 for a product that costs maybe only $1.50 to produce—a markup of over 2,500 percent! Assuming customers are willing to pay that much, is it a fair price?

Let's apply this thinking to your new AIDS cure. Your $1,000 product now goes to the pharmacy at $13,450 per treatment, and the customer pays approximately $25,000—all completely in line with industry guidelines.

But, perhaps we can calculate a formula that is more in line with what the market might be able to bear. Suppose we calculate that, on average, an AIDS patient will incur approximately $93,000 of health care costs from the time of diagnosis until the time of death. What would your cure be worth to the insurance company that is footing the health care bill? Wouldn't $75,000 be a reasonable price? This would save the insurance company nearly $20,000, increase shareholder profits, and reduce the premiums of AIDS patients substantially. In addition, the life saved would eliminate many months of pain and suffering. You and your investors would reap great sums of money to do many other good things for yourself and society.

"But," says someone else, "how can you put a price on a life? The market can obviously handle more than this." Suppose this person claims that the average time of death after diagnosis is five years, but to keep a 45-year-old AIDS patient alive for 25 years with current technology would cost much more than $93,000. How much would customers pay if they were young, desperate, and wanted to leave the hospital soon? Is $1 million enough? What about $10 million? The sky is the limit now.

In this light, isn't $1 million per cure just as fair as $1,040? What about the $75,000 cure? Even when we supply all of this logical rationale, most people simply feel that these prices are exorbitant and unfair. Some even believe the $2,000 price is outrageous.

Whatever the Market Will Bear

Actually, our private enterprise system has an answer for this dilemma. We call it "supply and demand." It is an economic system driven by competition and "gaming ethics." In this system, suppliers offer to sell their products at a certain price. Those who are willing to pay the price make the purchase, which acknowledges the fair exchange of value. Those who are unwilling to pay the price do not make the purchase, so nothing unfair occurs. And, if suppliers can't make a sale at a certain price, they will reduce the price until a fair exchange occurs. So, "fair price" is simply whatever the market will bear. In a market economy, then, there is no such thing as a "fair" or "unfair" price. Whatever people are willing to pay is fair.

Some people, out of a sense of morality, may want to change the system. The communists tried such a system and, over the course of about 70 years, failed. The socialists are still trying to make a new system work. But, the people who believe that the market system is the fairest way to set prices say it's just a matter of economics—not morality. To them, whenever you insert ethics or morality into the mix you are changing to an inefficient system. So, to expect everyone to live by the Golden Rule in a market economy is, perhaps, expecting too much.

What about wages? What is a fair wage, in light of what has been discussed so far? Recently, President Bill Clinton approved an increase in the federal minimum wage. Why? The administration and other lawmakers considered $4.25 per hour "unfair" in the wake of the rising cost of living index. Many citizens applauded the move, perhaps in response to the media's recent focus on pay discrepancies between front-line workers and senior executives. Apparently, whenever the highest paid executive makes a certain number of times more than the lowest paid employee, society feels the discrepancy is unfair.

According to the U.S. Census Bureau: "In 1960, the average after-tax compensation for CEOs at the largest corporations was 12 times greater than the paycheck of the lowest paid factory worker. By 1975, CEO pay was 35 times greater. In 1995, CEO compensation will average about 117 times more than the earnings of the lowest paid American worker."[5] Some felt that the discrepancy was unfair in 1960. Today, many feel the situation is "becoming" unfair, while others are furious that it already is unfair. But what is "fair"? Is 5 times fair? How about 50 times? How about 500 times? No one seems to agree.

But equity does not necessarily mean equal. To the CEOs, nothing about their salaries is unfair at all. For them, the multiple is irrelevant. Certainly, CEOs deserve to get paid more than delivery people or janitors. After all, the CEO often has many years more experience and is not performing a job that is easily trained. Their decisions place extensive company assets at risk, and greater risk implies greater return—and greater penalties for making mistakes. The stress, alone, should be worth more.

On the other hand, equity dictates that we must see some reasonable relationship between the highest paid and the lowest paid people in a company. For example, it would not be equitable for CEOs to take an exorbitant share of the organization's proceeds even though they may have the authority and influence to do so—especially if a company is in a financial crisis, and doubly so if the CEO caused the crisis by making an unwise decision. So, for CEOs to increase their annual income by millions while others must cut their salaries or face getting laid off does real violence to the Golden Rule.

The Golden Rule calls for all to share and share alike—after all, if someone had something you wanted, wouldn't it be great if he or she willingly shared it with you? That's what "Do unto others . . ." means. Likewise, when the deprivations of bad times are shared from the top to the bottom of an organization, or when good fortune abounds and is shared throughout the company, people feel that equity is in play—"We're all in this together." Leaders who are perceived to be sharing in the pain of cutbacks have a real claim on moral authority. Those who do not, lose that authority.

Sharing the bounty as well as the pain is a good place to start, but we still haven't resolved the issue of how much disparity between highest paid and lowest paid is still considered fair. At this point, I again reiterate that open discussion on these issues will do much to strengthen the moral fiber of your group or organization. The simple act of leaders making these topics legitimate matters of discussion initially will send a positive signal to others in the organization that corporate management really does feel some sense of concern and responsibility for employees. Then, making some effort to implement the suggestions derived from such discussions will demonstrate that the discussions were not just talk. That is the Golden Rule in progress: trying to do what you would wish others to do for you if you were in their shoes.

Beware: Such open discussions could point out discrepancies between what is currently happening and what others would like to see happen. The debate can get emotional and sensitive about what is fair and what might have to change to make things more fair. On the other hand, you may develop a powerful synergy that otherwise may prove illusive.

An Honest Day's Work for an Honest Day's Pay

Another aspect of fairness relating to fair wages has to do with what employers pay their employees. We often hear parents, community leaders, preachers, and other moralists admonish workers to give their employers "an honest day's work for an honest day's pay." Without ever identifying what an "honest day's work" might be or what someone might get paid for it, these exhortations seem to say, "Work very hard, give your employer your full effort, and be willing to put forth extra effort," and by implication, "Don't show up to work late or leave early, cheat on your timecard, or take care of personal business on company time."

In contrast, when was the last time you heard someone admonish employers to pay an "honest wage" to their loyal employees? Somehow, it just doesn't seem fair for those in power to constantly urge the less powerful to put forth greater effort, while they plead for wages that are more fair. And, when they ask for raises, they feel intimidated and dispensable and are often turned down. One owner suggested in a light moment that discussing raises is like bargaining for a car: The salesman (the owner) sells you on all the benefits of the beautiful-looking car (company), overlooking all of the trouble spots (problems caused by management or the system), and ratcheting up the price for every additional option (what you would have to do to earn such privileges), while your trade-in (what the worker has done to deserve the raise) is overexamined by mechanics (performance evaluation) and devalued below the actual market value. It becomes a take-it-or-leave-it situation for the buyer (the employee). Certainly, in our society, it's easier and more socially and morally acceptable to demand harder work than it is to request higher pay.

And, because we find it so difficult to determine on our own what "an honest day's work" or "an honest day's pay" might be, we must turn again to the competition-based market system for help. According to this system, it is "fair" for employers to pay the lowest wage that would attract and retain a workforce capable of maintaining or growing current business at the rate expected of management. So, they can either hire top talent and face the risk that (1) the company can't afford to pay or (2) the talent won't perform as expected. Or, they can hire average or below average workers and face the risk that (1) the workers can't be trained as efficiently as expected or (2) that training might make the workers more marketable outside the company. These strategies are applied solely in the effort to maximize shareholder return on investment. Somehow in our system we regard such policies as fair.

This begs the question: If it's fair for employers to pay the minimum wage necessary for their purposes, isn't it also fair for employees to put forth the minimum effort necessary to obtain and keep their jobs? To most people, even asking the question seems out of line. But fairness would indicate that we can't have one without the other. Our work ethic is so deeply ingrained in our social psyche that management's minimal wage practices are looked upon as "good" business practice while employees who attempt a minimal work strategy are hounded by all sides.

Again, the problem is resolved by the market system. It's not a matter of morality or ethics but of simple economics—supply and demand. "Fairness" doesn't apply.

The market approach to fairness often causes the advocates of moral fairness to squeal and wince. Even if employers morally feel that their employees deserve higher pay, the system may not allow them to pay it, even if it seems unethical not to do so. This has to do with the competitive nature of businesses. If competitors can pay lower wages and thereby reduce the costs of products or services, then "moral" managers will be forced either to reduce pay or reduce jobs to stay in business. For instance, it may seem unfair for an employer to close a company plant in Kansas, where the company pays $6.00 per hour for labor, and move to Mexico where it can find adequately skilled workers for $.60 per hour. Sure, it may not be fair to the workers in Kansas, but the workers in Mexico, who now get jobs, find it fair. The plant's owners, who now enjoy increased profits, find it fair. Also, the company improves its competitive position in the market.

Many people feel a moral urgency to make things "fair" and to alter the system by imposing government subsidies, or imposing minimum wage restrictions or price controls. A negative stigma is attached to companies who look outside the nation's boundaries for solutions. But, eventually, the economic forces come into play, either on the companies or on the governments in the nations that try to limit the scope of economic pressures. If we find it impossible to live the Golden Rule in a competitive environment, or if we choose to ignore it as my CEO friend did, then we must stop touting it. Employers and employees alike eventually must abide by the amoral forces of competitive business practices in the market system or bail out of business altogether.

In Search of Fairness

1. Discuss about what "fairness" means at work, school, sports, government, etc., and identify behaviors that everyone agrees are fair and unfair, and where the laws or rules are specific. What are the forces that cause people to step over the legal line? What can be done to stop, counter, or restrain those forces?

2. Reinforce your commitment to being fair in the face of clearly accepted rules. Is your guideline to take advantage of all the law or rules will allow? If so, how does this impact your commitment to live the Golden Rule?

3. Consider the case at the end of this chapter. Does your group agree on what is fair or unfair? If you do, what would happen if another group agreed on the opposite conclusion? How does this influence your ability to succeed if success is based on financial prosperity? What about your ability to succeed based on "higher law" or moral prosperity?

4. What does it mean to live the Golden Rule in a competitive environment? Can it be done without self-deception? Can it be done without limiting or confining the definition of competition or the Golden Rule? What price are you and your group willing to pay to be "fair"—to live the Golden Rule?

5. Which is more appropriate to a competitive environment: "personal ethics" or "gaming ethics" (see Chapter 9)? Should we let the competitive forces of the market system determine what is "fair" for prices? For wages? What role should governments play in these questions?

CASE: Wal-Mart Pricing[6]

Wal-Mart, the nation's leading retailer, reached its number one perch in part by following a simple motto: "Always the low price. Always." But an Arkansas judge ruled that Wal-Mart's prices were too low, and that the chain had engaged in predatory pricing practices—illegally pricing drug and health care items below cost as a way of driving smaller competitors out of business.

Wal-Mart, with nearly 2,000 stores and revenues of $55.5 billion last year [1992], claims that it stands for free enterprise, while the independents assert that Wal-Mart's aim is to stifle competition and then jack up prices.

Retailers and distributors have long protested Wal-Mart's pricing policies. Small businesses everywhere have bitterly protested when a Wal-Mart has moved into town, underpriced competitors, and then driven out Mom and Pop stores. Although 22 states have laws banning predatory pricing, the cases are quite difficult to prove.

Table of Prices[7]

Products	Avg. Wholesale Price	Wal-Mart Price	Fred's (Discount Drugstore) Price
Mylanta Liquid (12 oz.)	3.99	2.93	3.49
Crest Toothpaste (6.4 oz.)	2.54	1.68	1.99
Listerine Mouthwash (32 oz.)	5.84	3.97	4.19
Anacin (100 tablets)	6.85	4.88	5.29
Colgate Shaving Cream (11 oz.)	1.24	0.78	1.19

Questions:

1. Is Wal-Mart's pricing "fair"?

2. Is Wal-Mart practicing the Golden Rule?

3. In the other 28 states, where there are no laws banning predatory pricing, would it be "unfair" to sell below cost?

4. If, because of its volume, Wal-Mart can justify wholesale purchases for lower prices than small Mom and Pop stores and still keep shelf prices above its cost—even if the prices are lower than cost at those stores—should it continue to do so? Is that fair?

5. Is Wal-Mart's low-pricing policy fair to employees who may take lower wages to keep prices down? Is it fair to consumers who can pay less? Is it fair to Wal-Mart stockholders? Suppliers and wholesalers?

6. What would be fair pricing in this case? Is there a better system than market economics for setting prices and wages?

7. If Wal-Mart were to drive all of the independent (non-chain) stores in an area out of business, will the retailer keep its prices the same? If not, how will prices change?

Chapter 14

Money, Power, Influence, and Corruption: The Frog Principle in Action

Vice is a monster of so frightful mien,
As to be hated needs but to be seen;
Yet seen too oft, familiar with her face,
We first endure, then pity, then embrace.

—Alexander Pope[1]

LATE ONE AFTERNOON early in the summer, Marc was attending one of the cash registers at the sandwich shop where he worked. Although his parents had promised to help him financially when he entered college in the fall, he had committed to save everything possible from his summer job to make sure he would have enough money to enroll and cover basic living expenses. Although he had earned a modest scholarship, he knew the first year would surprise him with many unforeseen costs. One technique he used to control impulsive spending was to carry as little cash as possible. It was good discipline. He even used the bus to get back and forth to work instead of his car.

This particular afternoon Marc suddenly realized that during his afternoon coffee break he had spent all but 25 cents of his pocket money for snacks. He needed bus fare to get home but was short 50 cents, and the employees he felt comfortable asking for such a small loan had already gone home. He felt bad and was too embarrassed to let the other employees who were still there know that he was short of cash by asking to borrow the money.

As he went to close the cash drawer after the last customer left, it dawned on him: No customers were waiting, and the other employees were in the back of the store cleaning up. He debated with himself for a moment, and then felt reassured that he would only borrow two quarters for the night. He could return it in the morning, and everything would be fine. Besides, 50 cents could be explained by a counting error. It was such a small amount.

But, the next day, Marc was not assigned to a cash register, and he had no opportunity to slip the money back. No one asked any questions; it was obviously too little to worry about.

After a week passed, Marc had let the whole matter slip from his mind. But one morning as he was working the cash register again, he began to feel hungry. He had forgotten to grab the five-dollar bill on his dresser that morning which he had set aside for lunch and bus fare. A small snack in the break room was 75 cents, and he would still need another 75 cents for bus fare. Then he remembered that he had borrowed the 50 cents the week before. "Oh well," he reasoned, "I'll just bring in $2.00 tomorrow and replace the money."

Again, he forgot. Many more times throughout the summer he found himself needing small amounts—10 cents, 25 cents, or sometimes as much as five dollars—but replenishing his borrowings the next day was difficult because he was not usually assigned to the cash register two days in a row. Also, he felt uncomfortable putting too much money back in the till.

Before he knew it the summer was almost over, and he was sure he had racked up quite a tab. At first he had kept track of his borrowings in his mind, but with all the times he had put a small amount back in the till, he couldn't remember what he owed. Besides, it would be hard to return that much money without being noticed, and he really didn't feel like cutting into his savings, which seemed barely sufficient to get him through his first year of school. Also, no one seemed to notice that any money was missing.

Although Marc felt guilty about borrowing so many times, he was surprised at how much less it bothered him at the end of the summer to take a dollar or two out of the till at the end of the day than it did when he started in June.

The Frog Principle

Nearly everyone has heard a version of this or similar stories. Sometimes it's a kid at the cash register, but other times it's a bookkeeper, cash manager, professional accountant, or financial officer. Sometimes it's even a CEO who uses corporate perquisites for personal use, such as traveling in company jets to vacation destinations. I call the series of justifications the "frog principle," and in one way or another, it makes criminals of everyone.

Apparently (I've never tried it), if you drop a frog into a pan of hot water, the shock causes it to jump out immediately to save its life.

But, if you place the frog in a pan of cool water and gradually turn up the heat, it will stay in the pan until it is cooked. Frogs are cold-blooded, meaning their body temperature is consistent with their environment. So, it doesn't ever realize what is happening—it simply adapts and adjusts as the temperature rises—until it's too late. No alarm goes off to say it is time to jump.

I believe that most people in a business setting face this same dilemma. Many times, young people are hired into organizations, bringing their lofty ideas about being totally honest with them. If a manager or mentor tells them to "work around the truth" or "tell them only what they need to know," the idea is abhorrent to them, and they often refuse to indulge. But, when it becomes a matter of losing a job or an opportunity to make a good impression, the pressure builds and a small rationalization begins: "Well, I just won't say anything as long as they don't *ask*," or, "It's not actually lying since what I've said is *technically* correct," or "I wouldn't want to jeopardize our negotiating position." Then, when the tactics work as planned, the employees notice that such a strategy gets results. Any guilt is swept away efficiently by the feeling of success.

If and when the situation comes up again, these young employees find it more difficult to resist. After all, "it's just a little exaggeration" or understatement, they reason. Or, if they try to resist this time, the manager might say, "What's wrong now? You did it before."

Those who have lost their awareness of such subtle dilemmas soon begin to believe that "it's not actually lying—just a little puffery." They begin the journey down that slippery slope—or, rather, they soon find themselves over their heads in hot water, usually without realizing it.

The pressure for results can make it hard to see any red flags or stop signs, if there are any, that might say "not one step further." Instead, each successive degree seems like only one little step from the last one—"What's the harm in this much more?"

For example, many politicians go to Washington or other state capitols on the strength of their idealism and the votes of their constituents. Often, they promise to avoid becoming victims of powerful lobbyists, but most of them soon change. As the pressure to get re-elected builds they soon see the need to resort to "common practice." They accept, or even begin to elicit, large campaign contributions from the lobbies so they can keep their campaigns alive. (This is what happened to the senator described in Chapter 8.)

The frog principle seems to be at play in every walk of life. I can still remember when basketball was a "non-contact" sport. I would get called for a foul for simply resting my hand on the back of an opposing player I was guarding so I could keep track of his movement while I watched the ball. Since then, the sport has allowed players to escalate such practices that now include pushing, shoving, and other aggressive moves that maintain an advantage, especially when going after the ball. Of course, these would not be called pushing and shoving anymore. Now, it's "blocking out," "setting the screen," "posting up," "incidental contact," and even "no harm, no foul." If the present course continues, basketball players will have to start wearing protective gear like that of hockey or football players.

The Slippery Slope

The path seems so obvious and clear to observers who compare before and after, but the incline is so slight, and the descending steps so small, that no alarm goes off or demands attention until the jailhouse doors clang and we wonder, "What happened? When did I step over the line?"

Most people agree that honesty is right and safe legal territory, and fraud is very unsafe and quite wrong. But, with so many steps and shades of unethical behavior in between the two extremes and so many of them used in a business setting, no one seems to be willing or able to identify where the ethical or legal lines are that would warn someone if he or she is about to overstep the bounds. Placing some of these on a continuum, we have:

Honesty

Withholding Information

"Little White" Lies

"Puffery" and Public Relations

Leading to Believe

Exaggeration and Understatement

Evading or Stretching the Truth

Saying Things That Are Not So

Fraud

Certainly we would say that fraud is wrong and punishable, but keep in mind, if one of your business associates or partners can prove that you withheld information with the intent to commit fraud, then perhaps only one step is necessary to punish dishonest behavior. If you add to this list natural unclarity, errors of communication, basic misunderstandings, and the constant pressures of self-interest and competition, it's easy to see how the mind can rationalize or become numb and not pick up the faint warning signs.

A few definitions might help convey the feeling that no clear "stop" signs exist on the slippery path to deception and fraud, at least not in the pressure-filled, competitive business world:

> ***Honesty:*** Fairness and straightforwardness of conduct, adherence to facts, ability and practice of conveying a true impression.
>
> ***Withhold:*** To hold or keep back; to not share or inform.
>
> ***"Little White" Lie:*** Deliberately misstated nonessential fact designed to flatter or impress.
>
> ***Puffery:*** Exaggerated commendations, especially for promotional purposes.
>
> ***Mislead:*** To lead in a wrong direction or into a mistaken action or belief, often by stratagem or design.
>
> ***Exaggerate:*** To enlarge or increase in scope by words, especially beyond the normal bounds of the truth.
>
> ***Understate:*** To play down the importance or relevance of an item or action.
>
> ***Evade:*** To elude by dexterity or stratagem; to avoid answering directly.
>
> ***Stretching the Truth:*** Carefully crafting words by stratagem to convey a false message or impression while remaining technically or mostly accurate.
>
> ***Lie/Deceive:*** To cause to accept as true or valid what is false or invalid.
>
> ***Fraud:*** The intentional perversion, distortion, or withholding of truth to induce a person or entity to part with or never obtain something of value that would otherwise rightfully belong to him, her, or it.

Using these notches along the honesty-to-fraud continuum as benchmarks, where would you categorize your accounting reports, financial statements, explanations for declining stock prices, sales pitches, press releases, conversations during courtship, answers to your spouse about recent undiscussed purchases or about weight or hairstyle, responses to your children about sex or where you are going, stories to associates at the water cooler or friends at the local hangout, comments about people's job performance, observations about others' lifestyle choices or personal habits, your resume or job application, taxes?

The key to managing our efforts on the slippery slope of deception is not just to determine where we are on the slope but to understand and control which direction we are going and how fast. Otherwise, we may find that if we say something enough it becomes true in our minds. We sincerely begin to believe a lie. Or, if we do something often enough it begins to feel right. And, although deliberate efforts to move back up the slope towards honesty may meet with initial resistance or discomfort—even competitive disadvantage and financial losses—over time these efforts can engender great respect and trust.

We must maintain a constant vigil to keep fraud and other forms of flagrant deception from occurring. This vigil must include the courage to stand up and say stop or at least to raise questions to the level of debate about questionable ethical practices—particularly when such practices are producing results. We must establish productive counter forces to help push us and our organizations back up the slope toward honesty.

The Seduction of Power

John was just 17 when he enlisted in the U.S. Marine Corps a year before World War II ended. Raised in a rural western farming town of about 500 people, he had never traveled more than 200 miles from his place of birth. Shortly after he turned 19 he was promoted to corporal and assigned to be the Marine Corps dispatcher for the motor pool on Treasure Island in San Francisco Bay—which proved to be an interesting eye-opener to the ways of the world.

Almost overnight, this unknown and insignificant enlisted man became someone of notice to many commissioned and non-commissioned officers. Many of these people began to approach him offering favors. For instance, the chief cook offered John a standing invitation to move to the head of the mess line at any meal and promised him fresh donuts and milk after hours. The manager at the theater made it easy for John to find a good seat, even if he arrived late, without having to stand in line. Duty officers suggested that he could have late night liberty whenever he desired without any hassle. And, even the quartermaster invited him to take advantage of "midnight requisitions" of clothing and equipment beyond what normal standards permitted.

The attention and "thoughtfulness" of these people impressed John, and he felt fortunate that so many persons of influence wanted to be his "friends." Some of them even began to point out to him what a nice guy he was and how they knew they always could count on him. Soon he began to receive many friendly requests from these generous new friends for rides to San Francisco or Oakland. No problem, he thought. He simply could ask the driver of a vehicle going that way to take the person along. All he had to do was coordinate the time and instruct the driver.

From time to time, John might instruct a driver to travel a few blocks or maybe a mile out of the assigned way to accommodate the needs of a special passenger. After all, it would only be fair since many of these special passengers had gone out of their way to accommodate his needs on occasion.

As time went on, these special friends began to be more and more generous. On the other hand, they also began to make more and more requests for transportation that was further and further away from couriers' routes. But it was quite easy to accommodate them since no one ever checked up, and he could always find ample ways to cover for the extra miles and time.

Looking back as a mature man, John felt pleased that he was discharged before things got out of hand. He hadn't noticed anything wrong at the time, but as he reflected on his time at Treasure Island he remembered that he had become confident and bold with his power to make decisions without supervision, sometimes stepping over the ethical line and often coming perilously close to stepping over the legal line. It would only have been a matter of time.

Money, Power, Influence, and Corruption

Money, power, and influence are fascinatingly intoxicating in modern society. They often push, seduce, entice, or consistently tempt people to step over ethical and legal lines. Reports describe incident after incident in which people have fallen victim to the corruptive processes of success. It seems that as soon as people get a little authority, they immediately begin to use it for their own personal benefit and to the detriment of others, often skirting higher authority or ethical and legal guidelines to do so.

"Power tends to corrupt, and absolute power corrupts absolutely," said Lord Acton.[2] Money, power, and influence are all in the same family—close siblings with similar traits and mannerisms. Money, as a form of power, can be exercised to influence and persuade others. People in positions of power can gain access to money and influence, and can increase their power by leveraging both tools. And those who come with built-in influence because of their connections to wealthy or powerful families or friends can obtain money and position more easily than others.

People who gain more power, money, and influence than they are accustomed to tend to use these forces to aggrandize their own private needs and desires for more power, more money, more influence, and more recognition. They become vulnerable to, and participators in, the corruption process. And, when the three tools are combined, they are almost guaranteed to push all but the strongest and most wary moral vigilants over the ethical line and eventually the legal line.

The life cycle of the corruption process can be charted through four stages: (1) aspiration, (2) intoxication, (3) addiction, and (4) maturation.

Aspiration. Success has become the widespread embodiment of today's modern entrepreneurial dream. Books, tapes, lectures, seminars, classrooms, and selling schemes all give the term its vibrancy and urgency: "How to make a million in real estate with nothing down," "How to earn thousands of dollars a month part-time," "How to earn $100,000 a year in network marketing," "God wants you to be rich." In modern society, success is spelled "$u¢¢e$$," and whenever we say someone is successful, we primarily refer to wealth or influence.

Young people coming out of school and many older people in the workforce are driven to accomplish in faster and more dramatic ways what their wealthy and influential predecessors did. They are easily tempted by increased wealth and improved position. They look for and often succumb to get-rich-quick schemes, and when they fail they blame themselves for not working hard enough or smart enough. They aspire, plan, and even connive to attain positions of power in organizations or to get as much experience as they can fast before they rush out to set up their own businesses and take full advantage of opportunities. They pursue elected office because of the potential influence it renders. They pursue their educations solely to improve their marketability and income—not for enriching and broadening their knowledge. Education becomes simply a tool to accumulate more material wealth and to practice "beating the system." They master the empty arts of networking, name-dropping, politicking, gamesmanship, posturing, and personal positioning—all to make the best possible impression and to rack up favors and obligations.

But, so far, there's nothing wrong with aspiration or with pursuing excellence. Striving for a better way of life and for effective ways of helping others is a good thing. The danger arises when the early results of these aspirations take hold and the intoxication of power sets in.

Intoxication. Once a person gains that first big goal—a significant amount of money, or an eagerly sought-for elective office, or a major athletic award or championship, intoxication often commences. One meaning of "intoxicate" is "to stimulate and excite." Another meaning is "to put poison in (by some toxin, drug, or narcotic)."[3] Frequently, money, power, and influence act like narcotics on the mental and emotional aspects of a person. They generate feelings of euphoria, invincibility, and oversensitivity to negative criticism. Self-deception, defensiveness, and low self-esteem are common side effects, but they do not necessarily attack all intoxicated individuals.

Consider what might happen to people—perhaps accountants, insurance agents, attorneys, small business owners, bankers, or salespeople—who are accustomed to working on a local level but suddenly end up in Washington, D.C., the state capitol, or the national press. Although they may have been used to interacting with a relatively small circle of associates, they are now sought after by people and organizations of high prestige. They now daily receive letters printed on the stationery of *Fortune* 500 companies and signed by people with titles such as executive vice president, president, or chairman. Phone calls from popular radio and television talk-show hosts, national magazine editors, and newspaper columnists crowd voicemail. Letters and invitations pour in from national and state legislators, well-known movie stars with causes, and advertising executives from popular brand-name companies. A phone call may even come in that begins with, "I'm calling from the White House. . . ." Officers of corporations, representatives from universities and other revered institutions call and ask for appointments. Many unknowns ask if they can meet to introduce their teenagers. People offer tickets to the symphony, professional ball games, and popular resorts. All-expense paid trips and honoraria are offered for keynote speeches at trade association conferences or executive seminars in places like Jackson Hole, Hilton Head, Park City, Orlando, Palm Springs, or Waikiki. Intoxication is well underway.

The effects of outside attention are reinforced by internal staffs and assistants who are anxious to please. Underlings become very skilled at paying great deference to "the boss's" mandates and demonstrating the "can-do" attitude. They want to curry the favor of the people in charge. Most, if not all, such underlings are unwilling to point out errors or problems—they wouldn't dare tell the emperor he has no clothes. They engage in blatant flattery and empty praise and express excessive gratitude. At first, people new to positions of power discount such statements as exaggerations, but as the words are repeated they begin to feel so good that the discounting ceases and the insincere statements are accepted at face value. Good staffers antici-pate the boss's desires and fulfill them without being asked. This feels good and builds a sense of self-importance, justification, and effi-ciency. The intoxication of power begins to take hold.

Soon, people in power begin to find great self-confidence and start to feel that they really know what's best. They speak with greater surety and notice the people trying to curry good favor, using their advantageous positions to gain favors from them. Orders are issued and carried out—no questions asked. Decision-making power increases the sense of self-importance. Self-awareness becomes dulled, and stepping over ethical lines is done with more confi-dence—after all, the noble ends justify almost any means, and "busi-ness is business." The feeling of power lulls them into believing that contractual violations and even illegal ventures won't get detected. The narcotic of power is showing its effects.

To a lesser degree, the appointment as a vice president of a cor-poration or similar institution, or an election to a prominent local office offers a similar experience. Outstanding high school athletes or beauty pageant winners may also experience this intoxication.

And so the frog principle works its magic, intoxicating its victims with power. Just like drunks who don't realize they are unfit to drive, neither do people intoxicated by power realize they are unfit to lead or make rational and ethical decisions.

Addiction. After they have been propelled to "stardom" and experience the joy and thrill of intoxication, people who are new to power begin to show evidence of addiction. To reassure themselves that they are worthy of such lavish attention, they become less tolerant of criticism and opposing ideas, and often block out negative criticism altogether. They begin to believe that their ideas are right and all opposing ideas are not only wrong, but dangerous or threatening or evidence of disloyalty. They become poor listeners. They use questions to attack rather than search out new or helpful information. They lose tolerance for others who disagree or try to raise a different point of view, as well as for those who take the new ideas seriously.

When addiction sets in, actions to preserve power begin to appear. Those in power begin to declare enemies and launch attacks to treat them as such. Those who would threaten the people in power must be "dealt with." This means, perhaps at first, that offenders have certain responsibilities or benefits taken away. Sometimes they are moved into isolation or transferred away or fired. If the offenders resist or fight back, more stringent measures may be indulged, possibly including unethical or illegal tactics, but certainly not in keeping with the Golden Rule. Preserving power—protecting assets and investments, keeping stockholders happy, keeping government regulators or investigative journalists away, or ensuring reelection— becomes such a noble end that deception, withholding information, and planting rumors designed to assassinate an enemy's character seem not only appropriate, but necessary. Corruption preserves power and feeds and intensifies the addiction to it.

Maturation. At this stage, some people in power often begin to recognize the dilemma and take steps to cure it. One way is to use their money, power, and influence as they originally intended, often overcompensating for past questionable behaviors by blowing the whistle on people who use the same tactics, lecturing to students about the "real world," or contributing generously to noble or gentle causes, as cynics might say, "to buy respectability."

However, with others, addictions may be unremitting. Any efforts to pull back are met with resistance from coat-tail followers and co-dependent power addicts, or at least those who might otherwise try to break the addiction feel hopeless or powerless to stop the power surge. The more power is obtained in the form of money, position, or influence, the more unethical or illegal actions are needed to ensure its growth and to keep competitors from challenging the power. And, the more such behaviors are engaged in, the more coverup is needed to keep the public and the media at bay. Eventually, unless someone pulls back, power addicts typically suffer a tragic fate: They may die at the hands of their enemies like Julius Caesar, or Benito Mussolini, or Nicolae Ceausescu; or commit suicide rather than face up to their acts like Adolf Hitler; or dramatically lose power as the story breaks or their weaknesses are exposed like those of Napoleon Bonaparte, Richard Nixon, Idi Amin of Uganda—or even more recently, Michael Milken or Ivan Boesky.

Power does, indeed, intoxicate and engender addictions. And addictions of this nature, just like illegal drugs, nearly always cause or entice people to cross ethical and legal lines.

CASE: A Bank with a History

Security Financial Bank commenced business in 1908 and had over two decades of financial prosperity. Then, like many other banks, the Great Depression took a heavy toll, eventually causing the bank to declare bankruptcy and close its doors in late 1932.

In 1952, Theodore Sebastian launched his own banking enterprise. As he tried to come up with an attractive name for his company, he came across the records of Security Financial Bank and learned of its demise. And, after much research and investigation, he legally obtained the right to use the name. Later that year he opened his new financial institution with the name.

Knowing how important trust, reliability, and security would be in the banking business, he wanted to convey an image of stability. The building's architecture and interior decorations conveyed a feeling of solid strength and financial prosperity. A sign on the front of the building read, "Security Financial Bank—Founded in 1908." The same message appeared on the bank's letterhead and in all advertisements. After the bank began to grow, other branches were opened, and each of them had the same sign out front: "Founded in 1908."

Questions:

1. Was the owner of the bank dishonest or deceitful? If so, was this just a small or inconsequential matter?

2. Are the banker's actions the first step down the slippery slope to blatant lying and fraud? Would you trust this banker if you knew what he had done to obtain the name or to place "Founded in 1908" on his sign?

3. Is stretching your age by a year or padding your resume an unimportant matter?

Chapter 15

Nine Suggestions for Improving Ethical Awareness and Behavior

"American business needs a lifting purpose greater than the struggle for materialism."

—*Herbert Hoover*

"OKAY," YOU SAY, "I see the traps, seductions, forces, and enticements that push or lure me and my company over the ethical line. But what can I do about it?"

Throughout this book I have focused on helping you develop an awareness of complex issues relating to honesty and ethics. If I only raise a few tough questions in your mind and cause you to carefully consider how you would handle the situation, my effort will have been worthwhile. I have not tried to convert you to my way of thinking, but I only hope to help you root out hypocrisy and double standards in your behavior, whether you knew about them before or not.

Naivete and unawareness are powerful factors in unethical behavior. Thus, simply discussing the problems, in and of itself, is a major step forward. For those who were already aware of most of these dilemmas and who would like to know how to pursue a path of greater honesty, I think I will address something like this in a future book. Nevertheless, I also do not want to leave you suspended in thinking that the cause of ethics is hopeless or that I see no solutions for these complex issues. That would be unfair.

Many people I have met with have thrown their hands in the air saying, "These problems are unsolvable," or "There is no right answer." They feel that the problems are so complicated it's best just to leave them to others while they go on to tackle another problem that perhaps has a more readily available solution. On the other hand, I have found that most people who give these issues serious thought simply cannot let them sit. They absolutely must discuss the questions with others and outline how they plan to proceed in the future.

I hope you fall into the second category. You will gain much more from your efforts.

Maintaining morality in our society is like maintaining a garden. If you allow the plants to go without water or if you fail to weed them regularly, they die. Or, if you allow them to grow unchecked, they become unsightly and may stop blooming. Failing to exert a little effort now and then eventually leads to deterioration or disintegration. Likewise, a society cannot maintain itself without a few commonly accepted values and behaviors. These values must be refined and discussed frequently, or they deteriorate, too. Any community, business, institution, work group, or family that does not share a critical mass of common values—commonly accepted standards of conduct that are regularly discussed and refined—will eventually collapse upon itself. Everybody is left to do their own thing, and that means anarchy. Anarchy is a characteristic of a nonviable society.

On the other hand, the more values a group shares, the more satisfying life will be for each of its members and the more support each member will receive when tough decisions are made. They enjoy more security, experience less frustration and conflict, and meet a basic human need for belonging. And, when values are not shared or lived up to, tension arises, distrust flourishes, fear grows, and relationships prove less satisfying.

Something can be done. It may not be easy, but the effort alone is worthwhile and the results can be long-lasting. Those who say there are no answers—that these ethical dilemmas have no solution—are wrong. Choices must eventually be made, and I believe that right and wrong, at least in terms of motive, are very real forces. Even refusing or failing to decide is a decision—perhaps default is the decision—and, as a decision, it leads to a certain outcome. Thus, it would be much more constructive for you to make a deliberate decision than to have some decision forced upon you or to allow others to make your ethical decisions for you.

Striving to elevate society's moral behavior is truly a noble cause. As frustrating as it can be at times, the lessons are of great value to those who are willing to search out answers and learn from experience.

Money First, Morality After?

As you search for ways to improve your honesty and ethical behavior, beware of the many cynical philosophies that would tell you it's impossible to be an honest person in business. One of these says, in essence, "You can't knock success." That is, if someone has achieved significant economic success, or a great position of power, or enormous popularity, no one should criticize how it was accomplished. Those who follow this guideline seem to believe that success or achievement is the acceptable moral end, or that prosperity in every case is a gift from God. They somehow believe that the means of achieving success will soon be forgotten or that no one will be concerned—only the result is important. After all, they were destined for greatness. In this philosophy, the only unethical thing is to fail to achieve the goal.

Another approach was expressed by the Greek philosopher Horace in 62 B.C. He said, "Money comes first. Morality after." Thus, we should make our money by whatever means necessary, use the money to live like royalty, and then behave morally afterward. Horace implied that morality and making money may not be compatible, but at least lack of morality can be made up for afterward. Or, once you're old, it's too late to get rich.

Although such approaches to ethics have aspects of practicality, they are spiced with cynicism. They have considerable attractiveness because of their simplicity when compared with seriously wrestling with complex moral dilemmas. Also, they are appealing because we don't want to believe that good guys can't become rich, or that they can't get rich as quickly as less honorable people.

On the other hand, although many corporations and institutions insist that the best way to create an ethical organization is to fill it with honorable people, research shows that this doesn't always cut it, either. For example, Tulane University released three studies showing that hiring managers with strong personal values or establishing ethics programs are not enough to make organizations ethical. In the studies, "Researchers watched to see whether results would differ when codes of corporate conduct and managers' high personal values were in place. Codes of corporate conduct, per se, do not appear to work, the researchers found. And personal values [in managers] seem to have little or no effect."[1]

Logic suggests that an organization's culture would be a more dominant influence on individual ethical behavior. Looking back at the introduction, the behavior of one's boss and the behavior of peers have a more powerful effect than the stated beliefs of those people or a company's written code of conduct. And, as I have discussed throughout the book, what is rewarded is what gets the attention.

Thus, whether they wholeheartedly endorse it or not, many business-people embrace the philosophy, compelled by self-interest and competition, that says: "I don't care how you accomplish the goal; just do it. And, if you plan to do anything unethical or illegal, don't tell me about it and don't get caught. It's easier to obtain forgiveness than permission, especially if you're successful." The steps to change such philosophy in an organization might be the subject of yet another book. But, in the meantime, these nine suggestions can help you take the ethical pulse of your company.

The Nine Suggestions

These nine suggestions, then, are simple starting points. I do not pretend to provide any magical step-by-step plan to an ethical nirvana. Instead, these recommendations are designed to help you and your organization, institution, work group, family, church group, or community to lift awareness and set new guidelines for ethical conduct, root out hypocrisy, and get on a new practice regimen for strengthening your honesty muscles. These steps can guide you to make wiser decisions and contribute to a more healthy moral fiber in our society.

I do not expect you individually to turn an immoral group into a moral group. But, you can nudge the group in the right direction rather than contribute to its decline by your participation or silence. You will find that others will seek out your opinion and respect your judgment because of your willingness to speak up for the cause of honesty and doing what is right over that which may be wrong or, more often, shady-but-successful.

The idea here is to help you inculcate in your group a commitment to maintain desirable moral values and ethical conduct. This sharing of values is *culture*: the beliefs and forces that govern individual behavior when supervision is not present. A culture can be morally elevating or morally degrading. So, with this in mind, you can help create a culture that embraces values of higher moral content and enhances respect for each individual member. Warning: It may take a long time, and the results may not be financially impressive for you or your organization, but I think you will be glad you made the choice.

If your experience trying these suggestions turns out to be anything like mine, you will find the exercises invigorating, refreshing, thought-provoking, challenging, and rewarding—even if you look at them only for the purpose of interpersonal communication.

1. Acknowledge "It Starts with Me"

The only way we can influence change in others is by changing ourselves. So often, people see unethical behavior in others but are unwilling to admit the same tendencies in themselves. They concentrate their attention on pointing fingers at "those people"—thieves, cheats, liars, and so on—thinking the problem is always "out there" rather than dormant or untested inside their own hearts in many cases.

The solution to solving other problems also seems to reside outside: "When those in government [or teachers, managers, preachers, etc.] get 'them' to stop 'their' unethical behavior, then we will be okay."

As I said at the beginning of the book, I have never met a dishonest or unethical person. Whenever I ask people if they consider themselves honest, I usually get a straightforward answer: Yes. Certainly, everybody wants to attest to their own honesty. At the same time, they point to colleagues and peers, managers and employees, competitors and customers who behave dishonestly.

Many studies have shown that people tend to see themselves as different from others around them. For instance, a poll conducted by the *Cincinnati Enquirer* found that 81 percent of area residents rated their own ethics as "excellent" or "very good," and nearly all—95 percent—agree that honesty is the best policy, and 93 percent said being ethical in all aspects of life was "very important." However, 37 percent of those polled also admitted to stealing something from work, and 33 percent said they would use a sister's address to get their child into a better school district.[2] So, which is it? Are the other people hiding something, or are only the 37 or 33 percent hypocrites? Or, does this phenomenon happen to everyone, and we simply don't see it?

We are all a part of society, and our performance affects the performance of the whole team—whether it's a ball team, a family, a work group, a department, a company, a community, or a nation. If you want to improve the performance of an athletic team, for example, you must practice your own skills and participate with the coach to coordinate the efforts of the whole team. Then, the improved performance of each individual makes for a stronger team—the poor players get more experience; the average players become good, and the good players become great. If you just focused on the people who were poor and neglected the practice of the team as a whole, your team would not improve. In fact, it might get worse. Those who are good can strengthen and coach those who are not, often in ways the coach can't see.

Pogo's wisdom is still true: We have found the enemy, and he is us. When we go on our witch hunts for "unethical people," don't be surprised if your own name comes up occasionally. We all have room for improvement.

Make the commitment to recognize and discuss with others the unethical tendencies you find in yourself.

2. Create a Meaningful Definition of Honesty

Many years ago during my graduate studies, I learned a lesson that really stuck. Our class had been given a business case study—an actual business situation in which the class felt that something definitely needed to be done. The night before, we reviewed and discussed the case individually and in small groups for the next day's discussion in the classroom. Then, the next day, everyone was eager to participate in the discussion and share possible solutions. The instructor orchestrated the discussion and wrote many pertinent things on the board, allowing people to make counter recommendations with their reasons. We came up with several proposed solutions to the case and modified each of them several times. After more than an hour of discussion, we began to run out of ideas. Near the end of class, during a brief lull in the discussion, the professor looked at the chalkboard with its proposals, calculations, and ideas, and asked, "What is the problem in this case?"

A long silence answered his query. No one had defined the problem. Most of us thought the problem was "obvious," and we assumed everyone else understood the same thing and agreed on the matter. Our first tentative attempts to define the problem immediately revealed the fuzziness of our understanding and how wide our disagreement had been with regard to the real problem.

In subsequent cases that year we focused first on articulating the problem before we looked for solutions. Once we knew what the problem was, we could make appropriate recommendations and offer stronger solutions much faster. Defining the problem first established a strong basis for discussing possible solutions together. Otherwise, it seemed the problems would never go away and any proposed solutions were wholly inadequate.

So it is with ethics or honesty. Without meaningful definitions, little progress toward improved ethics can occur. Such definitions must be general enough to cover many situations but specific enough to help individuals make appropriate decisions without second thoughts. Definitions that are too general may at first be valid and acceptable, but they tend to be so vague that they give little help in making decisions or taking specific actions.

The definition in Chapter 3 is a good place to start: "To tell the truth is not just to state the facts, but to convey a true impression." This allows us to ask ourselves, "Did I convey a true impression?" And, generally, we may want to answer yes, but we may also find it appropriate in some instances to convey a different impression—such as in competition or in trying to be nice instead of brutally honest with a friend or loved one. Search for and describe the rare instances when exceptions may be appropriate, and do your best to avoid making exceptions whenever you can.

If you don't like this definition, develop one of your own. But develop one and write it down. If you can't write it down, you have not thought it through enough. Ask for help and feedback from people around you—your work group, family, or church—to refine your definition. Try to reach a mutual understanding about what it means to have this definition. Dialogue not only creates clearer meanings, but also helps establish the foundation of ethical behavior in your organization.

3. Assess Your Ethical Position

Whenever an organization wants to improve, usually the first step is to gather information and assess where to improve. In the case of ethical improvements in a company, management may begin by asking, "How ethical are the people in this organization—owners, executives, managers, supervisors, front-line workers, staff, suppliers, partners?" "How much do these groups trust each other's honesty or ethics?" "Why would people in this organization have a reason to deliberately lie?" "How much important information is withheld from others in this organization?" "How does management set the standard for ethical behavior and provide incentives for others to be honest?"

Assessing the moral climate of an organization is useful for at least two reasons: First, it provides data that either confirms you already have an ethical organization or reveals problems that can be treated to improve the ethical climate. The information also gives clues about where to begin improvement efforts. Second, it provides solid, in-house data as the basis for internal discussions and education. It leads to involvement at the individual level and promotes buy-in and cooperative implementation.

Several tools to assess ethics on a more formal basis are available from many companies.[3] Regardless of the assessment method you choose, begin by candidly discussing your own, and then your organization's, ethical position.

4. Seek Agreement

Formal seminars, discussions, and training sessions are good vehicles to seek agreement on ethical issues. Rather than lecture on what is or is not acceptable, groups generally can invite candid input from everyone without finger pointing or preaching. Whereas lectures tend to become preachy, discussions nurture buy-in. Even potential antagonists can become active and eager participants responsible for the group's conclusions and recommendations. Discussions also help participants to clarify misunderstandings and encourage the involvement of everyone, while lecturers tend to make assumptions about audience background, and listeners don't always get to participate.

To be effective, discussion groups should get past sweeping generalities and look at a variety of circumstances and cases. Too often, we indicate our approval of ethical clichés and slogans without considering more difficult subjects, probably because discussions of more complex issues may lead to disagreements, misunderstandings, or cultural or religious clashes. But, it's true, "the devil is in the details." Spend time wrestling with specific situations drawn from public resources and familiar group experiences to minimize the flare-up of "loaded" issues.

Conclude your discussions by setting specific guidelines or even rules whenever possible. You may find that, after wrestling with complex ethical dilemmas for some time, people begin to say things like, "It is unsolvable," "Everybody should just do what their conscience tells them," or "Every case is different; it just depends on the situation." Don't allow formal conversations to end this way, for these do not represent moral or ethical standards. However, you may conclude with something like, "We recognize that people in this group see different and viable alternatives, but we agree that, from now on, [A, B, and C] behaviors will be acceptable and [X, Y, and Z] behaviors will not."

Explore such topics as:

*   In this company and industry, what forces pressure us or entice us to cross ethical and legal boundaries? How can we counter balance those forces?

- Under what circumstances might lying, or different forms of lying, be the right thing to do? Is withholding information a form of lying? If so, when is it appropriate to withhold information?
- In our activities, what noble goals might justify the use of ignoble means?
- If bribery is "common practice" should we engage in it?
- How do we use the law of obligation to attain our purposes, both individually and collectively? How *should* we use it?
- Do personal ethics or gaming ethics govern our activities? Which should predominate?
- Should honesty or loyalty be our top priority? If loyalty, then loyalty to whom or what?
- When is whistle-blowing appropriate in our organization or industry? How should we go about blowing the whistle when it is appropriate?
- In what circumstances are binding promises made? If circumstances change, when is it appropriate to back out of a deal or a promise? What changing circumstances might justify such action?
- How can this organization or group follow the Golden Rule? Under what circumstances would following the Golden Rule not be appropriate?
- How can our organization or industry keep from getting trapped in the frog principle?
- How can we keep people in the organization from becoming seduced and corrupted by newfound success, such as great wealth or influential positions?

Use the short cases at the end of each chapter as discussion materials. Make sure that everyone in your group is challenged to say specifically what he or she would do in each situation and why. The challenge and struggle serve to build the group's ethical muscle, enabling individuals in the group to be more ethical, and to help others in the group perform on a higher moral plane.

5. Build Ethical Thinking into Daily Activities

Profit-conscious organizations must continually talk of revenues, expenses, productivity, and competitive advantages. Each staff meeting, especially among top management, keeps these items on the agenda. The need and justification for these issues repeatedly are emphasized, and the group sets new goals. Progress constantly is measured, reported, and evaluated. Management puts incentives in place and regularly checks up on performance. But, even with all this attention and emphasis, profits still are hard to attain and sustain.

Charitable organizations find that raising funds requires the same attention, measurement, reporting, evaluation, correction, reward systems, and emphasis as other companies. Athletic teams go through the same process, only their "profits" are also measured by wins and losses or points earned versus points given up. Political campaigns measure their "profits" by votes and polls.

Organizations that desire to reach and maintain high ethical standards must apply the same vigilance—periodic memos, public announcements, a statement in the annual report, or new posters on lunchroom walls simply will not bring about results. However, day-to-day outward evidence of concern and urgency helps greatly. To make honesty an integral part of your family, work group, company, institution, or community, you must make it a primary and frequent topic for discussions and action plans.

Talk about ethics in the car or train, over dinner, on the factory floor, in casual conversation, and in staff meetings—not in safe and non-disturbing generalities, but in specific and even complex terms. When someone in your company or industry breaks a sales or performance record or gets promoted quickly, discuss the ethical challenges the person might have faced on the way to that goal. Discuss what corners might have been cut or what kind of sales pitch may have been used. If it comes up that someone used unethical or dishonest means to reach a goal, don't avoid discussing the moral concerns and, by that silence, give a stamp of approval to questionable behavior. Or, if someone gets caught violating corporate rules, don't just rattle off company policy as if it were scripture: "Oh, we have a written policy against that." Instead, acknowledge your own difficulties in wrestling with some ethical issue, maybe something different. If you let people know that you believe ethics to be important, many will be encouraged to share their insights and dilemmas.

6. Establish a Legend

Many nations, societies, institutions, and families have established and perpetuated their values and behaviors by establishing legends. Long ago, citizens in the United States adopted the legend of George Washington confessing to cutting down a cherry tree as one of their favorite moral stories, even though its history is speculative at best. Nevertheless, it still conveys a moral of honesty to schoolchildren nationwide. Similar legends about Abraham Lincoln won him the title "Honest Abe" and continue to reinforce the importance of honesty, even in politics. The poet Henry Wadsworth Longfellow enshrined duty and courage in his immortal poem, "The Midnight Ride of Paul Revere," romanticizing those values for many generations to come.

Many organizations have such legends prominent in their cultures. Usually, legends arise from people telling and retelling incidents in the life of a founder. The incidents often exemplify acts of courage, sacrifice, honor, or commitment to a cause. In America, the legend of Horatio Alger has perpetuated the values of industry and hope and the promise that success can be available to anyone in our society who desires it. And the legend of Thomas Edison's hundreds of attempts to find a filament for his light globe has inspired thousands to never give up. President Jimmy Carter may have been trying to establish a legend in one of his campaign speeches by promising never to lie to the American public. Families in the United States often have legends about ancestors who sacrificed friends, family, and possessions to make a new home in the land of the free.

Organizations that want to establish honesty and integrity in their companies' cultures may find that legends help. Sometimes these motivational stories just spring up. But, more often, they need help. A single exemplary incident is not enough. The story must be told repeatedly in an inspiring way to gain the attention of many listeners. I don't think this merits lying or exaggerating the facts, but the most effective way seems to be to tell the story in a way that people remember and desire to repeat it. It may help to write it down or have several different people write it down and then compare notes. Have the legend published in the company newsletter, an annual report, local newspapers, or perhaps a magazine or trade journal. Share the story in staff meetings and in celebration events to reinforce the values in longtime workers and to introduce the legend to new employees.

Identify potential legends and the values they communicate. Then, take deliberate steps to reinforce the legend until it becomes part of the culture. In particular, search for legends that convey a powerful sense of honesty, integrity, trustworthiness, and teamwork.

7. Be Willing to Pay the Price

Most good and worthy things in life have a high price to pay, and not always a financial price. For example, many people understand the resources, skill, vigilance, and personal sacrifice required to win an Olympic gold medal or a league championship, build a quality home, become a concert musician, or make a profit in a new venture. These successes often require foregoing, postponing, or thwarting other desires to gain the focus needed for sustained effort. In the world of achievement, people seem to understand this—I don't think I've ever heard a mentor say to a protege, "You should try to do it all—be a professional ballplayer in at least three sports, an expert financier and entrepreneur, a famous actor on both the stage and screen, a renowned ballet dancer and opera singer, a physician, and an accomplished trial judge—at some point in your life." Usually, wise advisors counsel that you may like to do all those things, but you generally must forego several of them to excel in one or two.

Likewise, we can't always have it both ways with ethics and honesty. Despite their good career advice regarding specialization and focus, parents, teachers, coaches, and mentors rarely counsel their charges about the price that must be paid for honesty: "If you are going to be honest, you might not make the sale, beat your competitor, get the promotion, keep your job, win the election, or improve your relationships. In fact, you may lose more than you think." Instead, we breed hypocrites by ingraining slogans like "honesty is the best policy" without explaining why or how it is the best. The price of honesty can be high, and we should not withhold such information from our children, students, and proteges.

The preparation and willingness to pay the price are essential for anyone to maintain basic morality. Gratefully, once ethical behavior is established with guidelines and commitments, the number of dilemmas are significantly reduced. You no longer face an ethical question every time you look at money or a new opportunity. Also, we can learn much from each other in discussions, and we can relate the stories of role models—such as the Maine lumber company in Chapter 12 that, despite the fire that destroyed its main warehouse, still kept its commitment to the charity.

Captain Kurt Carlsen is another role model, at least for me, who gave 100 percent to his principles regardless of the cost. On December 26, 1951, as his ship, the *Flying Enterprise*, sailed from Germany to the United States, a hurricane cracked its deck. The ship began taking on water 320 miles off the coast of England, and on the 29th, passengers and crew were removed from the vessel.

The ship began listing heavily to port, and seagoing tugs and other ships raced to render assistance. Each day, evening news reports and headline newspaper stories gave the degree of list, the number of miles from port, and the hours it would take to get there. Carlsen, the only man on the ship for over a week, refused to leave, wanting to keep a vigilant watch on the cable lines attached to the tugs that were pulling and straining to get the *Flying Enterprise* to safety.

The whole world watched, prayed, and cheered for Carlsen to make it into port. Many believed it was a lost cause and criticized the captain for his expensive efforts to save a sinking ship. But Carlsen still refused to leave the ship. He felt he had to do all he could to carry out his commission and responsibility—to save his ship. Through the days the tugs pulled and pulled, and the captain kept his lonely vigil.

On the morning of the 10th of January—over two weeks since the hurricane—the ship seemed all but capsized. Still, the tugs kept pulling. The world kept cheering and praying. One picture, taken when the boat was just 50 miles from port, showed Captain Carlsen clinging to the side of his ship. It appeared he was engaged in a battle of physical strength and sheer personal will to right his ship. Shortly after that, the captain was finally persuaded to leave. One tug's cable line had broken, and the other tugs would need to cut their tow lines to avoid being pulled under. After all the heroic effort, the battle was lost.

Shortly after the saga, motion picture companies offered Captain Carlsen $100,000 or more—all perfectly legal—to make a movie about the drama and capitalize on his newfound fame, but he would have none of it. As Carlsen saw it, he was only doing his professional duty as the honor of a ship's captain would dictate. He explained, "I most certainly do not want honest efforts to save my ship to be commercialized in any way."[4]

In today's spirit of grab all you can, Captain Carlsen may seem to be a fool to many people. Yet he exemplifies what we mean about honor and the preparation and willingness to pay the price for what we feel is right. Professional honor is what professional action defines, not what the letter of the law may permit without penalty.

8. Reward Ethical Behavior

Rewarding ethical behavior when it wins the contract or the customer or the prize is all well and good—such actions should be applauded, celebrated, and honored. For example, it's good to publicize the boy who turns in the wallet he finds, intact, and it gets returned to the owner. Maybe the police or the person who lost the wallet should contribute a small reward.

But, if you really want to raise the ethical standards of your organization, you must reward ethical behavior not just when it accompanies good results, but also when it is difficult—even when it accompanies painful results. If you only do the first, you reward results, not ethical behavior. If you really want to send a message that honesty is important, reward people whose honesty results in a lost contract or customer, or that leads to embarrassment to the company or its management. Reward the whistle-blower. These actions are signs of courage and depth of character, and rewarding them, even when it's difficult, signifies that the organization values honesty. On the other hand, if the organization doesn't value honesty above loyalty, then it shouldn't be dishonest by sending such a message in either case. If you value results, reward them. If you value honesty, reward it. But don't say you are rewarding honesty if you only mean to honor the results.

9. Designate an Ethical Conscience

Formally designate someone in your organization or work group, or your family, as an "ethical conscience." This person is separate and distinct from the "compliance officer" that many companies have.

A compliance officer is formally appointed and authorized to make sure that nobody in the organization violates governmental regulations. This person has the backing of federal, state, and local governments, along with the stamp of approval from the organization's top authority. The behaviors watched by the officer are spelled out clearly in manicured legal language, which is important because, when a compliance officer presses the company to change questionable behaviors, the company generally realizes that the officer is helping to protect management from expensive penalties and litigation. Even if the compliance officer points out something that, if changed, would have a negative influence on production, profits, or customer service, the company tends to acknowledge that making the change is for the best. The officer usually knows how the neglect of certain government mandates can have painful consequences.

However, the ethics officer would not typically enjoy such precision and clarity. Much of ethics is subtle and subject to controversy: "Are we conveying a true impression?" may not be the best question to ask an advertising executive, for example. Also, conveying something less than a true impression to a customer will not likely send anyone to jail or precipitate heavy fines and penalties.

Because of these pressure-filled ambiguities, such an officer easily could be rendered impotent. After all, the person would not be a legal officer, but a conscience—not there to enforce, but to prompt, prod, and preserve moral awareness when the demands of day-to-day business would otherwise push such concerns out of the way. And, even with great interpersonal and communication skills, such an officer could become an irritant even to those who appoint the person. So, the ethics officer must not be a typical subordinate subject to the whims and mandates of superiors. If the ethics officer has to worry constantly about offending others in the company or possibly getting fired every time he or she has an observation to make or a question to pose, then the person's position would be too tenuous to be of any real value.

First, the ethics officer needs some form of security from the fears of incurring the displeasure of the people in power, but absolute security is not likely reasonable. Some security, perhaps in the form of tenure, could be granted to a person of high stature and competence in the organization who is regarded as a peer by people at all levels of the company. This means that the person can't be fired or reassigned except by the chairman of the board or an executive committee. Another fairly secure position is that of consultant, hired at the discretion of the company board or president, who could circulate freely with the employees and managers.

Second, the officer ought to have another position available with the company or one of its partners if something goes wrong. This way, the person does not feel the urgency to please the company powers that be at all costs. Without these precautions, the person is trapped in a position of being expected to speak the truth, but being driven to pay deference to loyalty or other concerns, which greatly compromises the value of any suggestions. The person should not be a person of authority given to taking actions but someone who would raise difficult questions, prompt appropriate answers, and generally view things with an ethical eye instead of a profit-centered or performance-centered eye.

Third, to be effective, the ethics officer must have easy access to people throughout the organization, including those at the top. Moral behavior is best influenced from the top down. For example, improving the moral awareness of the CEO will have much greater impact on the ethical behavior of the company than raising the moral awareness of a sales rep or foreman. Hopefully, by starting at the top, all are reached and influenced in an effective manner.

CASE: The $400 Suit

With experience, salespeople can become accurate judges of their prospective customers. So, when Sam Morris saw a breezy character striding into City Clothing Store, where he was employed, he identified the customer as someone who would say just what he wanted, make up his mind quickly, and depart with his purchase after the minimum delay.

He guessed right. The customer promptly informed Sam what type and color of suit he wanted and added that he had exactly $400 to spend on a suit and would not go a cent higher.

Sam loved these kinds of customers best. He could show them what was in stock and get a decision in a hurry, usually a sale, without having to drag everything off the racks and out of the back room. He hated doing something like that for customers who obviously came in to buy something, but then left without so much as expressing interest.

At the moment, though, Sam was troubled about his new customer. The store's inventory was temporarily low, and Sam did not have anything approaching what his customer wanted between $350 and $450. He knew he could not sell the man a $450 suit, and he was afraid that this type of customer might refuse to be sold on the economic advantages of an $350 suit. He did not want to lose the sale since he knew the customer had come in to buy.

So, as Sam went to the back of the store, he told the customer to look around for a moment. During the next few minutes, Sam removed the price tag from a $350 suit and substituted a $400 tag. The customer liked the suit and its price, and after some custom tailoring, he walked out of the store perfectly satisfied with his new suit.

Questions:

1. Was Sam honest or dishonest in his behavior? Was he justified in changing the price? Is there anything wrong with charging what the market will bear (or with sending away a satisfied customer)?

2. If you were Sam's department manager and you found out about this deal, would you promote him? Commend him? Say nothing? Reprimand him? Fire him?

3. If you were the customer and found out you had been overcharged, what would you do?

4. If Sam was your best salesman, would your response be the same?

5. As Sam's department manager, suppose you hear that Sam has been discussing his prowess in making sales to other employees in the break room. Do you say anything to the other employees? What do your words and actions (or your saying nothing) indicate about your company's standards of honesty?

Appendices

Appendix A

Ethical but Illegal:
The Dangerous World of Arena D

*"Atticus nodded, 'My dear Marcus, you will never
forget how dangerous it is to speak the truth, how
unpardonable. A liar leads a most comfortable life
under any form of government, and dies peacefully
in bed.'"*

—*Taylor Caldwell[1]*

IN CHAPTER 1, we discussed how self-interest and competition
constantly exert pressure, pushing people to step or jump over ethical
and legal lines.

Actually, there is also an Arena D, which governs actions that are
illegal but ethical. I determined to keep the discussion of Arena D out
of the first chapter to keep the topic of ethical decision making as
simple as possible. Generally, the decision to violate the law based on

Self-Interest and Ethics
Under Competition

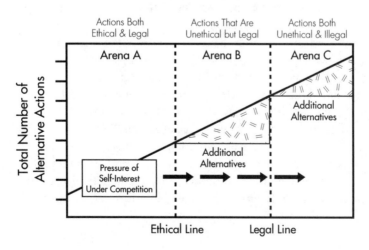

239

moral conscience or higher law is not driven by self-interest or competitive pressure. Therefore, the discussion of Arena D does not belong in a chapter called "Was He Pushed or Did He Jump," but merits separate treatment. In fact, the topic may be worthy of an entire book in its own right.

Making a decision to violate the law, even though the action is moral or justified by higher law or demanded by religious devotion, requires great courage and forethought with respect to the potential consequences. These decisions are even more weighty and rare in nations like the United States, where social intercourse is based on a code of laws written and enacted by elected citizens who represent the people, rather than the capricious judgments and decrees of an emperor, monarch or dictator. When everyone is governed by law based on the consent of the governed, the citizens are protected from the whims of self-serving totalitarians who can be very unjust or immoral.

Laws generally protect and perpetuate an orderly society. When everyone obeys the laws of a country, order prevails; and when people disobey laws, insecurity, unpredictability, and chaos raise their ugly heads, and the people suffer. Ideally, this means that everything that is legal is moral, and everything illegal is immoral. But, in real life, that is not always the case. It is almost impossible to enact laws that will be just and moral under all circumstances.

Consider the law that says you must wait for a traffic signal to turn from red to green before you can pass through an intersection. But, if someone in the back seat is in need of immediate and life-saving medical attention, wouldn't it be morally right to proceed with caution? Sure it's right, and even the nation's police or judges would tend to uphold such a decision.

But, what if the nation tends to punish harshly the violation of a certain law? In pre-World War II Germany, for example, it was illegal to harbor Jews to protect them from arrest. But, wouldn't it have been right to help hide such condemned people, even though it violated the law? In fact, wouldn't it have been immoral to turn them over to the authorities to face death or unjust confinement? Or, in pre-Civil War America, when slavery was legal, would it have been moral to help slaves who desired freedom to flee to the North, even though legally they were considered the "property" of slaveholders? In such a case, the action is not only against the law, but a form of stealing as well.

Is Violating the Law Morally Right?

With a little reflection, we can probably think of many situations in which violating the law would seem to be the morally right thing to do. In the American Declaration of Independence, the founders didn't just allow rebellion against an established government's unjust laws, but they admonished, "It is their right, it is their duty, to throw off such government." In fact, if the revolutionaries had failed, most would have been convicted of treason, yet they felt that throwing off the British government at the time was the moral thing to do. Many even felt that the laws were corrupt because the king and other legislators were corrupt, and therefore, even if the laws could be changed, it would be morally right to throw off the government.

Many also would argue that assassinating a ruthless dictator who had murdered, tortured, and enslaved others is morally right, even though it is against the law of the land and maybe even against God's law, "Thou shalt not kill." Even more people would agree that it is actually a government's responsibility to violate its own laws of homicide and put to death convicted murderers.

In consenting to such behaviors against the laws of the land, most people would justify some form of illegal behavior on the grounds that a law is unjust or immoral. But, who decides which laws are immoral, and when would someone be justified in violating those laws? If one person believes that violating a particular law is morally justifiable, does that license others to make similar decisions based on their own beliefs or values? If everyone felt morally justified in violating the laws of the land simply because they are unjust or because the government and legislators are immoral, doesn't this lead to anarchy? What would happen to government by law and order?

People in every land have experienced such dilemmas. Consider just a few examples from the United States in the past ten years: A woman feels morally justified in killing a medical doctor who performs legal abortions in a licensed hospital. A man refuses to pay taxes because he feels income taxes are morally wrong. Another man feels morally justified in taking more than one wife and claims God told him to do so. A family hires illegal immigrants for housekeeping and gardening duties, feeling that it is morally right to provide income to help them and their families live. A doctor prescribes marijuana for terminally ill patients to help them relieve pain.

As we can see from such controversial examples, those who decide to break the law based on moral conscience or higher law are not always supported by public opinion or sentiment. So, although we can all think of circumstances that would motivate us to violate the law, such decisions should be approached with great caution. I argue that such circumstances are extremely rare. Only the laws that grossly violate the most widely held common values would justify "moral actions" that fly in the face of established law. To do otherwise, we "take the law into our own hands" and let loose a cascade of lawlessness and self-righteousness that threatens the very foundations of society and prevents a government from providing basic protections to its citizens.

In a diverse society, we find infinite variation among people regarding what is moral and what is not. And, for that reason alone, a society with laws established by the voice of its citizens must maintain order by punishing the violation of law, whether or not it is done according to moral conscience. Requiring adherence to law is what keeps a society functioning.

Appendix B

Economic Espionage: Corporate Spying or Competitive Analysis?

"The man who tells the truth should have one foot in the stirrup."

—Turkish Proverb

THE PRACTICE OF economic espionage is fraught with moral challenges. Depending on their point of view, observers call this activity either "corporate spying" or "competitive analysis," and the ethics of this practice are always hotly debated.

I have not included this section in the main body of the book because, in my opinion, the debate does not center on the debate between "personal ethics" and competitive "gaming ethics" like the rest of the book. For the purposes of this short treatment, I assume the reader has decided gaming ethics are appropriate to business and that the Golden Rule does not govern market economics. I also assume that the reader's company tends to operate within Arena B much of the time. In fact, the discussion here centers on Arena B as the playing field itself and on the tactics companies use to advance "down field." Arena B, then, has a mid-field line where some believe certain actions are fair while others cry "foul." Thus, I will not focus on the legality of the practice, but only on the "fairness" or appropriateness of the behavior as debated by those who accept competition and gaming ethics as natural and inseparable components of our economic system. Those who live by personal ethics likely would not engage in economic espionage at all except for reviewing materials in the public domain that are produced by other companies or by the media.

In Search of a Competitive Edge

Athletes do not have to run a perfect race or play a perfect game to win. They must only outperform their competitors one game at a time. Therefore, knowing what the competition is going to do and how it is going to do it helps in preparing a strategy. In fact, leading a competitor to believe you are going to execute one strategy while you exercise another is a good way to reach the goal. Nevertheless, winning is based on performance, and many feel that with or without such knowledge they still must perform the essential tasks well to win.

Likewise, in business, companies do not have to produce a perfect product or deliver a perfect service to be successful, but only outperform their competition one customer at a time. Customers typically look for the best buy before they make a purchase—factoring in price, quality, and volume. Therefore, knowing what the competition is up to can be a helpful advantage in business, but satisfying the customer demands is still the main objective.

Nevertheless, information is power—and not just any information, but information that is not available to other competitors, and information that is accurate, complete, and timely. Such information can arm a company with great competitive advantage. However, the desire for such information can create enormous pressure and temptation for stepping over ethical and legal lines.

Now, the legal lines that mark the turf with respect to information gathering are fairly clear. Even though a competitive environment may press competitors to go after "all the law will allow," the law certainly does not allow some ways of obtaining information. For instance, breaking into a competitor's office to duplicate or steal documents is clearly over the legal line. Or, bribing a competitor's employee to obtain specific data is also a recognizable violation. But these actions may represent only the outside fringes of the competitive playing field—"out of bounds" as the sports world would say.

The challenge is to determine what other means are legal, and hopefully "fair," to obtain information about a competitor's planned strategy. Certain sources are obviously fair game, such as information gathered from public sources including news media, corporate annual reports, or company brochures and advertising. But, page for page, such information is not as useful as other data because everyone else has the same facts at the same time. In sports, we might compare the use of these sources to running a play "up the middle," where the majority of the players are defending and where sheer skill and strength are still the main determinants of advantage.

But, for smaller companies looking to break into "the big leagues," or for average companies to "win," or for large companies to thwart the creative efforts of small companies, any information that is not widely distributed or available will have much greater value. The efforts to obtain or develop such information and to create and implement new strategies based on this intelligence make up the rest of the corporate playing field. In this area, great creativity is exerted in forming strategies that won't be recognized or successfully defended by more dominant opponents. But, not surprisingly, it is also where all competitors, large and small, face temptations to cross the ethical and legal lines to obtain that information and gain or maintain an advantage. The main worry, then, is not to find out how everyone feels about the practice, but determining where the lines are—or, sometimes, what the odds and penalties are for getting caught.

In this large part of the playing field, the ethical rules are either not established or the lines are so fuzzy that people sometimes do not recognize them. And, because the playing field is so large, many practices and behaviors can't be judged well from a distance. Many employers seem to solve the problem by applying a version of the Golden Rule that says, "Do not gather information about a competitor from a source that you would not want your competitors using to gather information about you." But this philosophy has more to do with how much you can trust a sneaky middleman than how much you respect a competitor's wishes to keep some information confidential. The question is often not one of ethics but of good business practice based on trust.

Hot Potato

For example, in 1987, a Boston advertising agency learned that Microsoft was about to launch its new spreadsheet software package, Excel. Since the agency had experience working with Lotus, one of Microsoft's chief competitors, and had recently hired some people from Lotus' advertising agency to improve its ability to market products to the computer industry, company president Neal Hill knew he would have a shot to land the $20 million account. However, after making a few phone calls and sending a query letter, he learned that Microsoft had already closed the door to suitors for the advertising budget, and was preparing to make its decision.

Nevertheless, Hill fired off one last-ditch effort to put his company back in the running: He express-mailed a brochure to Rob Lebow, Microsoft's director of marketing communications, along with a round-trip ticket to Boston. The brochure played on the agency's behind-the-scenes knowledge about Lotus and said, "Since we know your competition's plans, isn't it worth taking a flier?" It went on to describe how people at the agency were "intimately acquainted with Lotus" and how this knowledge presented an important opportunity for Microsoft.

But Lebow wanted no part of it. He sent the letter, brochure, and airplane ticket directly to Microsoft's legal department, which forwarded the materials to Lotus. Lotus promptly filed suit against the agency. He explained, "You might consider it my moment of truth, but I didn't. At the time, it was a reflexive action. . . . My job wasn't to debate the higher principles of morality, but I could smell a dead fish when the wax paper was opened."

As it turns out, Hill's agency may not have had access to the trade secrets implied in the brochure, and the suit was resolved within a month. However, Microsoft's reaction to the proposal was swift—as valuable as such inside information could be, company executives could see no way to trust such an agency with the account. Imagine what Microsoft, the darling of the computer industry at the time, would have been risking by exposing itself to people who might shop their trade secrets around. This goes beyond the question of fairness to the driving concern presented in the introduction: trust.

Fairness Versus Trust

Consider the following examples of how some companies have gone about obtaining information about their competitors. Although in each example the people are acting within the law, they may test your sense of fairness. As you consider the fairness of each situation, look also at how trust impacts the people involved. Which practices are ethical, and which are not? How would you combat the tactics if you were the president of the company being spied upon and you found out about the behaviors? Would you use the information to your advantage if you were the president of the company that was spying? How?

1. A large retail chain regularly sends an employee to "shop" a competitor's store. The employee may buy a few things, but he or she mostly notes prices of popular items. The competition often spots the "spy" and finds it irritating.

2. The investment officer for the trust department of a large bank is asked by the bank's president to call a competing bank and pretend to be a potential customer. The officer is to inquire about forecasted interest rates and conditions in the industry. Although most other banks seem to be doing the same thing, the investment officer feels terribly guilty and hates having to do it.

3. A manufacturer hires away a key employee from a competitor. After she arrives on the job, the new employer asks her to attend a staff meeting where she is quizzed about her former employer's manufacturing processes, marketing techniques, employee benefits, and weaknesses in the competitor's products. She is also asked to identify which of the competitor's customers are most vulnerable to be won away.

4. A corporate vice president in charge of exports visits the U.S. Embassy in a country that has high potential for new sales. He asks the ambassador if his staff could gather information about three major companies in the industry already doing business in the country. It seems he could use the information to determine how financially strong or weak each one is.

5. A company often buys a competing product and disassembles it for detailed analysis and to discover possible structural secrets or secret formulas.

6. An employer requests an employee to take a competitor's strategically positioned secretary to dinner to ask specific questions about the competitor's company. The employee and the secretary happen to be close friends.

7. A senior executive parks a car across the street from the entrance of a competitor's corporate headquarters. He hides a video camera inside a stuffed Garfield cat attached to the car's rear passenger window. He says, "It's surprising how much you can learn by just observing who goes in and out, especially if you suspect a potential merger is in the works." He also learns who the company's key clients and suppliers are. (If this is ethical, why must he conceal the camera?)

8. The sales rep of a manufacturer has a personal friend in the purchasing department of a client company. Before bidding on a contract, the friend frequently volunteers the amount other competitors have already bid.

9. An executive sometimes hires a part-time janitor to rummage through a competitor's trash cans. (Modify this by considering what you would do if someone had already rummaged through a competitor's trash and was offering unsolicited information.) Is it ethical to use the information as long as it is not patented or trademarked?

10. An enterprising young man learns from a trusted friend that he could make money by erecting high power electric structures to transport electricity. For two weeks the entrepreneur sits on a hill with high-powered binoculars studying how another contractor set up his power stations on another hill. He takes extensive notes on how he could make the process more efficient. With that knowledge, he bids on the next contract and wins it. (If this is ethical, why does he indulge in distant "spying"?)

11. A service company regularly retains a consultant who happens to specialize in "competitor information services." Is this an ethical business arrangement?

Discuss these and other similar cases in your work groups, families, and among your friends and associates. You can find out much about the ethics or competitive instincts of the people around you by openly discussing how they would handle such situations. You can make the conversation more interesting by bringing up the Golden Rule or reminding them that you expect your company to become number one in its industry.

Notes

Introduction

1. The quotes at the heads of chapters that do not include notes are taken from Michael Josephson, ed., "Ethical Obligations and Opportunities in Business: Ethical Decision Making in the Trenches," monograph (Marina Del Rey, CA: The Joseph and Edna Josephson Institute for the Advancement of Ethics, 1988), 34-36.

2. Patricia Edmonds and Ann Oldenburg, "Morality Issues Matter More—Especially in this Election Year," including a CNN/Gallup Poll, *USA Today* (August 6, 1996): 4A.

3. Warren H. Schmidt and Barry Z. Posner, "Managerial Values in Perspective: An AMA Survey Report," monograph (New York: American Management Association, 1983), 34-35.

4. See Raymond Baumhart, "How Ethical Are Businessmen?" *Harvard Business Review* (Winter 1961): 6-9; and Steve Brenner and Earl Mollander, "Is the Ethics of Business Changing?" *Harvard Business Review* (Winter 1977): 57-63; both articles are cited in ibid, 34-36.

Chapter One

1. John Steinbeck, *Cannery Row* (New York: Viking Press, 1945), 150.

2. Barbara Wood, cited in an Associated Press article, "Win-At-All-Costs Mentality Plaguing Livestock Shows," in *Deseret News* (Salt Lake City, March 20, 1994): A-11.

3. Some people advocate greater refinements, arguing that there are some actions which may be illegal but still ethical. And although I agree such situations exist, they are extremely rare. Also, I wanted to keep the book focused purely on behavior that is both legal and ethical rather than help people find ways around the law in the name of so-called "ethical behavior." However, I have prepared a short summary of "Arena D" in Appendix A.

4. Karen Thomas, "Cheating, American Anthem: Land of the Fleece, Home of the Knave," a *USA Today* article in *Salt Lake Tribune* (August 2, 1995): A-1.

5. Chuck Gates, "S[alt] L[ake] Didn't Have a Moose's Chance for Games," *Deseret News* (June 18, 1985): B-1.

6. Herbert Johnston, *Business Ethics*, 2nd ed. rev. (New York: Pitman Publishing Corp., 1961 [1956]), 94-95.

Chapter Two

1. Thomas V. Newmark, "Treasures of Provence," previously unpublished short story in the author's possession, used with permission.

2. Robert Louis Stevenson, "Truth of Intercourse," part four of "Virginibus Puerisque," in *Virginibus Puerisque and Other Papers* (New York: Charles Scribner's Sons, 1924 [1887]), 56.

3. Herbert Johnston, *Business Ethics*, 2nd ed. rev. (New York: Pitman Publishing Corp., 1961 [1956]), 154.

Chapter Three

1. Tylenol's advertisement appeared in *Time* (May 16, 1977): 62.

2. Bayer's advertisement appeared in *Time* (June 27, 1977): ii (inside front cover); Tylenol's ad is included within the same advertisement.

3. *The Tormont Webster's Illustrated Encyclopedic Dictionary* (Montreal, QB: Tormont Publications, 1990), "deception."

4. *Time* (June 27, 1977): ii.

5. The overstatement of rate of return is shown in a comparison study of two banks by Tom L. Beauchamp, "Manipulative Advertising," *Business and Professional Ethics Journal* (Spring-Summer 1984): 12.

6. Jane Bryant Quinn, "New Handcuffs on the Cops," *Newsweek* (September 3, 1984): 62.

7. Michael Deaver, as cited in Edward T. Pound, "White House Aide's Family Finances Brighten After Political Associates Help Wife Start Career," *Wall Street Journal* (January 3, 1985): A-36.

8. Beauchamp, "Manipulative Advertising," 12.

9. Lee Berton, "Many Firms Hide Debt to Give Them an Aura of Financial Strength: Accounting Tactics Confuse Bank Lenders and Investors," *Wall Street Journal* (December 13, 1983): A-1.

10. Herbert Johnston, *Business Ethics*, 2nd ed. rev. (New York: Pitman Publishing Corp., 1961 [1956]), 113-14.

Chapter Four

1. S. Leonard Rubenstein, "Points to Ponder," *Reader's Digest* (April 1985)

2. Political cartoon, "Walk Talk," of the Register and Tribune Syndicate, February 19, 1953, copy in the author's possession.

Chapter Five

1. Edgar A. Guest, "The True Man," *Collected Verse of Edgar A. Guest*, 12th ed. (Chicago, IL: The Reilly & Lee Co., 1947 [1934]), 400.

2. Stephanie Anderson Forest, Peter Burrows, Kathy Rebello, and Catherine Arnst, "The Education of Michael Dell," *Business Week* (March 22, 1993): 85.

3. Arthur Kaplan, "Doctors Need to Lie Sometimes," *Salt Lake Tribune* (June 11, 1989): A-27.

4. Excerpt from a 1980 speech written and presented by Cyril Figuerres, notes in the author's possession, used with permission.

5. Merle Miller, *Ike the Soldier: As They Knew Him* (New York: G. P. Putnam's Sons, 1987), 114.

Chapter Six

1. Reverend Sun Myong Moon, as cited in John B. Judis, "Rev[erend] Moon's Rising Political Influence," *U.S. News & World Report* (March 27, 1989): 28.

2. Gregory L. Vistica and Evan Thomas, "The Man Who Spied Too Long," *Newsweek* (April 29, 1996): 26.

Chapter Seven

1. Louis Fischer, *The Life of Mahatma [Mohandas Karamchand] Gandhi*, reprint (New York: Harper & Row, 1983 [1950]), 33.

2. Robert A. Caro, *The Years of Lyndon Johnson,* 2 vols. (New York: Alfred Knopf, 1983 and 1990), vol. 1, "The Path to Power," cited in Peter S. Prescott, "The Power and Dubious Glory of Lyndon Johnson," *Newsweek* (November 29, 1982): 47-48.

3. Lorenzo Gracian [Baltasar Gracian y Morales], *Oráculo manual y arte de prudencia* [The Oracle Manual and Art of Prudence], Emilio Blanco, ed. (Madrid: Cátedra, 1995 [1647]); see also the English translation: *The Art of Worldly Wisdom*, Joseph Jacob, trans. (New York: Macmillan, 1956), cited in ibid, 47.

4. George Melloan, "Business Ethics and the Competitive Urge," *Wall Street Journal* (August 9, 1988): A-23.

5. Coleman Lollar, "Travel and Money: Car Rental Add-Ons," *Travel & Leisure* (August 1988): 36, cited in ibid.

6. William B. Glaberson, "Why Wasn't $1 Million a Year Enough?" *Business Week* (August 25, 1986): 73-74.

7. Skip Kaltenhauser, "When Bribery Is a Budget Item," *World Business* (in-house magazine of KPMG, March-April 1996): 11.

8. Carlo DeBenedetti, as cited in an Associated Press article, "Anti-Graft Probers Arrest Italian Tycoon," in *Deseret News* (October 31, 1993): A-8.

9. Alfredo Vito, as cited in Alexander Stille, "A Scandal Too Big to Ignore," *U.S. News & World Report* (April 19, 1993): 44.

10. Alexander Stille, "The Scandal That Is Rocking Italy," *US News & World Report* (May 25, 1992): 54.

11. Herbert Johnston, *Business Ethics*, 2nd ed. rev. (New York: Pitman Publishing Corp., 1961 [1956]), 114.

Chapter Eight

1. *The Tormont Webster's Illustrated Encyclopedic Dictionary* (Montreal, QB: Tormont Publications, 1990), "obligation" and "duty."

2. The death of Joseph Mengele, "The Angel of Death," was confirmed by genetic testing in 1992. See an Associated Press article, "Genetic Testing Confirms That Mengele Died in '79," in *Deseret News* (April 8, 1992): A-1.

3. Margaret Loeb, "Church Stirs Debate over Tobacco," *Wall Street Journal* (May 8, 1984): B-37.

4. Mario Puzo, *The Godfather* (New York: Signet, 1978 [1969]).

5. Eugene M. Bricker, "Sounding Board: Industrial Marketing and Medical Ethics, *New England Journal of Medicine* (June 22, 1989): 1691.

6. Doug Podolsky and Richard J. Newman, "Prescription Prizes," *U.S. News & World Report* (March 29, 1993): insert on 58-59.

7. David Rogers, "Senator [David] Durenberger Got Huge Campaign Gifts from Firms He Aided," *Wall Street Journal* (April 24, 1984): A-1.

8. David Ivor Young, Lord Young, as cited in George Gedda, "Anti-Bribery Worldwide Effort to Clean-Up Greased Palms," *Salt Lake Tribune* (February 13, 1996): A-1.

9. Peter Schnuck, "The Curious Case of the Indicted Meat Inspectors," *Harper's Magazine* (September 1972): 81.

10. Joseph B. White, "Comfy Ride: Car Magazine Writers Sometimes Moonlight for Firms They Review," *Wall Street Journal* (May 15, 1990): A-1.

11. Ellen E. Schultz, "More Crooked Planners Play on Fear, Scare Up Cash," *Wall Street Journal* (June 15, 1990): C-1.

12. Todd Mason, "When Buying a Home, Beware of Hidden Incentives to Brokers," *Wall Street Journal* (April 26, 1991): C-1.

13. Michael Mewshaw, *The Short Circuit* (New York: Atheneum, 1983), as cited in Spencer Reiss with Andrew Nagorski, "Dirty Pool on Center Court," *Newsweek* (May 30, 1983): 59.

14. Paraphrase from a 1995 speech by David J. Cherrington at Brigham Young University, Provo, Utah, used with permission. See Jay Owen and David J. Cherrington, *Moral Leadership and Ethical Decision Making* (Orem, UT: Legacy Foundation, 1997); see also Quinn G. McKay, "Red Flags Missed, Wrong Man Hired," *Business Horizons* (Summer 1963): 47-52.

15. *The Tormont Webster's Illustrated Encyclopedic Dictionary* (Montreal, QB: Tormont Publications, 1990), "bribery."

16. Herbert Johnston, *Business Ethics*, 2nd ed. rev. (New York: Pitman Publishing Corp., 1961 [1956]), 282.

Chapter Nine

1. Benjamin Selekman, *A Moral Philosophy for Management* (New York: McGraw-Hill, 1959), 101-2.

2. Edward P. Learned, "Multi-Products, Inc," case study 307-114 (Boston, MA: Harvard Business School, 1959).

3. Albert Z. Carr, "Is Business Bluffing Ethical?" *Harvard Business Review* (January-February 1968): 143-53.

4. Milton Friedman, "The Social Responsibility of Business Is to Increase Its Profits," *New York Times Magazine* (September 13, 1970): 32-33, 122, 124, 126.

5. *The Tormont Webster's Illustrated Encyclopedic Dictionary* (Montreal, QB: Tormont Publications, 1990), "amoral."

Chapter Ten

1. Eleanor Johnson Tracy, Peter Vanderwicken, Susie G. Nayem, and Sydney L. Stern, "In Love With 'Sweet Sixteen,' " *Fortune* (February 1975): 21.

2. Benjamin Selekman, *A Moral Philosophy for Management* (New York: McGraw-Hill, 1959), 101-2. See epigraph of Chapter 9 for the quote. Compare this with Jesus' teaching in the Bible: "Ye cannot serve God and mammon [wealth or riches]" (Luke 16—read the whole chapter for an interesting dialogue about business stewardship.)

3. David Halberstam, "Their Call to Duty," *Parade* (July 7, 1985): 4-7.

4. Ralph Nader, Peter J. Petkas, and Kate Blackwell, eds., *Whistle Blowing: The Report of the Conference on Professional Responsibility* (New York: Grossman Publishers, 1972).

5. Rich Jaroslovsky and Paul Blustein, "Feldstein Is Put Under Intense Pressure for Publicly Voicing Qualms on Economy," *Wall Street Journal* (December 1, 1983): A-3.

Chapter Eleven

1. The anguish David Kaczymnski felt about reporting his brother was detailed in an Associated Press Article, "Dilemma: Duty to Country or Family Loyalty?" in *Salt Lake Tribune* (April 5, 1996): A-17.

2. Roger T. Nazeley, Philadelphia, Pennsylvania, in "Letters to the Editor," *CFO: The Magazine for Senior Financial Executives* (November 1992): 9.

3. [Name withheld], Jessup, Georgia, in ibid, 5 and 7.

4. [Name and city withheld], in ibid, 7.

5. Herbert Johnston, *Business Ethics*, 2nd ed. rev. (New York: Pitman Publishing Corp., 1961 [1956]), 112.

Chapter Twelve

1. David O. McKay, from a 1950 speech in Salt Lake City, Utah; see also David O. McKay, *True to the Faith: From the Sermons and Discourses of David O. McKay*, Llewelyn R. McKay, comp. (Salt Lake City, UT: Bookcraft, 1966), 272.

2. See an Associated Press article, "North Says He Misled Probers But Didn't Lie," in *Deseret News* (October 6, 1994): A-19.

Chapter Thirteen

1. Justice Learned Hand, "The Spirit of Liberty," in *Papers and Addresses of Learned Hand*, Irving Dilliard, ed. (New York: Alfred A. Knopf, 1952), 38.

2. In the Christian tradition, the Golden Rule was given by Jesus in the Bible: "Therefore, all things whatsoever ye would that men should do to you, do ye even so to them: for this is the law and the prophets" (Matthew 7:12). However, the same principle in the Jewish tradition likely goes back to Moses: "Thou shalt love thy neighbor as thyself" (Leviticus 19:18, 34; see also Matthew 5:43-44 for Jesus' reference to Moses' writings). The philosophy of "reciprocity" also goes back to ancient China and Greece and is not unique to the Bible.

3. Michael Josephson, ed., "Ethical Obligations and Opportunities in Business: Ethical Decision Making In the Trenches," monograph (Marina Del Rey, CA: The Joseph and Edna Josephson Institute for the Advancement of Ethics, 1988), 13.

4. Joseph Weber with Catherine Yang, "Can a 1,245% Markup on Drugs Really Be Legal?" *Business Week* (November 1, 1993): 34.

5. Ronald E. Yates, "Fat Corporations Have Grim Underbelly," a *Chicago Tribune* article in *Salt Lake Tribune* (October 15, 1995): F-1.

6. Thom Geier, "Outlook: Wal-Mart's Price War: David Versus Goliath." *U.S. News & World Report* (October 25, 1993): 14.

7. David S. Merrill chart in ibid. Figures are based on prices gathered for litigation: *American Association of Retail Druggists v. Wal-Mart*, 1992. Matthew Adlong, attorney for the plaintiffs.

Chapter Fourteen

1. Alexander Pope, "An Essay on Man in Four Epistles to Henry St. John, Lord Bollingbroke," in *Poetry and Prose of Alexander Pope*, Aubrey Williams, ed. (Boston, MA: Houghton Mifflin, 1969 [1733-34]), 136 (epistle II, part V).

2. John Emerith Edward Dallberg-Acton, Lord Acton to Bishop Mandell Creighton, April 24, 1881, as cited in John Bartlett, comp., *Bartlett's Familiar Quotations*, Justin Kaplan, ed., 16th ed. (Boston, MA: Little, Brown and Co., 1992 [1855]), 521.

3. *The Tormont Webster's Illustrated Encylopedic Dictionary* (Montreal, QB: Tormont Publications, 1990), "intoxicate."

Chapter Fifteen

1. Dale Kurschner, "Ethics Programs and Personal Values Are Still Not Enough," *Business Ethics* (May-June 1996): 12.

2. Julie Irwin, "Poll: Everyone Else Is Lying," *Cincinnati Enquirer* (December 8, 1996): A-1.

3. The Synthesis Consulting Group provides an ethics survey that can be completed over the phone without pencil or paper. (But, if you prefer to use them, you may.) Each participant takes the survey anonymously using a specialized phone number and access code, and the data are processed within an hour of the last person's call. Individual assessments are also available. For more information, call 1-800-416-0699.

4. See the Associated Press account: "Gale Seals Ship's Fate, Spares Skipper, Mate," *Salt Lake Tribune* (January 11, 1952): A-1; and an anonymous editorial in *Deseret News* (January 15, 1952): B-2.

Appendix A

1. Taylor Caldwell, *A Pillar of Iron* (Garden City, NY: Doubleday, 1965), 311.

Appendix B

1. N. Craig Smith with John A. Quelch, "Rossin, Greenburg, Seronick, and Hill, Inc.," case studies (A-C) 9-589-124-26, rev. (Boston, MA: Harvard Business School, 1993 [1989]); and Robert Jay Lebow to Ken Shelton (editor of *Executive Excellence*), December 27, 1993, copy in the author's possession, used with permission.

Index

About Quinn G. McKay

QUINN G. MCKAY is a partner in the Synthesis Consulting Group and recently an adjunct professor of business ethics at the University of Utah. He holds a doctorate in business administration from Harvard University and has extensive academic and professional credentials.

Academically, he has held an endowed chair at Texas Christian University, was the first MBA program director at Brigham Young University, and has been a visiting professor at the Universities of Lausanne, Switzerland; Ahmadu Bello, Nigeria; and Rangoon, Burma. Professionally, he has been a senior executive in many organizations, including the American Cancer Society (Utah division), Praxis Institute, Tracy Collins Bank & Trust, American Stores, and Utah Health Cost Management Foundation.

McKay has been speaking and teaching about the principles of business and political ethics for over 30 years. He lives in Kaysville, Utah.